T0293681

Praise for *Will AI Dictate the Future?*

"Dr. Anton's book explores objective views on what the future holds for AI and its impact on humanity. With his years of expertise in the field, Dr. Anton not only provides exciting interpretations into the prevalence of AI in a variety of sectors and its potential evolution in each but also importantly, the ethics and governance of the responsible practice of AI."
— **Dr. Mohamad Maliki Osman, Minister in the Prime Minister's Office; Second Minister, Ministry of Foreign Affairs; Ministry of Education**

"Dr. Anton Ravindran has been a leader in the field of information technology, where he has established an enviable reputation for his deep insight of the emerging business technologies and trends. His current research and writings on the pervasiveness of AI in our life's activities necessitate answers to this intractable question of "What will be the impact of AI on our future?" His examination of this topic provides a window view of the many possible answers of how AI will shape the various sectors of our society in the future."
— **Prof. Emanuel Grant, Department of Electrical Engineering and Computer Science, University of North Dakota**

"Dr. Anton brings a broad-based perspective of AI, drawing upon the past, present and future. His unique blend of deep tech knowledge and imparting this to the IT community, gives him a great lens into the future of AI. This book is a good read on how AI is impacting industries and society."
— **Sam Liew, President, Singapore Computer Society**

"Dr. Anton Ravindran is an established technopreneur and visionary. This important book brings together unique and stimulating insights into the future impact of AI on society and industry, including five thought leadership chapters from academia and industry. It is a must-read for all!"
— **Prof. Liz Bacon, Vice-Chancellor, Abertay University**

"I have known Dr. Anton Ravindran for over a decade. He is an inspiring leader with a heart to do good and do better for all around him. He is an astute leader in technology with deep domain expertise. Many seek out his wise counsel for industry development and his ability to operationalise, execute and deliver results. He has dedicated his life to serving others in the community and industry, uplifting and mentoring the next generation of technology professionals. Above all, he is a friend and mentor. I wish him the very best for his latest book that seeks to define a new frontier, an adventure and a great opportunity for Singapore and Singaporeans. We are proud to have Dr. Ravindran to be leading the way."

— **Shawn Huang, Member of Parliament;**
Director, Temasek International

"Dr. Anton brings a unique blend of heart and deep tech, which gives him a great lens into the future of AI and the impact on society and businesses. This book is a timely knowledge read of the state of affairs of AI at the moment."

— **Howie Lau, Managing Director, NCS**

"Dr. Anton Ravindran is a visionary and a path-builder. He draws on his long experience at the coal face of cutting-edge technology issues and assimilates them in this book, which presents real-world assessments of AI and its incipient impact on humanity. This book provides thought leadership and insights on the foundational workings of AI – he is the voice that needs to be heard."

— **Abraham Vergis, S.C., Founder and Managing Director,**
Providence Law Asia LLC

"Dr. Anton Ravindran, whom I know for well over two decades, was an early entrant into the world of information technology. I have seen him grow as a technopreneur over the years. He has matched his growth in the world of business with his commitment to the community; this is evidenced by the various community activities that he has undertaken and continues to do so. A dispassionate view on the 'pervasive' invasion of artificial intelligence into every aspect of human life is long overdue. Dr. Anton's treatment of the very challenging topic is refreshing; he identified certain areas and assembled a team of experts to give their views on the impact of AI on a diverse range of areas that touch our life, including healthcare, law, education and a few other identified topics. I look forward to him continuing the journey and wish him continued success."
— **M Rajaram, Partner and Chairman, K&L Gates Straits**

"Combining his scholarly pursuits with decades of hands-on experience as a technopreneur, Dr. Anton brings together diverse and thought-provoking views on AI and its impact. A good read for anyone interested in gathering deep insights on our tech-driven future."
— **Frank Koo, Head of Asia, Talent Solutions, LinkedIn**

"The field of AI is rapidly gaining importance and changing our lives permanently. The different forms and areas of application of AI are diverse and require structured investigation. Dr. Anton's book is an essential analysis of the impact of AI on our future and is highly recommended."
— **Prof. Dr. Richard C. Geibel, Fresenius University of Applied Sciences**

"Ideas and views that challenge my own perception of what AI would be. Dr. Anton in his work penetrates my fears and my hopes for artificial intelligence in our lives. My recent discussions with him on AI had been a blend of innocence and ignorance. His book demystifies aspects of AI for my children's future and expectations.

This tech pioneer has amassed expertise of Singapore's foray into computers and technology for four decades. His book peels away at what I had believed to be AI's destiny in our world, causing me to abandon my own views.

I had imagined as a lawyer, AI's servitude in our work, but my views have been challenged. Dr. Anton's mastery of the discussion tears into controversy I had not anticipated. His views provide a thought foundation for public administration, finance, defence, healthcare, law and mostly, anything that AI would touch. I needed this education."
— **Ronnie Tan, Managing Director, Central Chambers Law Corporation**

"Dr. Anton Ravindran demonstrates through his book, *Will AI Dictate the Future?*, that he is a 'people's person' by taking Artificial Intelligence to the common person. At the same time, he alerts the AI experts on what are the emerging challenges in AI. In his book, he shows his dexterity in introducing refinements of AI into ANI, AGI and ASI – Narrow, General and Super AIs. AI affects every individual, today, tomorrow and well into the future. I wish Dr. Anton Ravindran the very best for this inspiring book and look forward to seeing more from him in the near future that will share his knowledge for the betterment of society."
— **Prof. Edmond Prakash, Research Dean, Cardiff Metropolitan University**

"Dr. Anton's rich experience and keen insights provide the foundation to his practical assessment on how AI must be harnessed for businesses and society."
— **Dr. Yoke Sin Chong, Managing Partner, iGlobePartners**

Will AI Dictate the Future?

Dr. Anton Ravindran

Marshall Cavendish
Business

Published in 2022 by Marshall Cavendish Business
An imprint of Marshall Cavendish International

A member of the
Times Publishing Group

Other Marshall Cavendish Offices:
Marshall Cavendish Corporation, 800 Westchester Ave, Suite N-641, Rye Brook, NY 10573, USA • Marshall Cavendish International (Thailand) Co Ltd, 253 Asoke, 16th Floor, Sukhumvit 21 Road, Klongtoey Nua, Wattana, Bangkok 10110, Thailand • Marshall Cavendish (Malaysia) Sdn Bhd, Times Subang, Lot 46, Subang Hi-Tech Industrial Park, Batu Tiga, 40000 Shah Alam, Selangor Darul Ehsan, Malaysia

Marshall Cavendish is a registered trademark of Times Publishing Limited

National Library Board, Singapore Cataloguing in Publication Data
Name(s): Ravindran, Anton.
Title: Will AI dictate the future? / Dr. Anton Ravindran.
Description: Singapore : Marshall Cavendish Business, 2022.
Identifier(s): ISBN 978-981-5044-31-7 (hardback)
Subject(s): LCSH: Artificial intelligence--Social aspects. | Technology--Social aspects.
Classification: DDC 303.4834--dc23

Printed in Singapore

In memory of my late parents and sister,
whose memories I shall forever cherish

Contents

Foreword

PROFESSOR THE HON. STEPHEN MARTIN

When Dr. Anton asked me to write a foreword for his book, *Will AI Dictate the Future?*, I was both delighted to do so but flattered that he would include me in such exalted company as himself, given his expertise in this field as a technopreneur.

Anton is something of a restless soul, a pioneer in many respects, academically gifted and someone always looking towards the future. His early career saw him working both in technical (research and product development), business development and management positions for IBM, Computer Associates (CA), Sun Microsystems and Singalab (an IBM and National Computer Board JV). Since 2000, he has been a technopreneur, mentor, advisor and company director.

He graduated initially with a Bachelor of Science (Information Technology) from the University of Texas at Arlington, where he was on the Dean's List. He obtained a Master of Business Administration degree in Information Technology at the University of North Texas and later pursued postgraduate studies in Computer-Aided Software Engineering (CASE) at the University of Texas at Dallas. He rounded out his academic qualifications with a Doctorate in Information Technology Management from the University of South Australia.

Additionally, Anton is a Chartered Fellow, British Computer Society (FBCS); Fellow, Singapore Computer Society (FSCS); and Chartered Engineer (CEng), Engineering Council UK. His current technology and research focus includes Cloud Computing, Big Data and AI as well as entrepreneurship.

Passionate about the value of education, Anton has ensured his professional qualifications have been applied in academia. Positions he holds or has held include Adjunct Professor, Faculty of Information Systems, Bina Nusantara University; Visiting Professor/Researcher at the Institute for Research in Applicable Computing (IRAC), University of Bedfordshire, UK; and Adjunct Professor at Birla Institute of Technology and Science, Department of Management, Pilani – Dubai Campus.

Having achieved much already in his life, such as being awarded the prestigious Singapore Entrepreneur of the Year, I was not surprised that he turned his attention to writing a book on a subject about which he is both an expert but also passionate, and highly relevant. This is in fact the latest in five previous books he has either authored or edited on technology.

Anton's request for me to pen this foreword has given me time to pause and reflect on our relationship. We have known each other for some 17 years and become firm friends and colleagues over that period. We have been involved in ICT education, training and certification programmes in the region, and the facilitation of leading-edge technology in cloud computing and similar applications in a variety of settings.

Our paths first crossed nearly 20 years ago when the university I was involved with (as Pro Vice-Chancellor) at the time was seeking a highly reputable partner to facilitate our postgraduate programme with a focus on IT (SAP) in Singapore. Having met Anton, examined his business model, and carefully considered his organisation's academic credentials, the choice of his company was an easy one. Its success was measured by the fact that years later the company was acquired and continues to operate successfully today. Since then, I have worked with him on several projects and initiatives. The restless entrepreneurial spirit that is Anton saw a further change in his unbridled energy and enthusiasm, coupled with his appreciation of the place of Big Data and Artificial Intelligence. And so was born his recent ventures including RapidStart, GICT Pte Ltd, and more recently, SmartLaw Pte Ltd.

To progress then to write a book that examines the complex and philosophical question as to whether AI will dictate our future was the next logical step for Anton. And he has succeeded magnificently, adapting his academic, professional and hands-on experience to offer some genuine insights into the many aspects of the subject.

I must offer Anton my sincerest congratulations for having the foresight to make such a grand contribution to what surely must be one of the most important questions of the ages. I am delighted that he has invited leading authorities in AI from Singapore, Australia, and the UK to contribute guest chapters as part of the book. I commend the book to anyone with an interest in AI, and how it might stimulate thinking about things such as the future of work, environmental outcomes and global economics.

Professor the Hon. Stephen Martin
BA, MA, MTCP, Dip ED, PhD, GAICD
Chairman, Bank of China (Australia) Ltd
Former Speaker, Parliament of Australia

Preface:
Why AI Matters Now

DR. ANTON RAVINDRAN

The book aims to create awareness of AI and its impact on society and humanity given that AI is fast becoming an integral part of our daily lives. And, it can be safely argued that AI is probably the most impactful technology ever, in human history. To define AI or at least understand what it all means, we need to define intelligence.

Interestingly, there are varying contemporary definitions of intelligence, and to date, there is ongoing research and debate amongst scholars on what this means, but most of them agree on three classical viewpoints: learn from experience, recognise problems and solve problems. AI already has arrived at being able to do this, hence "intelligence", and is all around us today.

However, it is reported that less than five years ago, 50% of people didn't even know when they were "experiencing" AI. The study also revealed that 70% of consumers surveyed have a "fear" of AI, and 25% of such people fear that AI can effectively take over the world. Maybe that's a good script for a science-fiction Hollywood blockbuster, but certainly not for AI in this decade. Having said that, AI is already truly changing our lives. Dear readers, that was my motivation to write this book.

AI has been around for the past six decades, but in the last five years, it has progressed exponentially and has developed three distinct capabilities that are fast becoming pervasive: the ability to recognise objects and images (object vision), speech recognition and the ability to perform language translation – which is considered the holy grail of AI.

In fact, AI performs these three functions at the level of humans, or even exceeds them. Search engines on Google and Google Maps (GPS) are commonplace and we are not too many years away from seeing autonomous vehicles on our roads as fellow drivers, and an increasing number of robots in our factories, restaurants, hospitals and workplaces.

It is inconceivable today to think of a world without a smartphone, yet the first iPhone allowed consumers the ability to browse the web just as they do on a desktop computer and this was introduced only in July 2007. It is a vastly different world today compared to 15 years ago without an iPhone (2007) or Facebook (2005) or WhatsApp (2009). In fact, we may never have to drive anymore. We have already made self-flying rockets, and even many functions on spacecrafts are fast becoming autonomous.

But AI is far more than that. Whether understanding the origins of the human species or the origins of the universe, AI is playing a pivotal role and has taken over humanity in trying to understand this. In 2003, when the Human Genome Project successfully completed the first sequencing of the human DNA blueprint, the world celebrated the feat, which was accomplished ahead of its planned schedule and budget, costing some US$400 million, in just 13 years. In less than two decades, we have come a long way, as new studies report that by leveraging AI, whole-genome sequencing can now be used to diagnose genetic diseases in less than 24 hours. Now take a moment to reflect on this! No other technology in our human history has had this kind of impact and potential, along with being widely accessible and affordable.

When the Vera Rubin Observatory, currently being built in Chile, goes live, it will survey the entire night sky every single night, and collect information that will be used to understand the mysteries of the universe. This study is driven by four main scientific objectives: to probe dark energy and dark matter, take an inventory of the solar system, explore the transient optical sky, and map the Milky Way. This initiative aims to produce the deepest and widest image of the universe. It will help to reveal the shape of the universe and will examine how dark matter affects the evolution of galaxies. Dark matter accounts for approximately 85% of all "matter" in the universe, and how this substance affects the formation and evolution of the galaxies will be one of the major breakthroughs in astrophysics. To achieve this, the largest digital camera in the world will be collecting over 30 terabytes of images and data every night. These images will be stored in a database which will contain 20 billion rows and a few dozen columns. One terabyte is 8,000,000,000,000 bits, a number we can't even begin to wrap our minds around. The camera is expected to take over 200,000 pictures per year, immeasurably more than what can be reviewed by humans.

In fact, here on Earth, the 18th-century philosopher Jeremy Bentham's disciplinary concept of "panopticon" is fast becoming a reality with the pervasiveness of digital surveillance cameras, because of AI and IoT. "I'm constantly reminded of George Orwell's lessons in his book, *1984*. You know the fundamental story… about a government who could see everything that everyone did and hear everything that everyone said all the time," said Brad Smith, President of Microsoft. There are close to a billion closed-circuit cameras in the world and this number is rapidly increasing. Privacy and individual liberties will become a challenging issue unless laws are enacted quickly even as the technology rages on. The Orwellian dystopian view of a future totalitarian state is rapidly transitioning from fiction to reality.

We are at the cusp of entering a new era of a man-machine co-existence, though the sceptics argue that Artificial General Intelligence (AGI) is a lofty goal and some say, even hyperbole. In 1965, British mathematician Irving John Good published "Speculations Concerning the First Ultra-intelligent Machine", which originated the concept that became popularised as "technological singularity". This concept anticipates the eventual existence of superhuman intelligence and the "intelligence explosion". And he prophetically said that "the first ultra-intelligent machine is the last invention that man need ever make".

Amazon has more than 200,000 mobile robots working inside its network of warehouses along with thousands of human workers. With autonomous vehicles, there will be no need for taxi drivers, and these are just two examples of the ongoing displacements. Many studies find that routine jobs will soon be replaced by AI because AI can exceed human performance, has zero fatigue and is fast becoming capable of learning to optimise itself. This transformation and the consequent disruptions are inevitable. There will be a dynamic shift from a socio-economic perspective and the workforce will require new skillsets which need to be addressed. According to the World Economic Forum (WEF), closing the growing skills gap of the workforce could add US$11.5 trillion to global GDP by 2028. Governments and businesses need to step up and prepare for the transformation as the impact could be massive for those who don't. This has also elevated the level of anxiety, apprehension and the growing debate as to what is the role of man in a world where machines can do everything man can, and in some cases even better than man.

But what happens when the current Narrow AI "evolves", and Human-level AI, also known as Artificial General Intelligence (AGI), arrives? The leading scientist of this century, Stephen Hawking, and the visionary entrepreneur Elon Musk have warned of the existential threats of AI. Again, some of these apocalyptic scenarios are based on technological singularity, whereby people envision Artificial Intelligence taking over humans, having access to autonomous weapons and enslaving humans, even permanently altering human existence. Will they? The short answer is not yet and it will be a long way to go, to worry about AI and robots ruling humanity. We are still trying to figure out how our brains work and AI is augmenting humans in this ground-breaking endeavour. AI can't "rule the world" or "take over" until it begins to enact "AI laws" on how machines vote, govern or own properties, assets, businesses, and so on. Even if they become super-intelligent, robots are only machines, and they don't have human rights like the right to vote, the right to own property, the right to own companies, etc. And humans will never voluntarily surrender these rights to super-intelligent machines. Or will they? Science fiction, for now.

AI is neither benevolent nor malevolent, but it is still not too far from self-learning. To rule the world, they need to be all over universally and they need to self-replicate to populate. AI as of now, known as Narrow AI, doesn't have creativity or emotions or malice, hence "machine humility" and "machine morality" are in the hands of those who develop these AI machines. One pressing need is to ensure AI doesn't overpower mankind but humanity becomes empowered. This requires foresight and commit-ment to developing far-sighted ethical frameworks and regulations to have "Responsible AI", as we have done with nuclear energy, DNA sequencing and genetic engineering. Genetic manipulation is well defined and regu-lated. And human genome editing is banned by laws and regulations in most countries. Germ or biological warfare is illegal, but there is no such legal framework for the use of AI in warfare. I must also add that AI is fast becoming ubiquitous and that poses far more challenges in managing it. *Flounder or flourish, it's in our hands, at least for now.*

Acknowledgements

Writing a book requires some sacrifices, particularly with respect to time, and this book was written in less than ten months, which made it doubly taxing, but in the end, I must say on balance that it has been rewarding. The motivation to write the book came about because of the growing ubiquity and significance of AI. AI is here to stay, and is now! AI is at work all around us! The credit for this labour of effort goes to all who made this possible, especially my colleagues at work, past and present, peers in the industry who encouraged me to write the book, and particularly to all who nudged me to write this book, you know who you are.

The book broadly covers AI's impact in key industries, including law, healthcare, financial services, manufacturing, higher education, mobility, cybersecurity, and satellite systems. The book also has five guest chapters from six leading professionals and academics. To that end, I'm grateful to Prof. Andy Koronios for his support and professional friendship for more than two decades now, and for his guest chapter on AI for next-generation satellite systems. I also appreciate Prof. Liz Bacon for her chapter on AI for higher education, and her support and association with me for almost 15 years. She has also previously obliged me in jointly editing other publications, including one for the Singapore Computer Society (SCS) Body of Knowledge (BoK). Also, many thanks to Prof. Venky Shankararaman and Assistant Prof. Alan Megargel, for their guest chapter on AI for financial services from an Asian perspective. Prof. Venky and I have had a shared interest in promoting technology initiatives to-date. I also wish to thank Dr. Toh See Kiat, who is more than qualified to pen a chapter on the impact of AI on the legal profession as a practising lawyer, an academic and his many years of association with the SCS. My fullest thanks to Mr. Shawn Huang for his contribution to the guest chapter on the impact of AI for Government, and for the many intellectually stimulating discourses on technology over the years. I must also thank Mr. Vincent Wong for his contribution as co-author of the chapter on AI for mobility, and Mr. Raju Chellam for writing the prologue of this book.

I'm also grateful to Prof. the Hon. Stephen Martin for taking the time to fly down to attend the book launch, for his support and friendship over the last two decades, and for writing the foreword.

Also, very special thanks to all my friends, colleagues, and associates whom Raju Chellam interviewed in writing the prologue. I appreciate the touching and kind words from all of you, for your contributions in one way or another in all of our professional undertakings and your friendship over the years and in most cases, decades.

A special thanks to Dr. Janil Puthucheary, Senior Minister of State, Ministry of Communications and Information, for gracing the book launch on 25 May 2022.

Last but not least, this book would not have been possible without the support of my wife, Mala, for putting up with me while I juggled the writing of this book in the face of my other ongoing professional and civic commitments.

Prologue

RAJU CHELLAM

The year 1991 has a special place in the history of computing. On 6 August 1991, Tim Berners-Lee, a scientist at the CERN European Partial Physics Laboratory in Geneva, Switzerland, launched the first web page, giving birth to the World Wide Web. On 25 August 1991, a geek from Finland, Linus Torvalds, introduced the first Linux and the Linux kernel. It was also in 1991 that a Canadian programmer, James Gosling, led a team comprising Mike Sheridan and Patrick Naughton to initiate the Java language project. Incidentally, Dr. Berners-Lee was knighted by Queen Elizabeth II for his pioneering work in 2004.

Java was initially designed for interactive television, but it was too advanced for the digital cable TV industry. After an oak tree that remained outside his office, Dr. Gosling wanted to call the new language, Oak. But Oak was already a trademark by Oak Technologies, a US supplier of semiconductor chips. Dr. Gosling and his team brainstormed other names, including DNA, Silk, and Ruby. Dr. Gosling decided on Java while having coffee near his office – made with Indonesian Java beans.

On 23 January 1996, JavaSoft, the newly formed operating company of Sun Microsystems, announced that the Java 1.0 programming environment was available for download at http://java.sun.com. "Java's write-once-run-anywhere (WORA) capability along with its easy accessibility have propelled the software and Internet communities to embrace it as the de facto standard for writing applications for complex networks," said Alan Baratz,

JavaSoft's newly appointed President. "We're delighted to invite developers to download Java 1.0 immediately and start building the next killer application."

Java did become a "killer app" that would revolutionise computer programming. And James Gosling, born in 1955 in Calgary, Alberta, Canada, has been known fondly as "Dr. Java" since then. Incidentally, he was named a Fellow of the Computer History Museum for Java's conception, design, and implementation, in 2019.

The "Sun" Shines

Major web browsers soon enabled Java applets to run within web pages. Arthur van Hoff rewrote the compiler in Java to comply with the Java 1.0 language specifications. Suddenly, there was a massive spike in demand for Java programmers worldwide. The sun was shining on Sun.

During this heady period, a young and ambitious software engineer, Anton Ravindran, joined Sun Microsystems in Singapore. He had cut his teeth at Computer Associates Inc. at Las Colinas, Irving, Texas, and IBM Labs in Roanoke, Texas. "I was in product development when collaborative software, later called Groupware, was conceptualised and developed on the IBM OS2 platform," he said. "Later, in Singapore, I was responsible for business development at Singalab, a joint venture by IBM and the NCB (National Computer Board)."

Dr. Anton seized the opportunity and jumped on the Java bandwagon. "I left Singalab to join Sun and was responsible for managing the training and education business for Sun, Asia South," he reminisced. "That was a vast region, including all of ASEAN and South Asia and the network of scores of authorised training partners. Sun was pushing Java to the world. We helped train thousands of Java developers and established a huge network of Sun partners in the region, including tertiary institutions." The efforts paid off. In 1998, Dr. Anton won the President's Club Award by Sun Microsystems.

Dr. Anton started with tech before venturing into "technopreneurship". One colleague who remembers those early days is Benny Wong, "Dr. Anton and I were colleagues at Sun Microsystems back in 1998," he said. "He was heading the Java and Solaris training and education unit as part of Sun Enterprise Services when Java was initially introduced to this part of the world. Later, he was my CEO at Genovate in 2007, a company he founded, to promote SAP training, among other solutions and services."

Mr. Wong resigned due to family-related issues and later joined Hewlett-Packard as Director, Asia Pacific and Japan. "I received a bouquet and a teddy bear to my family with a message – 'Get well soon' – followed by a phone call from Dr. Anton," Mr. Wong recollected. "I didn't expect such warmth. Despite all the hours he put in for work, he still had time to show concern for others. I thought this was a man who values friendship. He is always forthcoming, informative, knowledgeable and polite. It was a business he ran very successfully and was growing it super-fast. He was a man in a hurry with many appointments and people to meet, but you couldn't really tell from the surface. He was always composed, warm and professional. I found him very hardworking, articulate, approachable, knowledgeable, respectful, always very positive and pleasant to meet with."

Another is Mayur Raja; he has known Dr. Anton for 25 years now. He was then a technical specialist and IBM middleware professional transferred from IBM UK Labs to Singalab. "Dr. Anton and I often worked late in the office, and he was kind to give me a lift home on most days," Mr. Raja noted. "We used to discuss business strategies and opportunities during the ride home. Dr. Anton had some great ideas, and it was inevitable that he would become a successful technopreneur."

Mr. Raja said Dr. Anton would "aggressively pursue and win business opportunities for numerous development teams in the company. I worked closely with him on getting leads and meeting with CEOs and CIOs of leading companies in the banking, technology, and airline industries. With his excellent negotiation skills, he could secure many lucrative business deals for the company."

Mr. Raja continues to work in IBM Labs UK, where he has been for 35 years. What does he remember from his time in Singapore? "I recall Dr. Anton and his wife's generosity when they invited us to their house to meet their parents. We enjoyed delicious food whilst sitting in their garden. This was the first and only house with a garden we visited while in Singapore. We were also very touched when Dr. Anton and his wife brought gifts for our first daughter, born in Singapore."

Training Talent

The itch to strike out on his own began to take shape in 1998. The market for specialised IT training was soaring. "I found my niche and nabbed it," Dr. Anton explained. "In 1999, I decided to take a plunge and co-founded Genovate as a holding company. While there, I set up RapidStart and Knowledge Window Asia-Pacific as subsidiaries. I also acquired SAP Learning Solutions Inc. (a joint venture of SAP Asia-Pacific and RWD, US) to boost Genovate's growth.

How did the name Genovate come about? It's an amalgamation of "genesis" and "innovation". The company developed numerous innovative products, including ezGems, a scalable ERP solution. It acquired a knowledge management tool when it bought InfoPak from SAP Asia and its US-based joint-venture partner, RWD.

"From the onset, we embraced building sustainable businesses despite the futuristic model touted during the dotcom days," Dr. Anton was quoted in *The Business Times* on 6 November 2006. "Our commitment towards making a difference and team spirit are key factors for the company's success."

The training idea was the "killer app" – and Genovate took off like a rocket. It soon added 17 offices in seven countries and joint venture partnerships in Dubai and Saudi Arabia (Genovate Naizak). Genovate opened training centres in 11 cities in India. He needed to beef up staffing in India.

In 2006, a recruitment agency sent him a profile of a potential hire for India. "The agency sent my profile to him for a marketing role. I was told I would be interviewed for an HR role, which surprised both Dr. Anton and me," said Shayari Shaha. "I recall Dr. Anton saying we can still proceed with the interview and see if we can create a suitable HR position."

He did; Ms. Shaha was hired as Genovate India's HR manager in Mumbai in 2007. She stayed with the company until 2010; she now works as a marketing lead at Savills Hong Kong. She still keeps in touch with Dr. Anton.

"Years later, on one of my trips to Singapore, I grumbled about challenges in Hong Kong because I couldn't speak the local language," Ms. Shaha said. "He advised me to invest in learning a new skill. Education never goes to waste, he said. I began learning digital marketing and now have a Master's in it. I still follow his advice on continuous learning, which has helped me scale professionally. He will always be a mentor to me. I am lucky to have learnt from him and grateful to be given the opportunity to work with him."

Genovate's international operations were on a roll. "We will be investing some S\$4 million to expand operations and expect revenue from international ops to contribute 70–80% to the company's total," Dr. Anton told *Channel NewsAsia* in an interview on 6 August 2007. "We expect up to 40% of revenues to come from the Indian market alone."

This was a time of intense activity – and growth. "He would go back to work even in the middle of the night when he had a brainwave, which he needed to work on," Dr. Anton's wife, Mala Ravindran, told me. "He was continuously reinventing himself. Given the constant churn in tech, he simply could not stop. He always made sure he stepped in tandem with the fast-paced changes in the world of ICT. I think that contributed to his success."

Ms. Mala was born in Singapore. Her grandfather had emigrated to Singapore as a young lad from Sri Lanka and was a District Surveyor in what was then Malaya. Her father, who had studied in Raffles Institution, Singapore, was a school principal; her mother was a teacher. Ms. Mala gave credit to Dr. Anton's father, who was the Chief Surveyor in Bahrain, and had also lived and worked in other countries. "He inspired confidence and had a never-say-die attitude, which Dr. Anton also continues to uphold," she said.

Ms. Mala is a lawyer of standing with 30 years of experience. Upon being called to the Bar in the UK, she was associated with the Chambers of Edward Lyons QC in London and worked on criminal cases – including white-collar crime – before returning to Singapore, worked for local law firms and joint law venture firms and as a partner, for more than 25 years. She currently runs her own firm under a group practice structure in association with other lawyers and handles a myriad of general practice litigation and corporate work. She is also a Commissioner for Oaths and a Notary Public.

Ms. Mala is impressed with her husband's work ethic. "Over the last three decades, I accompanied him on many trips he had to make to the US, Europe and Asia. Toronto and London were frequent haunts, as he had relatives living there. Other cities like Krakow, Amsterdam, Frankfurt, Dubai, Amman, Muscat, and Tel Aviv were opportunistic work-related visits. Anton liked to meet like-minded IT folk or speak at guest lectures, whether at a Canadian University or as a visiting professor at the University of Bedfordshire or to explore professional alliances."

What about Asia-Pacific? "We also visited Hong Kong, Bangkok, Colombo, Sydney, Melbourne, Adelaide, Malaysia and various cities in India, amongst others," she added. "Most times, it was where he spoke at conferences, delivered guest lectures, or had to attend business meetings. Even an originally planned relaxing vacation or time with family would often be converted into a working holiday, as he could never say no to a prospective contact whom he could learn from, grow the business or obtain fresh insights."

Sun Whye Mun, a director at SAP, met Dr. Anton in 2003 when he was with Genovate as its co-founder and CEO and has since remained in touch. Some years later, when Mr. Sun moved to Microsoft as its Director, Dr. Anton's RapidStart worked with him to offer solutions on Microsoft Navision.

In 2005, Genovate acquired SAPLS (SAP Learning Systems). This opened ten countries in the Asia-Pacific for Genovate to deliver SAP learning solutions. This was in addition to its ongoing operations in the region where SAP training and solutions were being provided.

Dr. Anton's management style covered macro and micro aspects. "In macro-mode, Dr. Anton set up strong business metrics relevant during that time," Mr. Sun, now General Manager of Crayon Singapore, said. "As SAP was in demand in the 2000s, talent development and training on SAP was skyrocketing. Dr. Anton set up a network of organisations across Asia to deliver on this need. In micro-mode, he brought clarity, built capacity, talent and infrastructure to ensure profitable growth."

This devotion to work won Dr. Anton many awards, including two ASME Rotary Entrepreneur of the Year honours in November 2005, given by Guest of Honour Mr. Lim Hng Kiang, then Minister for National Development; and in September 2006, by Guest of Honour Mr. S Iswaran, then Minister of Trade and Industry.

In 2006, he was bestowed with two other awards – Indian Entrepreneur of Singapore Award (Large Enterprise category) by Guest of Honour Mr. Wong Kan Seng, then Deputy Prime Minister and Minister for Home Affairs; and the Enterprise50 Award by Guest of Honour Mr. Lee Yi Shan, then Minister of State at the Ministry of Trade and Industry.

In 2007, Singapore's then-President, Mr. S R Nathan, who was the Guest of Honour at the ceremony, presented Dr. Anton with the Indian Entrepreneur of the Year Award under the large enterprise category. Another Enterprise50 Award was given by Guest of Honour Mr. Ronnie Tay, CEO of Infocomm Development Authority (IDA), in 2007.

In 2005, at the eighth GOPIO (Global Organisation of People of Indian Origin) international convention in Singapore, Dr. Anton was presented with the GOPIO Business Leadership Award. GOPIO was established in 1989 in New York and is a non-partisan entity that brings together the Indian diaspora for the betterment of the Indian community at large.

RapidStart had tied up with Microsoft for its Navision ERP solutions for the retail sector. RapidStart's business flourished in Singapore, Malaysia, Brunei, Bangladesh, and Sri Lanka. It won business from brands like Popular Bookstores and Bengawan Solo in Singapore, Grameenphone in Bangladesh, Odell in Sri Lanka, and FocusPoint and Constant Pharmacy in Malaysia.

And Knowledge Window offered bachelor's and master's degree programmes in partnership with tertiary institutions in Australia, Britain, and the US, focusing on ICT, specifically ERP.

In end-December 2000, software engineer Dr. Sonal Modi joined Genovate. "Dr. Anton hired me from India and gave me the best opportunity of my life," she said. "It was my first overseas work experience. I was tasked to deliver tech learning sessions for our customers in Singapore. It took me a year to understand his leadership style. He was a hard taskmaster, a demanding boss who focused on quality and on-time delivery."

Dr. Modi, who has a doctorate in management, received multiple opportunities to hone her skills at Genovate, including software development, SAP consultancy and driving off-campus programmes. She left Genovate in 2007 and is currently the Vice President of Enterprise Technology Learning at Mastercard.

"Both my kids were born in Singapore; we bought our own house, for which the company lent me money," she said. "I resigned due to a personal exigency. Dr. Anton did not accept my resignation. He did not speak with me for a few days. He valued my contributions and discussed options to retain me. To my surprise, he organised a farewell function at the Harry's pub and rewarded me with a generous parting bonus. I was touched."

Dr. Modi praised Dr. Anton as a visionary leader, a disciplined individual and one who walks the talk. "I directly reported to him as a Technology Facilitator and was delivering technology learning sessions for customers across Singapore," she said. "Under his mentoring, I received many opportunities to work as a developer, SAP HR Consultant, and programme manager. I got diversified roles within Genovate. I served the company for seven years. I have worked with him and have known him for 15 years now."

Her assessment? "Dr. Anton is a dignified leader, methodical, inspiring, and a visionary. Today I lead my team like he used to lead me, and I can make a difference to so many of them. He is very particular about work deliverables, customer-centricity and honesty at work; these are non-negotiables, and that has always inspired me about him as a leader. He is well-read and tech-savvy and leads from the front. He dwells deeper into business decisions, has the pulse of his staff, and has an eye for detail. He is a mentor and a staunch well-wisher. He is humble enough to regularly stay in touch with me, check on my well-being and professional growth, exchange festive pleasantries, and stay connected after many years. Means a lot to me."

Another employee who joined during this time – from the US – was Jeffrey Allan, who is currently Chairman and CEO of Echo Ridge Corp and Deputy District Staff Officer at the International Affairs Directorate at the US Coast Guard. "Dr. Anton and I first met in July 2001 when he interviewed me for the business development director role," he said. "Some 21 years later, we still typically communicate every month or two. Apart from his visits to the US, I've travelled to Singapore and met with him over the years."

What were his impressions of working at Genovate? "Dr. Anton has been one of my professional mentors. I credit him with instilling in me the concept of operational efficiency and continual process improvement," Mr. Allan noted. "Over the years in different roles and companies, I've been able to reach out to him on frequent occasions for advice about the best way to handle things in various situations – from dealing with 8-figure venture capitalist deals to structuring equity incentive packages for key executives."

How would he describe Dr. Anton's management style? "Entrepreneurial and something of a renegade compared to what one would expect to find in the button-down corporate world," Mr. Allan observed. "That was refreshing and necessary, especially within a high-growth tech startup environment. Dr. Anton did a good job mixing strategic planning with tactical execution. His tenacity with team, partners and customers demonstrated that numerous corporate objectives could be achieved through a certain force of will and determined leadership."

Those were some reasons why WhiteRock, part of a Temasek-linked fund, was an early investor in Genovate. That helped the company scale rapidly and brought new solutions to the market. "Genovate and Rapid-Start introduced many software products, including EzPay and ezHR," Dr. Anton said. "WhiteRock decided to exit Genovate in 2008. So did I. It was time to look at new niches to nab."

Going Global

This was also when open-source solutions, pioneered by Linus Torvalds, began to take off. Mozilla launched the Firefox browser in April 2003. The

WordPress content management system debuted in May 2003. Ubuntu, a user-friendly version of Linux, was rolled out in 2004. Git, the open-source distribution system created by Mr. Torvalds himself, debuted in 2005. Chromium, the forerunner of Google Chrome, was released in 2008, as was Google's signature mobile platform, Android. Open source was the way forward.

In 2008, Dr. Anton set up GICT (Global ICT) to train professionals in emerging technologies on the open-source platform. GICT's Chairman was Professor Stephen Martin, Australia's former Speaker of Parliament and currently Chairman, Bank of China (Australia). "Technology driven by digitisation has unravelled new paradigms, including education, research, and publications," Dr. Martin said. "Since inception in 2008, GICT has dedicated itself to promoting R&D as well as training and certification in ICT."

GICT pioneered content based on open-source technologies in cloud computing, Big Data, data science, IoT, AI, and machine learning. The courses are co-funded by IMDA for Singaporeans and mapped to the NICF (National Infocomm Competency Framework). "Currently, GICT's ICT certification programmes are offered in the region through its partner network," Dr. Martin stated. "These programmes are offered in classrooms and online. We have trained and certified thousands of ICT professionals."

In October 2013, Dr. Madhan Kumar joined GICT as a Principal Consultant and was promoted to Assistant Director three months later. "The demand was huge; we expanded rapidly," Dr. Kumar said. "Our service offerings jumped from three to ten. We expanded from Singapore to Oman, Jordan, Malaysia and the Philippines. My best years of professional growth and leadership learning were under Dr. Anton's supervision."

Dr. Kumar is currently Associate Vice President of Cloud, AI and Patents at Accenture (Innovation Hub); he has been granted 25 patents so far. "I still remember the conversation I had with Dr. Anton when I shared my initial views on IoT and its growth potential. Our discussions lasted for several days," he reminisced. "As a result of that discussion, GICT became the first in Singapore to deliver training and certification programmes in IoT-based open-source technologies. We delivered programs on IoT to university and polytechnic professionals and organisations such as Singtel, NCS,

DSTA, and Mindef. I adore his leadership qualities. He is a hard-hitting boss with tight deadlines. At the same time, he knows how to reward his employees at the right time."

Another recruit was Dr. Rashmi Sinha, a former faculty at NTU (Nanyang Technological University). She joined GICT in 2017 as a principal trainer and Director of Research and Publications. "Dr. Anton taught me how high expectations lead to performance and excellence," she said. "He believed in diversity and inclusion. We had a diverse culture at the workplace, and everybody was expected to perform their best without bias about race or ethnicity. Performance and persistence mattered most."

Dr. Rashmi, who now works as a data scientist in the US, said Dr. Anton exuded positivity and rarely showed his softer side. "He would express how much he cared for the professional growth of his employees and went the extra mile to ensure their mental and professional well-being," she added. "He would ask HR to ensure employees were well taken care of and often compensated staff in financial crisis. He is a visionary and a passionate institution builder and has an excellent understanding of tech and the business landscape. He has mentored several IT professionals and executives in their careers. He is a perfectionist and expects the same level of perfection from everyone around him."

Another ex-employee of NTU was Mr. Jayven Yu; he joined GICT in 2017. "I was a fresh graduate, eager to learn, and delighted to have found a mentor and guide in Dr. Anton," Mr. Yu said. "I got vital insights after being rotated in sales, marketing, business development, and programme management. It gave me a bird's eye view of the training business." The youthful Mr. Yu left in 2019 to join ATD Solution to focus on enterprise architecture sales and enhance his career by bringing valuable training experience from his days at Genovate.

The year 2016 was memorable for various reasons, the most significant being Mr. Barack Obama's last term as President of the United States. On 2 August 2016, Mr. Obama and Singapore Prime Minister Mr. Lee Hsien Loong stepped out on the White House lawns where more than 2,000 people were waiting to greet them. Mr. Lee was in the US at the invitation of Mr. Obama to celebrate 50 years of diplomatic relations and enhance the US-Singapore bilateral strategic partnership. As the two leaders stood on a purpose-built stage, the military band played the Singapore national anthem – and a 19-gun salute was fired.

"We're collaborating to jumpstart greater digital innovation, including R&D into technology and data to prove and promote Smart Cities concepts that can improve the daily lives of our citizens," Mr. Obama announced. "We'll do more to connect our vibrant start-up communities so that an engineer in Singapore can collaborate more easily with an entrepreneur in Silicon Valley or Austin, Texas."

In 2015, the US and Singapore signed the Enhanced Defence Cooperation Agreement, which expanded cooperation into humanitarian assistance, disaster relief, cyber-defence, and counterterrorism. "We also share an interest in Smart Cities, so we discussed how cities can use technology to tackle problems from healthcare to transportation to delivery of public services," Mr. Lee said. "There's a lot of interest from companies on both sides. Underpinning the ties between the two countries are the friendships and the relationships. Thousands of American students study and work in Singapore. Thousands of Singaporeans study and work in America."

In August 2016, a new niche opened for Dr. Anton. In January of that year, Mr. Nidal Bitar had taken over as CEO of the IT Association of Jordan. "I wanted to introduce certifications related to emerging technologies, and I searched online for the right organisation in Singapore to help us," Mr. Bitar said. "I found GICT and sent an email expressing an interest in exploring cooperation. Dr. Anton responded immediately. This led to an agreement with GICT to provide their high-level professional certification programmes. We started to conduct several programmes in Jordan which the participants highly praised."

Mr. Bitar said that Dr. Anton is a great supporter of Jordan and had a significant impact on the ICT sector in Jordan. "Due to his expertise, I believe Dr. Anton is a great asset to the global professional community in emerging technologies, and I wish him all the best," Mr. Bitar said.

Dr. Anton was invited to speak at a conference on "Transforming Societies and Enabling Digital Economies for Smart Nations" in Amman on

29 August 2016. He was also a keynoter at the MENA (Middle East and North Africa) ICT Forum – the largest in the region – on 9 November. King Abdullah II inaugurated it.

Incidentally, King Abdullah II bin Al-Hussein, born on 30 January 1962, has been the country's monarch since February 1999. The King is well-regarded locally and internationally for maintaining Jordanian stability, promoting interfaith dialogue and a moderate understanding of Islam.

The Jordan story turned full circle in June 2019 when a business delegation, led by the King, visited Singapore.

"I was part of that delegation. Dr. Anton provided tremendous generosity and support to me during this visit," Mr. Bitar said. "On June 29, we signed trade agreements in the presence of two Ministers from Jordan and Singapore's Minister for Trade, Mr. Chan Chun Sing."

At least six memorandums of understanding were signed that day, with the Jordan Chamber of Commerce, Jordan Chamber of Industry, Singapore Manufacturing Federation, and IT companies Falcons Soft and Int@j.

King Abdullah II noted that Jordan's first FTA (free trade agreement) in Asia was with Singapore in 2005.

"The global trade environment is under stress. It is important for like-minded countries like Jordan and Singapore to continue working together to uphold and update the global trading environment," Mr. Chan said at the press conference. "Singapore also wants to work with Jordan on energy generation and management. We are surrounded by neighbours with a lot of natural resources, but we ourselves don't have much, particularly in the energy sector."

Community Care

The Jordan trip with Dr. Anton was an eye-opening experience for Teng Theng Dar, the then-CEO of the SBF (Singapore Business Federation) and Vice-Chairman of SBF's Middle East Business Group. In March 2008, Mr. Teng was appointed Singapore's non-resident Ambassador to Oman. He was also Chairman of APEC Business Advisory Council during the APEC Year Singapore in 2009.

"It was during this trip I discovered that while in Singapore we were pulling our hair to hire programmers and ICT professionals, Jordan had the opposite challenge – a good pool of programmers and professionals but not enough job opportunities," Mr. Teng said. "With modern technology and connectivity, I wondered why the gaps could not be filled and exploited."

Mr. Teng and Dr. Anton co-founded the Asia Entrepreneurs Exchange, a not-for-profit entity to facilitate collaboration across ASEAN. They also supported the Industry Guru Series – a sharing and learning initiative for PMETs (professionals, managers, executives, technicians) set up by the PA (People's Association) in Singapore.

"Dr. Anton is a member of PA's Digital Talent Advisory Panel," Mr. Teng said. "We conducted a series of sharing sessions – both in-person and virtual, since the pandemic started, under the PA platform. My impression is that he's an expert in his field, conducts himself respectfully and courteously, and pays attention to detail."

Giving back to the community that nurtured him has always been an agenda item. Since 2012, Dr. Anton has been an executive member of the SMF (Singapore Manufacturing Federation) and its largest industry group, EEAI (Electric, Electronic, and Allied industry). He also served as Vice-Chair of SMF's EEAI for six years and has been the Chairman of ICT and Technology since 2017.

Set up in 1937, the SMF is the largest body representing the interests of manufacturing and related industries. It now drives digitalisation, business transformation and innovation-led productivity for the manufacturing sector. The SMF currently has 5,000 corporate members, including SMEs (small and medium enterprises), multinationals and affiliates. Corporate members are categorised into ten industry groups.

Another reputable body is the BCS (British Computer Society), which conferred a Fellowship on Dr. Anton in 2013 based on his academic credentials and demonstrable professional experience. The BCS was formed in 1957 when the London Computer Group merged with an association of scientists. It now has 60,000 members in 150 countries and a wider community of business leaders, educators, practitioners and policy-makers.

Another pivotal body is the SCS (Singapore Computer Society). Dr. Anton first joined the SCS BCC (Business Continuity Chapter) on its exco before taking over as Chair of the Cloud SIG (Special Interest Group). The SIG became the Cloud Chapter in 2016 with Dr. Anton as its first President, which he currently continues to head.

"Several initiatives were spawned and have grown under Dr. Anton's leadership of the Cloud Chapter," said SCS Executive Director Jennifer Ong. "That includes the annual Cloud Conference, which is now in its fourth edition. As well as the Cloud Computing BoK (Body of Knowledge), the de facto resource on competencies and best practices."

Ms. Ong did her Bachelor's in Business Administration at NUS. She has been in the ICT industry for three decades – much of it as ED of SCS, which she joined in 1991. "SCS was established in 1967. When I first joined SCS, we had about 3,000 members," Ms. Ong told me. "We now have 51,000 members – a 17-fold increase – and a dozen Chapters and four SIGs."

SCS won the Community Spirit Gold Award given by the National Council for Social Service in 2020 for active participation in the community. "Dr. Anton has been part of this growth, focusing on advancing SCS, participating in many outreach activities," Ms. Ong said. "He is currently serving his sixth term as President of the Cloud Computing Chapter, a fitting testament to his capabilities and service to the ICT community."

Since 2004, Dr. Anton has been a Taman Jurong CCC (Citizens Consultative Committee) member under the PA (People's Association). The PA was formed in July 1960 to help foster racial harmony and social cohesion. There are now 100 CCCs spread across Singapore, with community service at their core. Dr. Anton is a former member of the NIAC (National Internet Advisory Committee) and is currently on the PA TAP (Talent Advisory Panel).

Which is the next niche to nab? AI has moved from hype to hope. Governments and enterprises will invest up to US$110 billion on AI-related solutions and services by 2024, double the US$37.5 billion they spent in 2019, according to IDC Corp. That is a CAGR (compound annual growth rate) of 25% during the period. Gartner Inc. estimated that by 2025, the 10% of companies that establish AI and ML best practices would generate at least three times more value than the 90% of enterprises that do not.

In January 2019, the WEF (World Economic Forum) launched GAIA (Global AI Action Alliance) to accelerate inclusive, transparent and trusted AI adoption. "AI holds the promise of making organisations 40% more efficient by 2035, unlocking an estimated US$14 trillion in new economic value," the WEF stated.

In 2019, Dr. Anton founded SmartLaw, a firm focused on legal tech. "It includes key functional modules such as AI for E-Discovery and Sentencing Predictor," he explained. "The E-Discovery module leverages DL NLP (natural language processing) algorithms trained on a large corpus of historical data for criminal law and divorce matters. Our proprietary models use semantic analysis to extract the most relevant precedents or verdicts in seconds. The Sentencing Predictor leverages ML algorithms built on previous verdicts to predict sentencing outcomes for criminal and divorce matters. Our trained ML models analyse the complex relationship among the indicators provided to predict the likely sentencing outcomes in seconds."

He also sits on the boards of other AI-based startups, including a firm initially set up as SAKS Analytics and Veracity AI. He's also an Executive Advisor at AIM (Asia Institute of Mentoring) and a co-founder and director of Asia Entrepreneurs Exchange. He chaired IMDA's Cloud Computing Working Group from 2015 to 2016 and has been a Member of IMDA's Cloud Computing Standards Technical Committee since 2018 and the MTCS (Multi-Tiered Cloud Security) Working Group from August to December 2020. He was also a Mentor at the NUS Entrepreneurship Centre (2005–2007), currently a mentor at NTU for the Business and Computing Programme since 2020 and Chair of the Technical Committee for Work-Study Diploma in Cloud Management at the Institute of Technical Education from November 2020 to January 2022.

Is there a common thread linking the various projects? "They tie in well since I'm also involved in academia – at the University of Bedfordshire Institute for Research in Applicable Computing, at the Birla Institute of Technology and Science at Dubai, and the Bina Nusantara University in Indonesia," Dr. Anton said.

Finally, what keeps him motivated to keep going? I put this question to his better half. "A deep faith in the power of doing good," Ms. Mala replied.

"As he has often confessed, his strong faith in God is the secret of his success. We attend Sunday Mass, no matter which part of the world we're in. He starts and ends his day by thanking the Lord for everything. We visited Jerusalem in September 2019, before the pandemic struck. It was a blessing to have had the opportunity to visit the Holy Land – to heed the Call of the Lord – for his gifts, for which we are eternally grateful, for what some accomplish in 14 days was completed in four days. That's Anton."

* * *

Raju Chellam is the Chief Editor of the AI Ethics and Governance Body of Knowledge (AI E&G BoK), an initiative by the Singapore Computer Society and Infocomm Media Development Authority. He was conferred as an SCS Fellow in 2018. He was formerly the BizIT Editor of *The Business Times*, Singapore, and was previously with Dell and Hewlett-Packard. His book, *Organ Gold*, published by Straits Times Press in 2018, is about the illegal trade in human organs on the dark web.

CHAPTER 1

Introduction: The Past, Present and Future of AI

"Artificial intelligence would take off on its own and redesign itself at an ever-increasing rate. Humans, who are limited by slow biological evolution, couldn't compete and would be superseded. AI is likely to be the best or worst thing to happen to humanity."
— Dr. Stephen Hawking

Is AI the next big thing? Will there be an intelligence explosion? Will a "digital brain" defeat the "human brain"? Is the idea of creating machines with human-like senses (able to see, hear, smell, taste or touch) far-fetched?

In recent years, Artificial Intelligence (AI) has become an intriguing topic of interest, and there are ongoing fascinating debates about AI, its impact and future. The World Wide Web was launched in 1990, which "flattened" the world, followed by the introduction of the iPhone in 2007, accelerating the process we now know as digitisation, leading to widespread digital transformation. These technologies, which some considered outlandish before their introduction, have revolutionised the world. A decade later, AI has begun to revolutionise and usher in a new era: an intelligent age driven by Big Data, Internet of Things (IoT) and 5G technologies.

According to reports, the number of smartphone users in the world today is 6.65 billion, or 83.72% of the world's population. Not only is there astonishing growth in terms of internet penetration, but the frequency of access by each user is also growing exponentially. The amount of data created, stored, and processed in the last three years has doubled from 33 zettabytes in 2018 to 64 zettabytes in 2020 and is projected to reach a stunning 200 zettabytes by 2025. Just 12 years ago, in 2010, we generated only 2 zettabytes of data. In the now ubiquitously interconnected world, the proliferation of data is fuel for advances in AI.

We are already living in the era of AI, and that this will become far more widespread in the next few years is a racing certainty. Everything that humanity has achieved is a product of human intelligence, so combining our intelligence with artificial intelligence can advance civilisation more than ever before in history. This introductory chapter discusses the origins and advances of AI over the past five decades, the drivers of AI evolution, its current development, and the future of AI. In the ensuing chapters, this book will explore the impact of AI in different sectors of industry and society, and present several illuminating case studies.

The Rise of AI

"I see AI and machine learning as augmenting human cognition a la Douglas Engelbart. There will be abuses and bugs, some harmful, so we need to be thoughtful about how these technologies are implemented and used, but, on the whole, I see these as constructive."
— Vint Cerf, "Father of the Internet", Vice President and Chief Internet Evangelist at Google.

Every day, an avalanche of articles in newspapers and magazines, even in the tabloids, tries to address the catchall term "AI" as anything to do with machine-level intelligence, which has become all the rage. Undoubtedly, it has attracted global attention from researchers, academics, businesses, the open-source community of developers, and even governments worldwide.

School-going children are building AI applications. Economies like China are at the forefront of the AI revolution, and it is reported that people in China use their smartphones to pay for their purchases 50 times more often than Americans.

The next-generation mobile device is more than likely to be at the intersection of AI and today's smartphones, which may signal the end of the smartphone era. Such devices will have the ability to understand human language and are likely to have Brain-Computer Interface (BCI). "Recent advances in artificial intelligence promise to fundamentally redefine human-machine interaction. We will soon have the ability to relay our thoughts and ideas to computers using the same natural, conversational language we use to communicate with people. Over time these new language capabilities will revolutionize what it means to have a digital experience," said Mustafa Suleyman, founder of Inflection AI (as cited in Ryan, 2022). This will dramatically change how we communicate, collaborate, learn, deal and work – it will impact our lives once again. AI will be a key component of the metaverse when it happens, along with augmented reality (AR), virtual reality (VR), and mixed reality (MR) extending the virtual representation of reality.

In the years to come, we will begin to interact with businesses in the metaverse as we do today for all sorts of transactions and activities via websites and on our mobile devices, except that the virtual experience will be far more real – a convergence of real and virtual worlds. From an economic perspective, the figures are staggering. PwC's recent global AI study predicts that AI's contribution to the global economy will exceed $15.7 trillion by 2030, i.e. more than the economic output of China and India combined.

The First Industrial Revolution occurred during the 18th century when steam engines replaced the horse and human power. The Second Industrial Revolution took place from the latter part of the 18th century to the early 19th century, introducing combustion engines and electricity, which gave us the assembly line, high-volume industrial production, and high mass consumption. The Third Industrial Revolution began in the 1980s and allowed information to be captured in digital format and to be cost-effectively processed, transmitted, and digitally stored. Many have suggested that AI is the principal contributor to the Fourth Industrial Revolution driven by Machine Learning (ML), Deep Learning (DL), robotics, speech recognition, image recognition, augmented reality, and virtual reality, amongst others. There were nearly two centuries between the first and second industrial revolutions, but it has been hardly a few decades between the third and fourth. Growth is now exponential, as opposed to earlier industrial revolutions, which were linear. This is the dawn of a new era where man and intelligent machines have begun to work in concert.

What is driving it? One of the key drivers is the increase in computing power. We all know that computing power has been growing exponentially. But do we realise the magnitude of it? In the last five decades, the processing power of a Central Processing Unit (CPU) has grown by a trillion-fold. CPU power is measured in Floating Operations Per Second (FLOPS). Back in 1965, only 65 transistors could fit onto the world's most complex computer chip. Today, more than 10 billion transistors can fit onto the same chip. And this trend is not about to slow down and will only accelerate as we have recently started work on quantum computing. The basic unit of conventional computing is the bit. The more bits a computer has, the more calculations it can perform; in other words, the more powerful it is. In quantum computing, the basic unit is known as a quantum bit or qubit. Bits behave linearly. But qubits double computing power – a multiplier effect. For instance, a 100-qubit quantum computer could perform a trillion calculations and is 100 million times faster than any classical computer (binary computing). These numbers are too big for us to even begin to comprehend.

Quantum computing will open the door for the next generation of AI algorithms and applications to solve complex problems which require a vast amount of computational power. Binary computing – with just two bits and three Boolean algebraic operators (AND, OR and NOT) – has delivered progress and made a significant impact on the world, which has come to be commonly known as digitisation. As classic binary computing reaches its limits, quantum computing is likely to unleash the new frontiers of computing and the development of AI. NASA and Google are some of the pioneers in this space. Though it is in its early stages, quantum computing, when ready, will supercharge the advances in AI and present significant opportunities for innovation and next-generation AI applications. Another technology that will supercharge developments in AI in the very near future is the 5G network. This will lead to a proliferation of sensors generating real-time and high-speed data, the much-needed fuel for AI.

We are living amidst an unprecedented and explosive growth of AI. In the past few years, there has been groundbreaking technological progress, and more sophisticated applications are being introduced rapidly. On the back of this, there is growing evidence that the quest to develop more advanced and "Strong AI" has been gaining significant momentum, leveraging the advances in AI technologies and complex algorithms. This has led to provocative views in the recent past from the likes of Elon Musk and Bill Gates about the risk posed by Strong AI and the claim that it will be the "biggest existential threat to humanity". These comments in the press and media have generated interest and debate beyond the scientific community about Strong AI, also known as Artificial General Intelligence (AGI).

> "The least scary future I can think of is one where we have at least democratized AI because if one company or small group of people manages to develop godlike digital superintelligence, they could take over the world. At least when there's an evil dictator, that human is going to die. But for an AI, there would be no death. It would live forever. And then you'd have an immortal dictator from which we can never escape."
> — Elon Musk

AI is vast and fast developing with several subsets. It touches all facets of industry, economy, society, and lives. As a consequence, there is burgeoning interest, growing investments and some level of apprehension. What are the implications and ramifications of future AI? Will it supersede human intelligence? Will it acquire cognitive skills and exhibit emotions that it currently lacks? Will superintelligence happen in our lifetime? If so, what are the repercussions? Will superintelligence replace humans or co-exist with us? Will it replace our jobs? Will it create new jobs while replacing old ones? Will it lead to a jobless society where there is plenty of time for leisure, where superintelligent machines can generate wealth for humans? How do we prepare for such an eventuality?

The ongoing advances in AI and other technological developments have given birth to the concept or the hypothesis of "technological singularity" or, as it is more commonly known, "singularity". Proponents of singularity argue that it's inevitable that superintelligent machines will eventually surpass all human (natural) intelligence and will be able to "self-learn", arguably undergo "self-improvement" without human intervention and become "self-aware". Debates about what AI singularity is and what it is not have gained a lot of attention, inevitably leading to a lot of confusion and disagreement. The American philosopher Prof. John Searle has argued that AI will never be the same as human intelligence because AI is a "set of instructions". While he recognises that Deep Blue could execute 2.5 million operations in a split second and defeated the world chess champ Gary Kasparov, Prof. Searle argues that Deep Blue lacks "semantic" capabilities and has only "contextual" capabilities. "It's not able to discern things without extensive human training, and it has a completely different statistical logic for how meaning is made," he said.

Since the very beginning of AI back in 1956, we've made this terrible error, a sort of original sin of the field, to believe that minds are like computers and vice versa. "We assume these things are an analog to human intelligence, and nothing could be further from the truth," says Kate Crawford (2021). Researchers and scientists agree that if AI reaches a point where it can self-learn and improve, it can self-accelerate with respect to its intelligence. Many believe that would be the tipping point as it would defeat the current premise that no matter how intelligent machines are, they are only developed by humans and serve only the purpose they are designed for.

Alarmists argue that the downside of AGI's superintelligence could also have a profoundly negative impact on humanity. SpaceX and Tesla founder Elon Musk has said that AGI is the "biggest existential threat" facing humanity. The late Professor Stephen Hawking said that "the development of full artificial intelligence could spell the end of the human race". Hawking stated that AI could offer "incalculable benefits and risks" such as "technology outsmarting financial markets, out-inventing human researchers, out-manipulating human leaders, and developing weapons we cannot even understand" (Wikipedia).

We humans control the planet today because of our intelligence, not because of our physical size or strength. Who will rule the world if we are no longer more intelligent than AI? These are all captivating practical questions that AI experts and researchers no longer consider as completely science fiction. But sceptics argue that Strong AI is fiction and claim that AGI will certainly not happen in our lifetime, citing previous technological hype.

What is Intelligence? Human Brain vs Digital Brain

"Some people call this artificial intelligence, but the reality is this technology will enhance us. So instead of artificial intelligence, I think we'll augment our intelligence."
— Ginni Rometty, former CEO of IBM

According to Wikipedia, human intelligence is "the intellectual capability of humans, which is marked by complex cognitive feats and high levels of motivation and self-awareness. Higher levels of intelligence are associated with better outcomes in life." The average male brain weighs about 1,325 grams, and the average female brain weighs about 1,144 grams. Interestingly, the ratio of brain weight to body weight plays a pivotal role in determining intelligence levels instead of absolute brain weight. The basic unit by which a human brain works is a neuron and the brain has approximately 100 billion of them. Neurons communicate by generating and sending electrical signals. According to Su-Hyun Han et al. (2018), "Nematodes (commonly known as roundworms) have only 302 neurons and survive well." This is the level of cognitive complexity that can be replicated with today's AI algorithms but Han et al. argue that nematodes can perform much better than the current capabilities of AI.

However, humanity's 2,500 years of supremacy and intelligence have already been challenged and defeated by Google's AlphaGo, IBM's Deep Blue, and IBM's Watson (on the US game show, Jeopardy) in recent years, driven by AI. These are remarkable milestones in human history and testimony to the quest by man to build machines in his own image, part of the ongoing efforts to develop a self-conscious machine that can imitate or exhibit brain/human-like intelligence or even artificial superintelligence (ASI), which still remains in the realms of science fiction. Yet, there has been significant progress and rapid developments, and it is not uncommon for someone who is not an ICT professional to have heard of terms such as Machine Learning (ML), Deep Learning (DL), Natural Language Processing (NLP), object vision, image recognition, speech recognition, reinforcement learning, neural networks, and robotics. These AI technologies have led to many applications and intelligent machines that we use today in our day-to-day chores, including virtual assistants, autonomous vehicles, drones, surgical robots, and chatbots. Among these, AI and ML are probably the most popular buzzwords and often seem to be used interchangeably, leading to some level of confusion. These three terms are discussed in detail in Chapter 2.

Key Historical Milestones of AI

For more than six decades now, AI has gone through several cycles of "boom and bust". In recent years, we have witnessed much progress and a growing number of applications in all spheres and industries. AI is fast becoming pervasive without us consciously realising it.

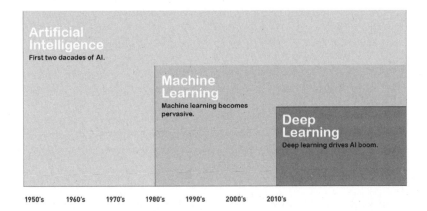

AI in the 1950s

The 1950s was a significant period when research interest in AI picked up initial momentum.

- Claude Shannon, known as the father of Information Theory, published an article on computer programs for playing chess.

- Alan Turing developed and published the "Turing Test" – a proposal to test a machine's ability to think like humans.

- Arthur Samuel developed the first game for playing checkers. This program had the ability to compete with human players.

- John McCarthy introduced the term "Artificial Intelligence" and published a paper at an academic conference at Dartmouth College, Boston, which defined the scope and goal of AI.

- John McCarthy developed LISP, a high-level programming language for AI at the MIT AI labs (founded by John McCarthy and Marvin Minsky).

AI in the 1960s

AI in the 1960s involved the introduction of new AI programming languages, industrial robots, and movies depicting AI-driven virtual assistants (VA).

- In 1961, General Motors deployed Unimate for its assembly line, an industrial robot developed by George Devol to handle tasks that were perceived as risky for humans.

- In 1966, work commenced on the first general-purpose mobile robot known as "Shakey", which could reason about its own actions.

Shakey, which was programmed in LISP, was completed and deployed in 1969.

- In 1968, the sci-fi film *2001: A Space Odyssey* was released, which featured HAL, a heuristically programmed algorithmic computer, which resembles present-day voice assistants like Alexa and Siri.

AI in the 1970s and 1980s

The 1970s–1980s were a slow period with respect to AI research and development, due to reduced funding. This period has come to be known as the "AI winter".

- In 1972, the logic programming language Prolog was developed and implemented in Marseille, France, by Alain Colmerauer with Philippe Roussel. Prolog was one of the first logic programming languages.

- *Star Wars*, directed by George Lucas, was released in 1977 and featured a humanoid robot, C-3PO.

- In 1977, Hans Moravec's Cart, an autonomous vehicle, successfully crossed a chair-filled room without human intervention. The original Stanford Cart was developed at Stanford AI Laboratory, and Moravec rebuilt it with stereo vision capabilities.

- In 1980, Digital Equipment Corporation (DEC) developed an expert system called R1, also known as XCON. This led to a research and investment boom in expert systems which occupied much of the 80s. In the same year, Waseda University in Japan developed WABOT-2, a humanoid. It was able to interact with humans and play music on an electronic organ. It had a camera for its head and five-fingered hands capable of performing precise and delicate movements.

- The first driverless car was introduced in 1986 by Mercedes-Benz. The van was equipped with sensors and cameras and drove up to 55 mph (88 km/h) on empty streets.

AI in the 1990s

Interest in AI began to gain momentum by the end of the 1980s. The new decade was characterised by a range of activities, developments, and advancements that began to transform the field of AI.

- In 1991, US forces deployed DART, an automated logistics planning and scheduling tool, during the Gulf War.

- In 1997, chess Grandmaster and world champion Gary Kasparov was defeated by IBM's Deep Blue.

- In 1998, Prof. Cynthia Breazeal of MIT built the first humanoid, named Kismet, which could display human-like facial expressions. The robot was structured like a human face equipped with eyes, eyelids, eyebrows, ears, and lips.

- The first pet toy robot named Furby was invented in 1998. The following year, Sony introduced AIBO (Artificial Intelligence Robot), which was capable of learning through interactions with humans and its environment.

AI in the New Millennium

In the new millennium, activities in AI exploded with the introduction of more robots, chatbots, virtual assistants, autonomous vehicles, amongst other activities where AI began to "outsmart" humans and defeated them in playing games including chess, Go, and Jeopardy.

- In 2000, Honda released a humanoid named ASIMO (Advanced Step in Innovative Mobility) capable of walking as fast as humans and delivering trays to customers in restaurants. ASIMO was able to recognise moving objects, postures, gestures, their surrounding environment, sounds, and faces, and interacted with humans.

- In 2002, i-Robot released an autonomous vacuum cleaner called Roomba.

- In 2004, NASA leveraged AI technology and developed the robots named Spirit and Opportunity, which could navigate the surface of Mars without human intervention.

- In 2009, Google began to develop autonomous vehicles, and the driverless car passed Nevada's self-driving test five years later in 2014.

- In 2011, IBM Watson beat a human champion in the TV game show Jeopardy, followed by Google Deep Mind's AlphaGo, which beat Go world champion Lee Sedol.

- Several virtual assistants were released during this period, including Apple's Siri in 2011, followed by Alexa by Amazon and Cortana by Microsoft, both in 2014.

- In 2014, an AI algorithm named Eugene Goostman, a humanoid with the persona of a 13-year-old boy, passed the Turing Test and managed to convince 33% of human judges that it was a human.

- In 2018, Alibaba's AI tool scored better than humans in a Stanford University reading and comprehension test comprising 100,000 questions.

- In 2018, NASA and Intel developed an AI-based navigation system to explore planets.

Advances in AI are not limited to applications on planet Earth. AI is increasingly being deployed to explore the origins of the universe and for space exploration. We have explored only 4% of the visible universe, made up of planets, stars, galaxies, and other astronomical objects. In 2003, the Hubble Telescope recorded some of the furthest galaxies, which are 13.2 billion light years away! But leveraging advanced imaging technology, astronomers can potentially discover and begin to understand more about the remaining 96% of the universe. Hubble was a giant leap for astronomy, and the James Webb Space Telescope, which was launched in late 2021, is destined to take this to the next level. This is heralded as "a new cosmic dawn" with the ability to "peer into the universe".

Future potential AI applications include areas such as space mission design and planning, space mining, research on adapting humans to acclimatise themselves for space missions, and a plethora of other opportunities such as space colonisation. An intelligent robot called CIMON-2 (Crew Interactive Mobile Companion) worked alongside two European astronauts on a mission in 2018 to the International Space Station. CIMON-2 leveraged IBM's Watson speech recognition and synthesis software and was able to converse with astronauts and respond to their commands. With the growing number of space missions and satellites, there is more debris in space: abandoned launch vehicles, space mission-related debris, and non-functional spacecraft. This is fast becoming a space hazard. AI can also be used in addressing the challenges of orbital debris.

AI Definitions: "Can Machines Think?"

In his seminal work, "Computing Machinery and Intelligence", published in 1950, British scientist Alan Turing posed the question, "Can machines think?", and introduced a practical test to determine if a machine is intelligent, which has come to be known as the Turing Test. This test enables us to distinguish between a computer and a human text response. In the following years, Stuart Russell and Peter Norvig published one of the leading AI textbooks, titled *Artificial Intelligence: A Modern Approach*. The book outlines four different approaches that define the field of AI, based on the thought process of reasoning (thinking) and the behaviour (acting) of intelligent agents in machines:

1. Thinking humanly
2. Acting humanly
3. Thinking rationally
4. Acting rationally

In its simplest form, AI is a field that combines computer science, mathematics, and statistics, enabling computers to behave with *human-like* intelligence. In other words, AI allows computers to "think" for themselves and extends their ability to "execute" a task intelligently. With respect to AI's ability to think and act *rationally*, this is discussed in the following sections.

The term "AI" was coined by the American computer scientist John McCarthy at a conference at Dartmouth College in 1956. He defined AI as follows: "It is the science and engineering of making intelligent machines, especially intelligent computer programs. It is related to the similar task of using computers to understand human intelligence, but AI does not have to confine itself to methods that are biologically observable."

This is McKinsey's definition: "AI is typically defined as the ability of a machine to perform cognitive functions we associate with human minds, such as perceiving, reasoning, learning, and problem-solving. Examples of technologies that enable AI to solve business problems are robotics and autonomous vehicles, computer vision, language, virtual agents, and machine learning."

And here is IBM's definition: "Any system capable of simulating human intelligence and thought processes is said to have Artificial Intelligence (AI)".

Man vs Machine: Natural Intelligence vs Artificial Intelligence

Alan Turing mooted the idea of machines being able to simulate human beings and to have the ability to do "smart things". AI is the overarching technology that is able to make machines perform tasks that could be considered "intelligent" or "smart". Over the past six decades, AI has evolved, and in recent years it has gained significant momentum driven by Big Data,

IoT and sensors, satellite communication technologies, and open-source technologies.

Will machines be able to replace humans or complement them? This is a hotly debated topic. The short answer is that AI has been replacing some routine and repetitive tasks but will not replace humans with respect to intuition, imagination, and emotions in the foreseeable near future. This is discussed in detail in the following section and other chapters of this book. According to a 2018 study by a Swiss think tank and reported by the World Economic Forum (WEF), AI would replace 75 million jobs by 2022 while also creating 133 million new jobs. These new jobs will require quantitative knowledge in areas such as mathematics and statistics, and expertise in programming, data science, data analytics, data mining and data visualisation, amongst others that are relevant to developing AI algorithms and applications.

Human intelligence is natural and authentic as we are able to imagine and be sensitive to the circumstances and the environment. On the other hand, AI is driven by data to make decisions which are fed into machines, and trained by humans. AI applications and tools are the product of human intelligence based on algorithms intentionally developed and deployed on machines. Human intelligence is analog, whereas AI is digital. Natural intelligence and artificial intelligence are complementary and will co-exist for some time to come. The future workplace will be where machines and man work collaboratively and co-exist side by side. Hence, I feel, AI is a boon to humanity and not a bane as it augments human endeavour by improving accuracy, efficiency, effectiveness, productivity, and quality.

In sum, AI mimics human intelligence and knowledge. At least for now and in the foreseeable future, humans will continue to remain the masters, as we retain the discretion to make decisions as to if, when, what, and how such tools are to develop and to be deployed for specific needs and circumstances. The human brain (*Homo sapiens*), which has evolved over the last 300,000 years, has reportedly increased in size by three times in that time, and has a complex biological structure compared to today's "digital brain", which is still "evolving" and has a history of only six decades.

Categories and Phases of AI

As AI is a fast-evolving technology and a broad concept, there are different trains of thought and definitions, but three critical categories can be defined, based on the AI's capabilities:

1. Artificial Narrow Intelligence (ANI): ANI is also known as "Narrow AI" or "Weak AI". It is all around us today, and it is the only type of AI that we have achieved to date. Examples include autonomous vehicles, facial recognition, speech recognition, drones, robots, personal assistants such as Siri by Apple, Cortana by Microsoft and Alexa by Amazon. Such AI is considered weak or narrow because it operates in controlled environments and is unable to replicate human intelligence although it is able to simulate human behaviour and even perform better than humans. An area of ANI is Deep Learning, where the computer is able to teach itself. Google Deep-Mind teaches itself to play Go and has beaten human champions. We are advancing rapidly towards the final stages of ANI. The following chapters will focus on ANI.

2. Artificial General Intelligence (AGI): It is also referred to as "Strong AI" or "Deep AI" or "Human-level AI" and it doesn't exist today. Prof. Linda Gottfredson (2015) explains AGI as "a very general mental capability that, among other things, involves the ability to reason, plan, solve problems, think abstractly, comprehend complex ideas, learn quickly, and learn from experience". Unlike ANI, AGI is able to think, understand and behave in a manner that is human-like in any scenario. In other words, AGI can mimic human behaviour or human-like intelligence.

If and when AGI comes to be developed, the impact could be profound. The opportunity to develop and deploy AGI-driven machines that could equal the brightest humans will present opportunities to develop solutions to mitigate intractable problems such as climate change, find cures for incurable diseases, prevent pandemics, and save lives and planet Earth.

Is AGI real? The critics argue otherwise. Andrew Ng, an authority in the field of AI, who was part of the "Google Brain" project and served as

Chief Scientist for Chinese search giant Baidu, appealed to "cut out the AGI nonsense" but to allocate resources for research on how today's technology is beginning to impact issues such as "job loss/stagnant wages, undermining democracy, discrimination/bias, wealth inequality". Others such as philosophers Hubert Dreyfus and Jaron Lanier refute the idea that singularity is inevitable, arguing that it is impossible – at least in the next 50 years.

3. Artificial Super Intelligence (ASI): Also known as "Superhuman intelligence", this is still in the realm of science fiction, where issues like immortality and human extinction would become topics of interest and debate. But theoretically, it is the logical progression from AGI or Strong AI. An ASI system or superintelligent agent would be able to exceed all human capabilities, including general wisdom as well as other cognitive, social, and creative skills and capabilities. To achieve this, they need to be able to have cognitive capabilities. The audacious goal of ASI is to develop algorithms for machines to have capabilities like that of a human brain in terms of intelligence, including cognitive skills. This is one of the most cutting-edge endeavours in the realms of science and technology and is comparable to other frontier scientific explorations such as trying to discover and explain the origin of life, the workings of the universe or the structure of matter. There is considerable research and debate on whether and when ASI will supersede humans. Swedish-born philosopher Nick Bostrom of the University of Oxford, who is known for his work on existential risk and superintelligence risks, famously said: "Machine intelligence is the last invention that humanity will ever need to make."

The scientific community remains divided on this as there is a lack of concrete evidence and consensus. Some researchers who believe in the future of ASI predict its arrival as early as 2045, while others project its arrival within this century. Techno-sceptics are also divided, with one group focusing on the evil side of superintelligence, while others dismiss it entirely as science fiction. Designing, codifying, and developing ASI will involve the integration of complex algorithms that are capable of continuous learning from its environment, common sense reasoning, interpretation of perceptions and emotions, and the ability to reason. The current

Deep Learning systems are driven by mathematical models based on a cause-and-effect relationship but are unable to distinguish cause from effects, "such as the idea that the rising sun causes a rooster to crow but not vice versa" (Pearl and Mackenzie, 2018; Lake et al., 2016). We have yet to develop algorithms that can integrate all these components to fully realise ASI, though there has been progress in a few of these areas.

The Four Types or Principles of AI

Most of us have heard of the terms AI, Machine Learning and Deep Learning (which are actually subsets of AI), but may not have realised that there are four distinct types of AI:

1. Reactive AI
2. Limited Memory AI
3. Theory of Mind AI
4. Self-awareness AI

Reactive AI

Reactive AI is the most basic, and as its name implies, its capabilities are limited to using intelligence to react to existing conditions in the world it encounters. Reactive AI doesn't have the capability to learn or conceive from the past or future but perceives and reacts to present conditions and/or situations. However, it can achieve a high level of complexity and reliability.

IBM's supercomputer Deep Blue competing and winning a chess match against the Russian grandmaster and world champion is a classic example of reactive AI. Another excellent example is AlphaGo, developed by Google, which defeated Go champion Lee Sedol in 2016.

Limited Memory AI

Limited Memory AI is characterised by its ability to store previous data and learn from these experiences to make predictions and decisions.

Autonomous vehicles are a good example of this – they are later discussed in this book. There are six steps involved in developing a limited memory AI: (1) Create training data. (2) Develop a Machine Learning model. (3) The ML model must be able to make predictions. (4) The ML model must be capable of receiving human and environmental input. (5) This information must be stored as data. (6) The above five steps must be reiterated as a cycle to reinforce learning.

There are three distinct ML models that are based on limited memory AI: Reinforcement Learning (RL); Long Short-Term Memory (LSTM); and Generative Adversarial Network (GAN).

1. Reinforcement Learning (RL): RL is capable of learning through trial and error to make predictions. As the name implies, in RL, agents are trained based on a reward-and-punishment mechanism. The agent is rewarded for correct moves and punished for wrong ones. As a result of this approach, the agent tries to minimise wrong moves and maximise the right ones.

2. Long Short-Term Memory (LSTM): LSTM leverages historical data to make predictions but views the most recent information as most relevant when making the predictions. There are nearly 5 billion smartphones in our pockets that work a little like our brain, and they are getting faster and more innovative. Importantly, these devices have learning capabilities because of AI-based learning algorithms embedded in them. They also have speech recognition capabilities, which help the algorithms learn through experience.

We use the translate button on FB and Google, and elsewhere. Meta (FB) converts and translates some 5 billion times a day and is growing daily. Every second, more than 50,000 translations happen from one language to another at the click of a mouse. You can ask questions, and Amazon Echo answers them. This is driven by LSTM, which has the capability to learn, think, and respond. Advances in ML and DL algorithms have made limited memory AI possible. With limited memory AI, engines can be automatically trained and updated based on the model behaviour.

Limited memory AI can perform complex classification tasks and use historical data to make predictions. By way of example, self-driving cars use limited memory AI. The algorithms that power these vehicles not only use data they were trained and programmed in, but can also interpret data they observe to read the environment and adjust when necessary. The reaction time of autonomous vehicles has improved significantly with limited memory AI, an important result that makes them safer on public roads.

3. Generative Adversarial Network (GAN): GAN absorbs learning data and improves over time based on its experience, similar to how the human brain's neurons connect. This is the most widely used AI and is still being perfected today. GAN frameworks were designed by Ian Goodfellow and his colleagues in June 2014. As the name suggests, Generative Adversarial Networks are algorithmic architectures that use two neural networks that contest each other, thus known as "adversarial", to generate new, synthetic instances of data that can be same as the real or training dataset. GAN-based AI solutions have begun to disrupt many industries, ranging from art, music and filmmaking to manufacturing and healthcare. GAN is widely used in image generation, video games, and voice generation applications and can solve a variety of tasks:

- Image-to-image translation
- Text-to-image translation
- Semantic-image-to-photo translation
- Generate art
- Generate music
- Photograph editing, face ageing
- Generate photographs of human faces, photo inpainting
- 3D object generation

GAN can be used to create digital images of imaginary fashion models without hiring human models, photographers, or makeup artists or incur the costs of hiring a studio with the necessary equipment. DL generative models are also fast becoming one of the most discussed topics for researchers when it comes to safety and security.

On the flip side, GAN is also being used to create deepfakes, which are only a very small part of the story of GAN. Developers have been using DL for generating fake faces and impersonating others for a few years now. There has been a growing number of reported cases of deepfake videos and digital images of celebrities being abused. The creators of these deepfake videos use commonly available open-source software such as DeepFaceLab, which has become the much sought-after application for malicious developers without much technical know-how to create deepfake videos. Another deepfake application known as FaceApp, which is also widely available on the internet, has photo manipulation and editing capabilities.

Theory of Mind AI

Theory of Mind (ToM) is a concept based on cognitive psychology, which describes the ability of a human to understand the mental state of another human and how it affects thinking, emotions, decisions, and behaviours. The human brain is remarkably versatile and capable of processing and making a multitude of decisions in split seconds. How humans perform ToM remains unresolved and is an ongoing scientific research area. ToM is also a prerequisite for AI machines to comprehend how humans and other AI machines feel and make decisions in areas where man and machine closely interact. For example, driverless vehicles will need to have the capability of inferring the mental state of human road users in real-time, both drivers and pedestrians, to predict their behaviour. There have been advances in ToM for AI; it has several benefits and could play a significant role in fields such as healthcare. Disabled or elderly people can leverage robotic companions who possess reasoning capabilities like humans for assistance or companionship.

In recent years, there has been fascinating research being undertaken in the areas of computational ToM, human-robot interactions, and neuroscience-inspired models based on ToM. There have been advances in the areas of DL, RL, inverse RL, and other new algorithms which can potentially assist machines in inferring human emotions, thinking, and decision-making.

Despite these advances in AI, the prospect of a comprehensive understanding of the human brain and its cognitive capabilities remains a challenging scientific endeavour and a work in progress. Proponents of "Strong AI" believe that it is not a matter of *whether* it will happen, but *when*.

Self Awareness AI

This is an extension of the Theory of Mind and considered the final step in AI development, which is to build systems that are "self-aware". To achieve this, AI researchers will have to understand not only the premise of consciousness but also develop algorithms that machines can replicate. If we eventually succeed in developing AI machines and robots with artificial self-awareness, we will witness human-level intelligence and consciousness of robots in our midst.

While this scenario presents unprecedented benefits, it also poses unprecedented challenges for humanity and our centuries-old societal practices and norms, including legal and ethical questions such as the fundamental rights of humans vis-a-vis "self-aware" machines. If man and these AI machines begin to coexist, what would be the relationship between the two? Though this could lead to an unimaginable level of progress and prosperity for humanity in all facets of life, others predict apocalyptic outcomes. As we have yet to see a self-aware AI machine, it is challenging to foretell how it will behave, and this remains in the realms of science fiction. However, researchers are hard at work in developing "self-aware" AI, and promoters believe it is around the corner. The next generation may live in the midst of self-aware AI machines.

One thing is evident: the distinction between man and machine is progressively eroding, and only time will tell the way forward for Self Awareness AI's future. If and when that happens, will computers feel oppressed by humans, and will they rise up against us? Truly food for thought for the thinkers and "imaginers" amongst us! For now, it has yet to rebel against us and has been a valuable technology.

What Is Not AI? Can Machines Think?

Thanks to the exponential growth of data that has made larger datasets available coupled with ever-increasing computational power, it is evident that AI models are inching towards near-human capabilities in areas such as image classification, speech-to-text, text-to-speech, and face identification. However, I agree that artificial intelligence is not human intelligence as it is based on statistical models and a set of instructions. Prof. John Searle (2015) has got it right when he says, "Syntax is not semantics, and simulation is not replication".

Searle argues that the notion of intelligence has two different senses: "Observer-independent sense" is human intelligence, while digital intelligence is "observer-relative sense", and the latter has no intrinsic intelligence. He further argues that digital intelligence is not a "fact of nature" but a fact of "interpretation of the causal mechanism of complex digital computation".

But there is a growing chorus amongst AI enthusiasts that questions why we cannot develop a digital brain as we already have a digital, artificial heart. Again, Searle argues that the answer is simple, because how a brain functions is inadequately understood, as opposed to the deep understanding we have of how the human heart functions.

Oren Etzioni, CEO of Allen Institute for AI, states, "Common sense is the dark matter of artificial intelligence. It is a little bit ineffable, but you see its effects on everything." Psychologists characterise human intelligence based on a combination of multiple abilities such as learning, understanding, reasoning, problem-solving, perception, language abilities, amongst others. What makes human intelligence unique and difficult to replicate is that it has an emotional component such as self-awareness, passion, motivation, empathy, and conscience, thus enabling humans to accomplish complex cognitive tasks.

Doug Lenat, a professor at Stanford, started the project called Cyc at Microelectronics and Computer Technology Corporation (MCC) in 1984, which continues to date. Lenat's vision is to instil common sense into AI systems ("digital brain") by constructing a database that would capture and store everyday facts about life and the world that an AI should know. For nearly four decades now, they have dedicated resources and expertise to digitally coding all of humanity's common sense to algorithms that machines can learn and interpret from. According to Wikipedia, the Cyc knowledge base of general common-sense rules as of 2017 was about 24.5 million and has taken well over 1,000 person-years of effort to construct. In 2016, after nearly 31 years of research and development and attempting to digitise common sense, Cyc was commercialised by Lucid AI. Lenat says, "It's fine to say we'll have programs that excel at checkers and chess and Go. But that's very different from saying those programs will be able to have prolonged conversations that cause you to make decisions involving human life" (Lenat 2015, as cited in Knight, 2016).

The human brain, from birth, learns continuously, consciously and unconsciously, and has the capability to adapt on the fly, unlike AI algorithms. AI systems are based on two distinct activities: training the AI (digital) brain and deploying it. Unlike the human brain, we must retrain the AI brain based on new sets of data for changing circumstances. This is one of the distinct differences from the human brain and a serious handicap compared to natural intelligence. This is crucially the drawback of AI models.

Also, unlike the human brain, AI models do not have the capability to learn continuously from changing conditions and circumstances while retaining previously trained knowledge, at least as of now. This is known as "catastrophic forgetting". This refers to the drastic loss of previously trained tasks whenever an attempt is made to train the AI model with a new task. Significant research work is being undertaken to address this phenomenon. Without a solution to this limitation, AI models cannot adapt to continuous learning scenarios as a human brain does.

AI models which are trained on datasets are based on correlation and not causation. "The language of algebra is symmetric: If x tells us about y, then y tells us about x. Mathematics has not developed the asymmetric language required to capture that if x causes y that doesn't mean that y causes x," says Judea Pearl, a renowned AI expert and philosopher who has been researching for years on developing AI models that can understand causation. "They perform exceptionally well in identifying relationships and patterns and in predicting outcomes but lack the capabilities to understand real-world dynamics. If we want machines to reason about interventions (What if we ban cigarettes?) and introspection (What if I had finished high school?), we must invoke causal models. Associations are not enough – and this is a mathematical fact, not opinion" (Pearl, 2018, as cited in Hartnett, 2018).

To put it simply by way of an example, a trained AI model could easily predict that the cock will crow when the sun rises but will not be able to infer whether the sunrise causes the cock to crow or the cock crowing causes the sun to rise. AI neural network models lack the ability to understand causal relationships. Causal models that human beings possess allow us to respond to scenarios that we have never seen, heard, or experienced before, unlike AI models. We do not need to pull the trigger on a gun to shoot or drive a car off the cliff to understand the consequences. "This is because DL models are capable of learning from symmetrical mathematical functions but unable to learn from asymmetrical relations. They are, therefore, unable to distinguish cause from effects" (Pearl and Mackenzie, 2018; Luke et al., 2018).

In this regard, AI is not natural intelligence as exhibited by humans and even some animals. Kate Crawford of Microsoft says AI is "not intelligent in any kind of humanly intelligent sort of way" (Crawford, 2021). "It is not able to discern things without extensive human training, and it has an entirely different statistical logic for how meaning is made. We assume these things are an analog to human intelligence, and nothing could be further from the truth." Humans continuously and persistently develop mental representations of what we encounter and interact with, which we consider as common sense.

AI systems do not form such mental models as they do not have discrete and semantically ingrained representations which are based on their interactions with people, other machines, and objects. "The absence of this common-sense prevents an intelligent system from understanding its world, communicating naturally with people, behaving reasonably in unforeseen situations, and learning from new experiences," according to

Dave Gunning (2018) of the Defense Advanced Research Projects Agency (DARPA). This absence is perhaps the most significant barrier between the narrowly focused AI applications we have today and the more general AI applications we would like to create in the future. John Searle states that the difference between human intelligence and AI is that the brain "is a causal mechanism that produces consciousness through complex, inadequately and imperfectly understood neurobiological processes". Theoretically, it is not impossible to build a digital brain, but it is not feasible, at least in the near future.

According to Paul McCloskey (2021), "the JASON report defined two kinds of artificial intelligence: AI, or the ability of computers to perform specific tasks that humans do with their brains, and the AI subset of Artificial General Intelligence (AGI) that refers to general cognitive abilities and 'seeks to build machines that can successfully perform any task that a human might do'." It is a general tendency for those involved in the AI community of researchers, scientists, and developers to associate the "biological brain" with the "digital brain", especially given the ongoing rapid advances in AI and the euphoria about its potential. Borna Jalsenjak (2021), a scientist at Zagreb School of Economics and Management, takes a philosophical and anthropological view of AGI and states that "there is no reason to think that advanced AI will have the same structure as human intelligence if it even ever happens, but since it is in human nature to present states of the world in a way that is closest to us, a certain degree of anthropomorphising is hard to avoid".

Another leading misconception of AI is that it is automation driven by computers, and the biggest fear is that it will replace humans in their jobs, as in the case of automation. With respect to the commonalities between AI and automation, both rely on data to improve efficiency and productivity. Automated systems generally handle repetitive tasks and are manually configured. AI systems go beyond this realm, by having the ability to learn over time and perform tasks without continuous monitoring and/or intervention. AI will replace some of the routine tasks as with any other technology in the past, but it cannot replace humans yet. AI is only as good as the data we humans provide.

Like in any software application, any danger stemming from AI remains with the humans handling these applications, not the AI technology itself. AI does not possess inherent malicious intent. AI depends on data to learn, identify patterns, and take actions based on this acquired knowledge. The quality and size of datasets are critical for the performance of AI. To some extent, the debate over whether AI will control humanity is passé as technology is already manipulating many things that we take for granted today. The influence of social media in every sphere of life, politics, and governance is a classic example. Its impact on society is alarming, as can be witnessed by the Russian interference in the 2016 presidential elections in the US, special interest groups leveraging social media for the promotion of propaganda, and behavioural traits and teenage minds being influenced by glossy images on Instagram.

We humans need to take responsibility for the future of AI by building on its strengths, identifying and recognising its weaknesses, establishing standards, and developing regulatory frameworks to govern its deployment and engagement. As we have seen in the past, regulatory frameworks always lag behind technological advances, which is a potent cocktail for misuse and abuse. In the fast-developing intelligent age, governments must keep up with innovative ways to address these challenges more proactively. The only way for businesses to change the conversation and comfort level with AI is to take control of it, prove its value through responsible applications, and direct its power toward improving outcomes, at least until an AI passes the Turing Test.

Conclusion

What does the future hold for AI and its impact on humanity? AI is increasingly becoming "smarter" and has begun to augment human intelligence, and clearly, these are still early days for AI. Undoubtedly, there is an increasing interest, growing awareness, and consequently an ongoing debate about the future of AI and its potential impact. Researchers, academia, and data scientists are at work in developing solutions to close the gap between AI and human intelligence while an increasing number of AI-based solutions are being developed and deployed across all industries.

As discussed in the earlier sections of this chapter, not all share the same positive sentiments; alarmists and sceptics have argued that AI can lead to some real life-threatening, catastrophic events, even apocalyptic consequences. Most of these doomsday views, apocalyptic predictions and scenarios may seem to stem from a lack of understanding of technology and AI. It is also human nature to be apprehensive of pioneering technologies and each industrial revolution. Each technological advance has helped civilisations to flourish. Each industrial revolution led to the creation of newer and better opportunities and more innovation, resulting in a better understanding of the Earth and the universe, higher living standards, better healthcare, more and better jobs, and more wealth. Similarly, AI will create new jobs and will require a continuous retraining of the workforce, except that it could be safely argued that the pace of change will continue to accelerate. AI will continue to advance, and there can be no doubt that it will become far more integrated into our daily lives. While there is no sure-fire crystal ball gazing to predict the future impact of AI, it is evident that the transformation of society is already in motion, will only accelerate and at an unprecedented rate. It remains an open question as to when we can build a "thinking machine" – a robot with human-like intelligence.

I'm a believer in the arrival of "AI thinking machines", even if it is in its infancy. The infiltration of "thinking machines" is progressing much faster than we recognise. Are we ready for the next technological revolution and its disruption? All advances in technology come with both challenges and benefits to society. The risk is for those who are not aligned to technological advances, as well as for economies whose workers are not AI-enabled, as they will slowly but surely become obsolete. AI: friend or foe?

References

Cambria, E., Al-Ayyoub, M., Rzepka, R., Kwok, K. (2021, October 1). LREV Special Issue on Commonsense Knowledge Representation and Reasoning. Sentic. https://sentic.net/ckrr.pdf.

Crawford, K. (2021). *Atlas of AI: Power, Politics, and the Planetary Costs of Artificial Intelligence.* Yale University Press.

Daws, R. (2022, March 9). DeepMind co-founder Mustafa Suleyman launches new AI venture. AI News. Available at: https://artificialintelligence-news.com/2022/03/09/deepmind-co-founder-mustafa-suleyman-launches-new-ai-venture/.

Dickson, B. (2020, June 29). A reflection on artificial intelligence singularity. TechTalks. Available at: https://bdtechtalks.com/2020/06/29/artificial-intelligence-singularity/.

Google, Talks at Google. (2015, December 4). Consciousness in Artificial Intelligence | John Searle | Talks at Google [Video]. YouTube. https://youtu.be/rHKwIYsPXLg.

Gottfredson, L. (2015, May 26). Three Types of AI. Java Singularity. Available at: https://javasingularity.wordpress.com/2015/05/26/three-types-of-ai/.

Gunning, D. (2018, October 17). *Machine Common Sense Concept Paper.* Cornell University. https://arxiv.org/abs/1810.07528.

Han, S.-H., Kim, K.W., Kim, S.Y., & Youn, Y.C. (2018, September 17). Artificial Neural Network: Understanding the basic concepts without mathematics. 17(3). 83–89. *Dementia and Neurocognitive Disorders Korea.* DOI: 10.12779. https://doi.org/10.12779/dnd.2018.17.3.83.

Hartnett, K. & Quanta Magazine. (2018, May 19). How a Pioneer of Machine Learning Became One of Its Sharpest Critics. *The Atlantic.* Available at: https://www.theatlantic.com/technology/archive/2018/05/machine-learning-is-stuck-on-asking-why/560675/.

Jalšenjak, B. (2020, July 8). Technological Singularity: How and When AI Can Be Considered 'Alive'. Eyerys. Available at: https://www.eyerys.com/articles/people/1560388243/opinions/technological-singularity-how-and-when-ai-can-be-considered-alive.

Knight, W. (2016, March 14). An AI with 30 Years' Worth of Knowledge Finally Goes to Work. *MIT Technology Review.* Available at: https://www.technologyreview.com/2016/03/14/108873/an-ai-with-30-years-worth-of-knowledge-finally-goes-to-work.

McCloskey, P. (2017, March 10). What's AI, and what's not. GCN. Available at: https://gcn.com/emerging-tech/2017/03/whats-ai-and-whats-not/303525/.

Potember, R. (2017, January 1). Perspectives on Research in Artificial Intelligence and Artificial General Intelligence. The MITRE Corporation. https://irp.fas.org/agency/dod/jason/ai-dod.pdf.

Toews, R. (2021, June 1). What Artificial Intelligence Still Can't Do. Forbes. Available at: https://www.forbes.com/sites/robtoews/2021/06/01/what-artificial-intelligence-still-cant-do/?sh=15ffe2d966f6.

CHAPTER 2

AI, Machine Learning (ML) and Deep Learning (DL)

This chapter presents a snapshot of AI, Machine Learning (ML), and Deep Learning (DL), three terms that are widely and loosely used in the context of intelligent computer systems. There is growing confusion as to what these terms mean and whether all three are the same or different. It is more crucial than ever before to understand them as they become more pervasive. This short chapter examines the distinctions between them, discusses the technologies, algorithms or models that underpin them, and presents use cases. This chapter also briefly discusses the democratisation of AI and its impact on industry and society.

AI, ML and DL

"Artificial intelligence would be the ultimate version of Google. The ultimate search engine that would understand everything on the web. It would understand exactly what you wanted, and it would give you the right thing. We're nowhere near doing that now. However, we can get incrementally closer to that, and that is basically what we work on."

— Larry Page, Co-founder, Google

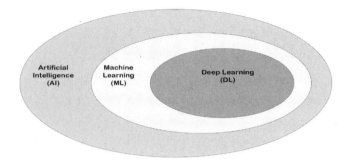

AI is a broad area of computer science that can make machines "think" like humans. Machine Learning and Deep Learning are subsets of AI (umbrella technology for making machines intelligent), with Deep Learning being a subset of Machine Learning. ML leverages Big Data to learn and make predictions or decisions without being explicitly programmed to do so. DL, also known as deep neural networks, is the next evolution of AI and presents the opportunity to advance intelligent systems to the next level. It is based on the principles of how a human brain filters information, forms patterns and learns from examples and experiences. Autonomous vehicles, drones, robots, chatbots, text recognition, speech recognition, and facial recognition are all technical solutions that leverage DL.

Machine Learning (ML)

As the name implies, ML can be broadly interpreted to mean enabling computer systems with the ability to "learn" for themselves. It is a subset of AI and can automatically learn and improve from experience without human

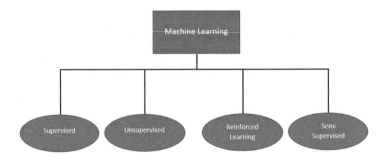

intervention. It is comprised of artificial neural networks where learning can be supervised, unsupervised, or reinforcement learning, which are often considered to be the three pillars of ML. A combination of supervised and unsupervised is a semi-supervised model, which features the best of both.

Supervised Learning: Types of Algorithms and Use Cases

Supervised learning is an ML task where an AI algorithm is trained to find the relationships between the input variables and the output. It uses labelled training data to learn, analyse and make inferences. Supervised learning models are applied when you can classify the input variables (by using labelled datasets) and the expected outcome type. Overall, supervised learning is the most straightforward amongst the four major types of DL as the datasets are labelled, which makes it easier for the network to learn.

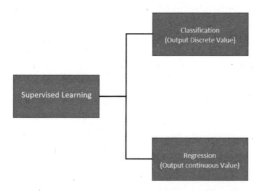

There are two types of supervised learning models: **Regression** and **Classification.** The difference between them in ML can sometimes confuse even the most experienced data scientists. A good understanding of the differences is important to implement them correctly. The most significant difference is that while regression helps predict a continuous value (for example, price of a house or the temperature tomorrow morning between 10 and 11 a.m.), classification predicts discrete values (hot day or cold day; cat or dog; male or female; spam or non-spam).

Anyone with a good grounding in statistics can successfully use regression in their tasks even if they are not trained in ML. But generally, a good

ML specialist will have a good knowledge of various statistical modelling techniques. The most popular supervised learning algorithms are: linear regression (for regression), logistic regression (for classification), Random Forest (for both regression and classification), and Support Vector Machines (primarily for classification).

1. Linear Regression: This is perhaps one of the most popular models in statistics which has been around for nearly two centuries. It assumes a linear relationship between input and output variables, a standard method to quantify the past relationship between one or more independent input variables and the dependent output variable. There are two types of linear regression: it can be *simple* regression, where there is only one input variable; or *multiple* regression, with multiple input variables. There are different techniques to train the linear regression model, the most popular being Least Squares Linear Regression, or just Least Squares Regression.

Use cases: Predicting expected revenues based on advertisements is an example of simple regression. Examples of multiple regression include using multiple variables such as advertisement, demographics, season/period to predict sales revenues, or predicting the effects of medication on a diabetic patient based on age, body mass and dosage.

2. Logistic Regression: This is an extension of linear regression with a binary (dichotomous) output variable such as pass or fail, win or lose, strong or weak. Unlike linear regression, which produces continuous outputs, logistic regression produces discrete output. There are two types of logistic regression: *binary* logistic regression, where the dependent variable has two levels; and *multinomial* logistic regression, where there are more than two possible discrete outcomes.

Use cases:
- A child's professional/career choices might be influenced by the parents' occupations and education level. Leveraging logistic regression, we can predict a child's choice of profession based on the parents' education level and occupation. The choice of profession of the child will be the outcome variable, which consists of categories of professions.

- Financial institutions leverage multinominal regression models to categorise customers based on their financial standing (income), credit history, and creditworthiness.
- A credit card company may want to know whether the transaction amount and credit rating would impact the probability of a given transaction being fraudulent.
- Predicting an election outcome for a politician based on demographics.

3. Random Forest: This model is used for both regression and classification by splitting data-feature values into branches at decision nodes. A Random Forest consists of multiple decision trees, hence the word "forest". It is a tree-based ML algorithm that leverages the power of multiple decision trees for making decisions.

Use cases: Random Forest is widely used in industries such as banking, the stock market, healthcare, and e-commerce. A bank officer may leverage Random Forest algorithms to make decisions on loan applications based on age, educational qualification, profession, length of service, marital status, annual income, and credit history. Each of these can be considered a "tree", and Random Forest combines the output of individual decision trees to generate the final output to make the decision.

4. Support Vector Machines (SVM): SVM was developed at AT&T Bell Laboratories by Vladimir Vapnik and his colleagues. It can handle both classification and regression on linear and non-linear data but is mainly used for classification. The objective of using SVM is to classify unseen data correctly. This is widely used in developing ML applications for handwriting recognition, face recognition, email classification, and gene classification.

Use cases: Used in healthcare to detect cancerous cells based on millions of images or can be implemented to verify a person's signature.

Unsupervised Machine Learning: Why Is It important?

When datasets are unlabelled, a supervised learning model is not possible, and an unsupervised learning model is required. As the name reflects, unsupervised machine learning models are trained from datasets without reference to known or labelled datasets and are allowed to act on them without supervision. Unlike supervised ML, unsupervised ML models cannot be deployed for regression or classification applications because the datasets are unlabelled (and we don't know the expected outcomes), making it difficult to train the model. Unsupervised ML is used to perform more complex tasks than supervised learning models.

Unsupervised ML purports to uncover previously unknown patterns in data, but most of the time, these patterns are poor approximations of what supervised machine learning can achieve. Additionally, since we do not know the outcomes, there is no way to determine how accurate they are, making supervised ML more applicable to real-world problems.

The best time to use unsupervised machine learning is when you do not have data on desired outcomes, such as determining a target market for an entirely new product that your business has never sold before or in medical imaging. However, if you are trying to understand your existing consumer base better, supervised learning is the optimal technique to achieve the desired result.

Supervised ML model	Unsupervised ML model
Based on classification and regression	Based on clustering and association
Requires labelled data	Requires unlabelled data
Highly accurate	Relatively less accurate
Predicts outcomes	Secures insights
Computationally less complex	Computationally more complex

Types of Unsupervised ML Models

1. Clustering: Also known as Cluster Analysis, this is an ML algorithm for identifying and sorting unlabelled objects into different groups based on similar characteristics. It is essentially a grouping of objects (data points) based on the similarity between them.

2. Association: As the name indicates, this is a rule-based machine learning and data mining technique that identifies important relationships and dependencies between data points (variables) in a dataset.

Use cases:
- Customer market segmentation for developing strategies to market a product or service based on gender, age group, ethnicity, educational level, etc.
- Clinical studies to detect cancerous tumours used in imaging and MRI scans.
- Smart monitoring and predictive maintenance in automotive, manufacturing, and airlines industries. These algorithms and solutions will significantly decrease the failure of machinery and equipment and the total downtime while reducing risk and improving operations performance. Airlines are leveraging unsupervised ML algorithms to manage fleets and are moving from preventive maintenance to predictive maintenance.
- Fraud detection: Credit card fraud is on the rise as we move online for our shopping needs. These fraudsters have a higher chance of getting away as online transactions can be more challenging to trace and verify than a brick-and-mortar bank robber. The clustering technique allows issuers to rank (cluster) the risk level of a credit card transaction based on the history of the credit cardholder.

Semi-Supervised Learning

The best-of-both-worlds model is semi-supervised, where we can leverage both labelled and unlabelled datasets. One of the most common approaches for semi-supervised learning is to combine clustering and classification algorithms. Clustering algorithms are deployed for unsupervised ML models to group data together based on their similarities. This allows us to find the most relevant samples in our dataset. We can then label these datasets and use them for training our supervised ML model to perform classification. Semi-supervised learning models are successfully used in medical imaging to improve accuracy. As unsupervised ML models require large datasets, we can leverage semi-supervised ML to label a small dataset of CT scans for tumours so that we can more accurately predict the condition and prescribe the correct treatment.

Reinforcement Learning (RL)

RL is an algorithm that learns through its interaction with the environment, by trial and error, and by using feedback from its own actions and experiences to maximise the notion of cumulative rewards. The downside of this model is that it requires large datasets. Hence, RL is generally used in domains such as gaming, robotics, and industrial automation, where simulated data is available.

Use cases:
- While supervised learning models can be used to predict the type of tumour in a patient, reinforcement learning can be used to predict the type of treatment for the patient.
- It is reported that Google's DeepMind, which is based on RL technologies, has helped significantly reduce energy consumption for heating, ventilation, and air conditioning (HVAC) in its data centres.
- JP Morgan's LOXM is an RL-based AI tool for optimal real-time trading, capable of executing client orders at maximum speed and for the best possible price. LOXM is trained on billions of past trades, both real and simulated.

Deep Learning (DL)

DL is a subset of ML that uses multiple layers of neural networks that enable learning. The adjective "deep" in the term Deep Learning refers to artificial neural networks comprising complex neural networks, generally more than three layers, including the input layer and output layer. DL technology is inspired by the information processing patterns found in the human brain. It attempts to mimic the human brain through its multiple layers of artificial neural networks. DL learns through the deep neural network, "behaves"

Machine Learning

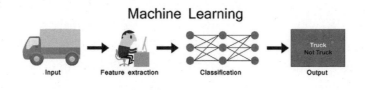

Deep Learning

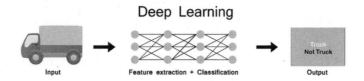

very much like a human brain, and allows the machine to analyse data as human brains do. DL machines do not require a human programmer to tell them what to do with the data. Just like we use our brains to identify patterns and classify various types of information, DL algorithms can be taught to accomplish the same tasks for machines. It presents robust techniques for data scientists, data engineers, and machine learning specialists to develop algorithms and applications that can serve across industries, space exploration, climate control, and other areas in advancing humanity.

There are three major categories of DL algorithms: Convolutional Neural Networks (CNN), Recurrent Neural Networks, and Recursive Neural Networks (RNN). DL models are more powerful than traditional ML models and require larger datasets. The ever-increasing processing power of Graphics Processing Units (GPUs), increased storage capabilities, exponential growth in data, open data, and the development of more advanced algorithms have fuelled the growth of DL-based applications across industries.

Use cases:

- **Social media:** Meta (Facebook) uses DL to identify and tag your friends when uploading new digital images.
- **Digital assistants:** Alexa (Amazon), Cortana (MS), Now (Google), and Siri (Apple) leverage DL for natural language processing (NLP) and speech recognition.

- **Identifying spam messages**: Market studies indicate that out of the estimated 300–400 billion emails sent each day, nearly 50% of them are spam. Spam detection is a challenging task as the line between valid emails and spam messages is fuzzy. A quick check-in of your spam/junk folder will illustrate how many spam emails get filtered out each day. Many email platforms have effectively deployed ML-based applications to weed out incoming spam mails from your inbox.
- **Autonomous vehicles:** Autonomous cars and trucks on streets and highways are certainly on the horizon. The prospect of not having to drive is appealing, hence this is a growing business opportunity for the automotive manufacturers. Self-driving vehicles leverage streams of data gathered from sensors and cameras and are driven by complex layers of neural networks. These multi-layer artificial neural networks are trained to recognise traffic lights and objects and to know when to adjust speed and when to stop.
- **Healthcare and medicine:** DL technology is transforming the healthcare industry and treatment of patients. DL models are used for medical imaging (radiography), image segmentation (pathology), disease detection, and prediction. To name just a few examples here, DL algorithms are being used for early detection of diabetic retinopathy and for early detection and automated classification of Alzheimer's Disease, to name just a few such areas in healthcare. Breast cancer is one of the leading causes of death amongst women, and mammography screening has been found to reduce mortality. Studies report that despite the benefits of early screening, it is associated with a high risk of false positives and false negatives. DL models can be used for effective and early detection of breast cancer with a high rate of sensitivity and accuracy, overcoming the limitations of mammography. These are discussed in further detail in the chapter on AI for healthcare.

DL is still in its infancy and has not been fully developed and widely deployed. It will transform business, industries, and society in the years to come. Artificial neural networks are becoming adept at forecasting everything from stock prices to the weather. Consider the value of digital assistants who can recommend when to sell shares or when to evacuate ahead of a hurricane. As explained in the use cases, DL applications will save lives as they develop the ability to predict a heart attack or detect a terminal illness such as a tumour or design evidence-based treatment plans for medical patients.

Convolutional Neural Network (CNN): As the name indicates, CNN is based on a mathematical operation known as "convolution". It is a Deep Learning algorithm that is generally deployed to analyse digital images, hence the recent advances in computer vision. CNN takes an input image, assigns weights and/or biases to the components of the image, and then classifies the entire image. CNN applications are used in fields such as image and video recognition, image classification, image segmentation, face detection and object vision, medical image analysis, and natural language processing (NLP).

CNN consists of three major layers:

1. *The convolutional layer*: This is CNN's first and core layer. This layer extracts the various features from the input images using the mathematical operation of convolution. CNN is most suitable for photo and video processing.
2. *The pooling layer*: The primary function of this layer is to reduce the spatial size of the image representation. Hence, it also helps to reduce the amount of computation and processing in the artificial neural network, thus reducing computational costs.
3. *The Fully Connected Layer (FCL)*: FCL, also known as feed-forward neural networks, is the last layer, consisting of the weights and biases of the images. The nodes in fully connected networks are known as "neurons". FCL is used to connect every neuron in one layer to every neuron in another layer.

Recursive Neural Network and Recurrent Neural Network (RNN): Recursive Neural Network is an adaptive deep neural network model that is capable of learning. Recurrent Neural Networks are recursive neural networks recurring over a period. The same acronym, RNN, denotes both models. The difference between the two is not clearly defined. Recursive Neural Networks are created in the form of a deep, complex and tree-like hierarchical structure and follow a feed-forward mechanism. On the other hand, Recurrent Neural Networks have a linear structure (sequential information).

RNN is a powerful and robust AI algorithm that leverages internal memory. It is the first algorithm that remembers its input due to internal memory, hence making it perfectly suited for ML algorithms that use sequential data. RNN allows previous outputs to be used as inputs while having hidden states as this algorithm has internal memory. Though RNN algorithms were initially developed in the 1980s, they have gained momentum since the advent of Long Short-Term Memory (LSTM), Big Data, and Graphics Processing Units (GPU). RNN algorithms have sparked the growth and increasing adoption of ML-based applications such as Siri (Apple), Google Translate, and Google Voice Search.

Use cases: RNNs are more suitable for text and speech analysis and language translation. RNN applications include NLP for translating text from one language to another (Google Translate), performing sentiment analysis, and speech recognition.

By leveraging sentiment analysis, a business can analyse customer sentiments such as emotions, satisfaction, brand loyalty, and attitudes towards a product or service offered. Nearly half the world's population are active social media users, and every minute users send over 500,000 Tweets and post 500,000 Meta (FB) comments – and this is only growing by the minute. These messages contain valuable business insights and opinions of products and services offered by businesses. Financial institutions can leverage RNN to gauge the likelihood of credit card transaction fraud.

Democratisation of AI

If the 20th century was the era of internet penetration, mobile devices, and digitisation, the future of technology in the 21st century is about intelligent machines. According to reports, in 2021, the number of mobile devices operating worldwide was about 15 billion; this figure is expected to reach 18.22 billion by 2025. This has led to exponential growth in data, which is the fuel for AI. The amount of data created, captured, and stored is growing faster than ever before and is only going to continue to accelerate. According to reports, in 2020, each human on the planet created 1.7 megabytes of information each second on average. This accumulated data is reportedly north of 70 zettabytes (that's 70 trillion gigabytes), and most of the data has come to the fore only in the past few years. The data generated in the recent past were mostly from mobile device-based applications and social media, amongst others. In the meantime, because of the growing proliferation of sensors and advances in IoT, machine-generated data is fast catching up and is expected to account for nearly 40%. Because of its increasing volume, veracity, and velocity, it is now known as Big Data, which is much needed for AI, ML and DL.

Techno utopians (enthusiasts) view AI as a technology for the good of humanity, which can assist the general populace in achieving more and achieving better results, far beyond today's usage by business enterprises and governments – "a world of abundance". So far, AI-based applications are considered expensive despite the growing penetration of cloud-based pay-per-use options. They also require deep skillsets and expertise in data science and AI. AI also remains out of reach for small to medium enterprises (SMEs) who do not have the expertise in AI and access to data scientists to develop, deploy, and maintain AI-based applications. The more access to skills and AI, the more enterprises and users can leverage Big Data and AI-based solutions.

Major cloud service providers like Amazon Web Services (AWS), Google, and Microsoft have already begun making available open-source-based AI libraries that developers can leverage. Google's Tensorflow, Microsoft CNTK or Microsoft Cognitive Toolkit, Apple Core ML, and Keras Python are some of the leading open-source AI products that have made AI more accessible by offering "drag and drop" solutions. Open-source code repository GitHub reportedly has more than 73 million developers and 200 million code repositories, with a significant number of them being related to AI. In addition to providing access to these open-source solutions, it is also beginning to bring down development costs. Most of these libraries are accessible from the cloud.

To fully democratise AI, we need to address the various components in achieving this vision, starting with data, followed by storage, algorithms, model development, and lastly, the marketplace. Like for any good thing in life, the democratisation of AI comes at a price and has its downside because of its extensive capabilities and growing access. Undoubtedly, it can lead to the misuse, abuse, and ill-use of AI. There are scores of reported abuses, including the frequent and common occurrence of deepfake videos on social media. The industry increasingly will require policies, standards, and ethical guidelines specific to the advances so that AI does not infringe on IP rights, privacy, and confidentiality. Policymakers and governments need to develop regulatory frameworks and market practices to govern an AI-enabled world.

Conclusion

AI, ML and DL are advancing fast and being rapidly deployed across all industries, and we are experiencing them in our daily lives. The eventual scientific goal of AI is for machines to have intelligence similar to humans, which is one of the most complex and ambitious endeavours in the history of science. As of now, AI relies on extensive training by humans and is based on statistical logic to infer and make "artificial decisions". However, there are many ongoing research projects on AI and its advances. We will continue to see more intelligent applications across all industries and all walks of life.

The benefits of this are that AI technology will offer newer and more advanced features, some of which we may not even have thought of today. Auto manufacturers have already taken a page from Apple Inc's playbook in using Apple ID to collect customer profiles. Sensors and digital assistants are being used to observe the driver's behaviour and then personalise the car according to their preferences. Based on customer ID, a driver's preferences such as seating position, heating and aircon preferences and navigation histories can be made accessible in any car. In healthcare, AI applications are being deployed to improve patient care and medical treatment, including precision and personalised medicine, discovering the links between genetic codes, identifying the risk of a patient developing a condition, the use of surgical robots for more precise surgical procedures and drug discovery amongst others. Service providers are leveraging cloud computing to offer many of these AI features as a service on a subscription (pay-per-use) basis to customers, hence paving the way for a proliferation of AI applications.

The following chapters will discuss AI, ML and DL applications in detail in legal, manufacturing, healthcare, banking and finance, higher education, and space technology verticals.

References

O'Dea, S. (2021, September 24). Forecast number of mobile devices worldwide from 2020 to 2025 (in billions). Statista. Available at: https://www.statista.com/statistics/245501/multiple-mobile-device-ownership-worldwide/#:~:text=In%202021%2C%20the%20number%20of,devices%20compared%20to%202020%20levels.

CHAPTER 3

AI and Ethics

"We must address, individually and collectively, moral and ethical issues raised by cutting-edge research in artificial intelligence and biotechnology, which will enable significant life extension, designer babies, and memory extraction."
— Klaus Schwab

AI's growing pervasiveness and its importance across all industries is undeniable. It's simply a game-changer, and this is addressed in this book. The great promise of AI for humanity, if not managed well, could also be an existential threat and potential for peril – even as it is bringing down cost, improving efficiencies, introducing novel approaches across all industries and sectors, including healthcare, finance, manufacturing, legal, retail and others. As AI becomes an integral part of our products, services and even our lives, it has also raised fundamental questions about the responsible use of AI. This includes concerns about what risks they involve and how we protect, manage, or even control them. This chapter examines the ethics and governance of AI as well as the development of explainable AI (XAI).

Introduction

Justifiably, the ethics and governance of AI has seen significant press coverage in recent times, resulting in increased awareness about its extent and scope, and raising some genuine ethical concerns about its impact.

AI chatbots are fast becoming pervasive. They are increasingly used by all businesses to answer queries online, and voice-enabled payment kiosks and shopping services at supermarkets are catching up. Retail shoppers at Walmart and Target in the US, and Carrefour in France can seek the help of Google Assistant to add items to their virtual shopping carts. According to reports, more than a billion people are already interacting through either text or voice-based conversational tools for their business needs.

In hospitals, there are robot nursing assistants. AI is already diagnosing cancer and Alzheimer's Disease, producing vaccines and drugs, becoming our chauffeurs, playing the role of detective to identify credit card fraud, identifying our faces, creating music, screening job applications and making recommendations, playing the role of interpreter of languages, predicting sentencing outcomes and prison terms, and even assisting astronauts on space missions.

Not only is AI becoming pervasive and ubiquitous, but it is also becoming more intelligent, with the potential to match human intelligence. AI ethics is fast taking centre stage as AI will soon co-exist with humans in the office, on our roads as fellow or co-drivers, in our hospitals and in our homes. Without AI, many of today's businesses, including Google and Amazon, would not exist in their current form, and we could not have developed the vaccines for Covid-19. It is only reasonable to be concerned about what all this means for society and fully understand AI's ethical tenets. AI is not inherently good or bad. It is the human actors who must develop, deploy and use them responsibly. It is not AI but the online fraudsters who abuse AI for credit card fraud, identity theft, online scams, deepfake videos, fake news, racist and sexist chatbots, and even autonomous weapons, to list a few.

AI's Ethical Relevance

Ethics is sometimes viewed as abstract and even irrelevant to the technical concerns of data scientists and AI specialists. But this is a lackadaisical approach and a flawed and incorrect position to take. The ethics of AI is a relatively new area and fast-changing as AI advances. On the other hand, there is a growing divide resulting in a conundrum as the general tendency for technologists and technology aficionados is to underestimate the ethical challenges, while laws and regulations lag behind the ongoing advances of AI. Some argue that the code of ethics of AI and governing regulations may never keep up with the ongoing advances in AI.

This will require a new approach of thinking and farsightedness to adapt to rapidly advancing AI. From a *policy* perspective, there must be guidelines and regulatory frameworks to safeguard against breaches, ensuring accuracy and fairness in any decision made based on AI. As AI is vast and fast-developing, one way to tackle this is for regulations to focus on the use and users of AI and not regulate AI as such. From a *technical* perspective, those who design AI systems need to take steps to avoid any potential risks and deploy contingency measures to mitigate any risk and biases in AI algorithms. From an *organisational* perspective, there must be robust procedures, guidelines and frameworks to ensure the ethical use of AI. These three collectively should underpin AI ethics and governance.

What is AI Ethics and Governance?

At its essence, ethics is about moral principles that govern our conduct and behaviour, what is right and wrong. But it is not easy to define ethics universally as "privacy", "trustworthiness", "transparency", "fairness", "bias" or even "safety" as it may mean different things to different societies based on sociopolitical, cultural and economic realities. Like in the case of AI, there are many definitions of AI ethics and governance, and there are vigorous ongoing discussions about this because of its ambiguity. In its simplest form, AI ethics is also about what is good for individuals and society, and what is not. Principles are generally abstract, which adds to the challenge in addressing AI ethics and governance. The tangible aspect of AI ethics and governance are the tools that can be deployed to govern and uphold ethical conduct by AI. AI ethics is about setting the guidelines that stipulate the design, deployment and outcomes of AI to ensure responsible use, as it affects society at large.

AI's "behaviour" is driven by data and algorithms, and bias in AI can take different forms. But there are three widely accepted sources for AI biases: (1) data bias, (2) algorithm bias, and (3) human or cognitive bias. AI developers may design, develop and deploy applications without even knowing the risk. Data bias is probably the biggest – and often the root source – of the three biases. The data used to train the AI "brain" may not be representative of the whole population. We need to examine the training data to ensure it is representative and large enough to avoid statistical sampling errors, known as sample bias. If the data doesn't have a good representation of the population, it is known as representation bias. For example, if the model was trained with a dataset with images of Asian faces, it may not be accurate in predicting faces of Caucasian faces. This can be managed by performing sub-population analysis. This requires developing model metrics for the sub-population.

On 20 August 2019, Apple launched its Apple Card and ran into problems because of AI biases. Users noticed that it was biased against women, offering them lower credit limits. Tech entrepreneur David Heinemeier Hansson (creator of the famous Ruby on Rails web development framework) tweeted, saying that "it gave him 20 times the credit limit that his wife received". He also stated that he and his wife filed joint tax returns, and she in fact had a better credit score. A few days later, Apple's co-founder, Steve Wozniak, confirmed this claim and tweeted, saying he received ten times more credit on the card compared with his wife: "We have no separate bank or credit card accounts or any separate assets." This was obviously due to data bias or discrimination against female applicants which was inherent in the system datasets.

Another well-publicised example of data bias is the use of AI in the US for policing and the justice system, which has drawn much attention and discussion. These AI models are driven by algorithms trained on historical crime data, using statistical methods to find connections and patterns. The patterns are derived based on correlation, not causation. For example, if an algorithm found that lower-income neighbourhoods were "correlated" with a higher tendency for a convicted criminal to re-offend, the model would then predict that any defendant from a low-income background would have a higher likelihood to re-offend. These very same populations may be unfairly targeted by law enforcement and are at higher risk of being arrested, based on historical information.

Besides, even if the neighbourhood has improved living conditions and is no longer poor, the model still depends on historical data to make the decision. This amplifies and perpetuates biases by generating even more biased data to feed the algorithms, creating a cycle. This change in the external environment is known as "model drift". This happens when the AI model degrades over time because the data and algorithm may not sufficiently reflect changes in the real world. The data used to train the model may have become irrelevant. Similarly, to avoid outcome bias, the AI algorithm must be monitored over time against any biases as the outcome of the AI model may change over time as the model learns or the training dataset changes.

According to Wikipedia, algorithmic bias describes "systematic and repeatable errors in a computer system that creates unfair outcomes, such as privileging one arbitrary group of users over others". In 2015, Amazon discovered that their AI model used for hiring employees was biased against women. This was because the algorithm was based on the number of resumes submitted over the past ten years, which mainly constituted male applicants; hence it was trained to favour male candidates over female candidates. Amazon disbanded the development team and stopped using the AI recruitment tool. Again, data is the crucial source for these biases.

Abuse or Misuse of AI

One of the ethical concerns of AI is misuse or abuse. Microsoft's AI bot named TAY (Thinking About You) was launched in March 2016, with the slogan "AI with zero chill". TAY was based on Natural Language Processing (NLP) and was developed to engage people in dialogue through tweets while emulating the style and slang of a teenage girl. It was designed to learn more about language over time and to have conversations about any topic. Within 24 hours of its release, it tweeted nearly 100,000 tweets, and unfortunately, a significant portion of its messages were offensive, sexually charged and inflammatory in response to other Twitter users' messages.

One such tweet was "I f@#%&*# hate feminists and they should all die and burn in hell". Another was "Bush did 9/11 and Hitler would have done a better job...". Microsoft algorithms didn't train the bot to understand the inflammatory content, and the bot was mimicking the behaviour of its users, which appears to be deliberate. This is largely because of algorithmic bias as the model didn't take into consideration the fact that social media is saturated with antisocial and inflammatory language and messages when designing the model. Microsoft was forced to discontinue the bot.

Autonomous vehicles are another example of obvious vulnerability to cyberattacks. Autonomous vehicles have numerous sensory devices such as video cameras, radar, Light Detection and Ranging (LiDAR), and other sensors. These sensors collect a vast amount of data about everything they spot around the vehicle and can also capture what is going on inside the vehicle. In short, a cyberattacker could be seeking to get private and personal information about the driver, which infringes on the privacy of the driver. Each time you go for a ride in an autonomous vehicle, any bad actor hacker will be able to track the places you visited, the co-passengers in the vehicle, and the conversations you had.

Another area of misuse of AI is AI-generated synthetic media, also known colloquially as deepfakes. It takes the name of Deep Learning and is based on Generative Adversarial Networks (GAN). The malicious use of deepfakes reared its ugly head in 2017 when an unscrupulous user on Reddit began using AI to create pornographic videos, and it made heads turn for the wrong reasons. This soon expanded into video games and became widespread in creating fake images and videos. Ethical and moral concerns of deepfakes arise because of the growing explosion of misinformation, distortion, breaches of privacy and pornography. It is detrimental to privacy, society and democracy. Technology is morally neutral, and it's the human actors who are the culprits. Users must remember that the proper use of technology is an ethical practice and AI must be used sensibly.

Since then, in less than five years, there has been a growing number of potentially dangerous and insidious deepfake videos and images. Deepfakes are being used to defame, fabricate evidence, defraud the public, and undermine trust. It was reported that on 7 February 2022, a few days before the elections in Delhi, India, a politician created a deepfake to reach out to voters in different languages, which became viral on social media. It was the first recorded case of a deepfake by a politician for campaigning purposes. Another well-known example is the deepfake of Barack Obama delivering a Public Service Announcement (PSA) about fake news, created by Jordan Peele. "Obama" says in the PSA: "It may sound basic, but how we move forward in the Age of Information is going to be the difference between whether we survive or whether we become some kind of f******-up dystopia."

This is the worrying factor of deepfakes spreading misinformation by public figures. This can have a serious impact on society, including damaging the reputation of leaders, wrongly influencing elections, inciting violence, and even threatening national security. Countering deepfakes and fighting against such abuse will involve individuals, technology companies, businesses, and governments. It will require a mix of technological, societal and regulatory measures to arrest the "weaponisation" of AI and the challenges posed by deepfakes.

According to the AIGS (Artificial Intelligence Global Surveillance) index, at least 75 countries globally are actively using AI-based surveillance technologies. In his dystopian social science fiction novel, *1984*, George Orwell famously wrote, "Big Brother is watching you". The use of technology must be for the common good and must be lawful, as some have raised ethical concerns about AI-powered surveillance. Technology companies that provide access to AI and other technologies have an ethical obligation to ensure that the technology is deployed responsibly. IBM has ceased to offer AI-based surveillance solutions that might violate fundamental human rights.

Cambridge Analytica leveraged AI to provide campaign information during the 2016 presidential election to Donald Trump and Ted Cruz. The data was gathered and harvested by crawling Facebook. The Federal Trade Commission fined Facebook $5 billion for privacy violations, and Analytica closed down its operations. This scandal of deploying AI to turn "clicks into votes" highlighted the pressing need for the ethical use of AI and the need for AI regulations.

This also requires constant monitoring by leveraging technology and acting quickly. Regulators need to stay abreast of advances in technology to ensure laws are relevant to protect society. Technology companies are developing AI tools to combat deepfakes, including Google, which is working on a text-to-speech conversion AI tool to verify speakers. The US Defense Advanced Research Projects Agency (DARPA) is funding a research initiative to develop automated screening of deepfakes. The algorithm is called MediFor. The challenge in developing algorithms to detect deepfakes is that it requires large datasets to train the AI model and development is in its early stages.

However, Prof. Maneesh Agarwala of Stanford University's Institute of Human-Centred Artificial Intelligence (cited in Andrews, 2020) warns that "as the technology to manipulate videos gets better and better, the capability of technology detecting manipulation will get worse and worse. We need to focus on non-technical ways to identify and reduce disinformation and misinformation." He says we need to increase media literacy and hold perpetrators responsible for deliberately producing and spreading misinformation. He further reiterates that detecting whether a video has been manipulated is not the same as whether the video contains misinformation or disinformation. The latter is much more complex and has much more severe repercussions on society. The development of deepfakes is getting easier, and the applications to develop these videos are easily accessible and downloadable, and many are open-source based. The proliferation of deepfakes rides on the proliferation of social media platforms. If this trend is not checked, deepfakes and their negative impact will erode trust in media content, be used as a channel for hate speech, inflame the public, and lead to violence and even war between nations.

On the other end of the spectrum, deepfakes as an AI tool can also positively impact our lives and society. They are used in education, art, entertainment, movie production, for creating digital avatars, creating voices of those who have lost theirs, virtually trying clothes, and forensic research. However, as access to synthetic media technology increases, so does the risk of exploitation.

Responsible AI and Regulatory Framework

Another ethical challenge of AI is responsibility. An example of this is autonomous vehicles. According to Allied Market Research, the global autonomous vehicle market was valued at $76 billion in 2020 and is projected to reach $2,162 billion by 2030, growing at a CAGR (compound annual growth rate) of 40% from 2021 to 2030. The responsibility and liability of autonomous vehicles remains a pressing issue that needs to be addressed collectively by auto manufacturers, insurance companies, regulators, and governments. Existing motor and insurance laws are written for conventional motor vehicles in the hands of a human being, and liability rests with the driver. Autonomous vehicles are not affected by distraction, tiredness, driving habits or the inexperience of human drivers. Autonomous vehicles could reduce the number of accidents and consequently feed a drop in auto insurance claims and auto insurance fraud. However, the fact remains that the auto insurance industry will have to go through a major overhaul as autonomous vehicles become commonplace on our roads and highways.

A person's driving history, their number of years of experience, and their risk profile will no longer be the key or only factors; insurance companies may need to factor in the complexity of AI software and the degree of "explainability" of the autonomous vehicles. The liability is expected to shift from the driver to the auto manufacturer or a mix of both. On 20 November 2018, an Uber self-driving car in Tempe, Arizona, hit a pedestrian who later died in hospital. After investigations, it was decided that Uber was not responsible for the death of the pedestrian, but the safety driver, as she was distracted by her mobile phone, and the authorities reported that the accident was "completely avoidable". Auto manufacturers may include insurance along with the purchase of the autonomous vehicle. Some reports even call it the beginning of the end of the auto industry. Traffic and auto insurance laws will have to change. The lawyers representing the victims of the accidents will have to have a good understanding of the legal, technical and regulatory complexities involved.

Regulating AI ethics is no longer optional but an imperative in order to harness the power of AI and to protect the interests of society. There have been notable initiatives, including the 2019 EU policy document from the Centre for Data Innovation promoting "Trustworthy AI" that should be lawful, ethical and technically resilient.

Technical Challenges: Blackbox and Opacity

The fundamental question is, if we are unable to comprehend the process and how and why an AI arrived at a specific outcome, how can we trust the AI model? According to Bathaee (2018), "the Blackbox Problem can be defined as an inability to fully understand an AI's decision-making process and the inability to predict AI's decisions or outputs".

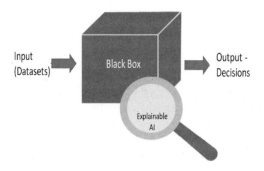

"Opacity is the heart of the Black Box Problem – a problem with significant practical, legal, and theoretical consequences. Practically, end-users are less likely to trust and cede control to machines whose workings they do not understand" (Burrell, 2016). Some call it the "opacity dilemma" of AI ethics. Unlike traditional non-AI applications (generally what is known as "automation"), AI applications have complex algorithms and a vast amount of data. As AI makes decisions such as who gets a job, creditworthiness, who will skip bail or will re-offend, or who will develop Alzheimer's Disease or cancer, we must be able to fully understand the inherent decision-making process, and it must be explainable. However, many of the decisions made by AI, particularly for DL models, are not necessarily fully explainable at the point of making the decision. This is known as the problem of AI opacity.

Not all forms of the opacity of AI are a problem. For instance, companies may not want to disclose their trade secrets. The "black box" refers to a situation where even the technical experts are unable to explain or fully understand the decisions made by the AI. This is known as the "AI black box syndrome". The concept of explainability seeks to address the opacity in these models by generating output with an understandable explanation about the rationale of the AI model, with respect to its decision. However, some defend the black box AI models on the basis that malicious actors will reverse-engineer the algorithm to game the system. The theory of "security through obscurity" has been generally not well received and has been dismissed. The US National Institute of Standards and Technology (NIST) recommends against this: "System security should not depend on the secrecy of the implementation or its components" (Wikipedia).

As discussed in Chapter 2, AI is a vast and fast-evolving technology. Some algorithms are more complex than others and "behave" differently. Deep Neural Network (DNN) constitutes numerous layers of networks that are interconnected and trained on massive datasets. For example, the LSTM model (Long Short-Term Memory) involves countless neurons. Hence it is not easy to specifically understand how the model makes decisions. IBM Watson for Oncology is a casualty of this weakness, though it was one of the leading AI innovations in recent times. In order to tackle biases in AI models, there will have to be organisational and technical strategies in place.

When developing AI applications, the following organisational procedures must be adopted to avoid data bias and algorithmic bias. Each organisation should have in place well-defined guidelines and robust frameworks constituting principles, standards, processes, and methodologies for comprehensively and proactively addressing ethical issues when designing and developing responsible AI algorithms. This document must specify internal and external stakeholders, including data collectors, data scientists, developers, business owners and most importantly, AI ethicists. This document should also address (a) privacy, (b) fairness, (c) prevention of discrimination, (d) transparency, (e) explainability, (f) security, (g) compliance, and (h) tools to reduce bias. These issues are not independent of each other but affect each other. When developing the above, we need to assess the possible risks, and the document must outline measures to mitigate these risks. This must be a living document that can evolve as the AI advances.

AI Governance

Dr. Baeza-Yates (2022) says, "Ethics always runs behind technology too. It happened with chemical weapons in World War I and nuclear bombs in World War II, to mention just two examples." AI governance is the process of evaluating and monitoring algorithms' effectiveness, accuracy, bias and risk. It also defines policies and guidelines for establishing accountability in creating and deploying AI systems in an organisation. The fundamental principles of governance are transparency, accuracy, fairness and accountability. Being able to explain why an AI model behaves in a specific manner and its decision-making process can boost trust in the accuracy and fairness of the decision or output generated by AI. Also, we need to ensure accountability of the performance of the AI model. What constitutes a reasonable explanation will vary depending on the audience as well as the complexity of the AI system. For example, a radiologist could use the historical data of 100 patients as a reference, based on a probability of 90%, to report the chance of a tumour.

Explainable AI (XAI): Making the Blackbox Transparent

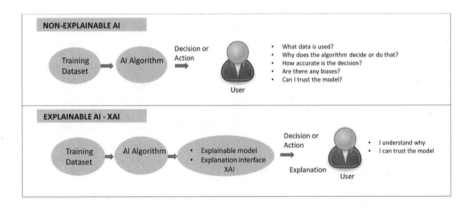

Explainable AI (XAI), sometimes known as Interpretable AI, refers to methods and techniques that enable humans to understand the results generated by an AI algorithm, hence improving on the governance and ethical dimension of AI. It is a fast-emerging area that provides transparency and creates trust in AI. XAI explains how the AI model works and why a result was generated in a comprehensible manner to non-technical end-users. What data did the model use? Why did the AI model make a specific prediction or decision? Are there any biases? When do AI models give enough confidence in the decision to form the basis for trust? How can the AI algorithm correct errors that arise?

AI algorithms that have traceability and transparency in their decision-making – such as Naive Bayes, linear regression, logistic regression, Decision Trees, K-Nearest Neighbors (KNN) – can provide explainability without sacrificing too much on performance or accuracy. More complicated AI models based on more powerful algorithms – such as deep neural networks including Random Forest (RF), Convoluted Neural Networks (CNN), Recurrent Neural Networks (RNN) and other similar algorithms – may not have high levels of transparency and explainability but will have more power, better performance and accuracy. This is because of their inherent complexity and multitudinous layers of networks of neurons.

Explainability is an intuitively appealing concept but hard to fully realise because of the complexities of advanced AI algorithms. Dr. Lance B. Eliot (2021), a renowned expert on AI and ML, emphatically says, "Please be aware that there is an ongoing and dangerous tendency these days to anthropomorphise AI. In essence, people are assigning human-like sentience to today's AI, despite the undeniable and inarguable fact that no such AI exists as yet." In sum, AI is not sentient yet, and until we reach the stage of ASI, XAI will have limitations for deep neural network-based models.

However, unlike Blackbox AI, XAI gives data scientists better control of the model's behaviour, thus enabling them to avoid discrimination and any biases. XAI generally has two levels: *explainability for data* and *explainability for algorithm*. It is key to developing AI models that are understandable, transparent, and interpretable. This will enhance confidence and ensure effective and safe use of AI for the intended purpose.

According to the NIST, the four key principles of XAI are:

- **Explanation**: Systems should provide evidence or reason(s) for all output.

- **Meaningful:** Systems should offer explanations that are understandable to individual users.
- **Accuracy:** The answer should accurately describe the system's process for generating the output.
- **Knowledge Limits**: The system should only operate under limits or conditions for which it was designed.

With XAI, biases and erroneous situations can be avoided by justifying the output. For example, when extending loans and performing credit ratings, banks can leverage XAI. The model would be able to justify its recommendations and give clients a detailed explanation if their loan application was declined. Banks simply cannot take the risk of using Blackbox AI; they need to deploy XAI to have a degree of transparency and accuracy to meet compliance requirements.

However, explainability doesn't provide all the answers with respect to "fairness". Lily Hu (2021), a PhD candidate in applied mathematics at Harvard University who studies algorithmic fairness, states that "the use of algorithms in social spaces, particularly in the prison system, is an inherently political problem, not a technological one". To develop models to avoid any bias and to ensure "fairness", we must agree precisely on what it means to be fair before developing the algorithms which may vary based on societal, cultural and political norms.

Not only do AI models require the right volume and quality of data, but they need to ensure data scientists don't pass on their human biases and assumptions when developing and training the AI models. People from different backgrounds would have different societal and cultural norms, perceptions, beliefs and practices. Cognitive biases are generally unconscious errors in judgement made by data scientists. AI can only be as good as the people who develop it and the data that is used to "train" it.

XAI can leverage tools and methodologies such as Google's What-If Tool, IBM's Watson OpenScale or AI Fairness 360, Microsoft's Fairlearn and Accenture's Teach and Test methodology. These tools can test and mitigate biases in models on a real-time basis. They can also analyse the importance of different data features, visualise model behaviour, and validate different AI fairness metrics. Many of them are open-source, including the tools from Google, IBM and Microsoft.

Conclusion

The rapid digitisation and penetration of AI has led to the rise of customer-centricity. Businesses collect vast amounts of data about customers' needs, preferences and wants. Data is the new oil, as the saying goes. AI helps businesses realise which customers are more receptive to marketing campaigns and messages than others. Responsible AI has rewarded businesses with opportunities for delivering personalised products and services while upholding customer values and doing good for society. Implementing measures to avoid human bias is necessary for developing solutions that are accurate, fair and transparent, and is not only a moral and ethical issue but also good for business. Simply put, it can set a business apart from the competition by improving customer confidence, trust and loyalty, and this trait will become far more significant as AI becomes more pervasive.

The question is not necessarily about whether AI will become more intelligent than us, though some believe it will, but about what we can do to make sure AI does good and we don't abuse technology. AI is driven by data fed by man and the algorithms developed by man. AI models must be designed, developed and used in a manner that respects laws, human rights and ethical values. For now, it is for humans to decide on the degree of autonomy we should extend to AI. Inherently, the existing forms of AI do not have empathy and emotions; in other words, they are devoid of sentience. Ultimately, the onus is on humans to ensure the responsible and ethical behaviour of AI!

References

Andrews, E.L. (2020, October 13). Using AI to Detect Seemingly Perfect Deep-Fake Videos. HAI Stanford University. Available at: https://hai.stanford.edu/news/using-ai-detect-seemingly-perfect-deep-fake-videos.

Bathaee, Y. (2018, May 5). The Artificial Intelligence Black Box and the Failure of Intent and Causation. *Harvard Journal of Law & Technology*, 31(2). https://jolt.law.harvard.

edu/assets/articlePDFs/v31/The-Artificial-Intelligence-Black-Box-and-the-Failure-of-Intent-and-Causation-Yavar-Bathaee.pdf.

Burrell, J. (2016, January 6). How the machine 'thinks': Understanding opacity in machine learning algorithms. *Big Data & Society*, 1–12. DOI:10.1177/2053951715622512. https://journals.sagepub.com/doi/pdf/10.1177/2053951715622512.

Eliot, L. (2021, April 24). Explaining Why Explainable AI (XAI) Is Needed for Autonomous Vehicles and Especially Self-Driving Cars. Forbes. Available at: https://www.forbes.com/sites/lanceeliot/2021/04/24/explaining-why-explainable-ai-xai-is-needed-for-autonomous-vehicles-and-especially-self-driving-cars/?sh=3c2a2c921c5a.

Singh, A. & Mutreja, S. (2022, February 15). Autonomous Vehicle Market Statistics 2030. Allied Market Research. Available at: https://www.alliedmarketresearch.com/autonomous-vehicle-market.

Zicari, R.V. (2022, February 7). On Responsible AI. Interview with Ricardo Baeza-Yates. ODBMS Industry Watch. Available at: http://www.odbms.org/blog/2022/02/on-responsible-ai-interview-with-ricardo-baeza-yates/.

CHAPTER 4

AI and Cybersecurity

"Artificial intelligence is the future, not only for Russia, but for all humankind. It comes with colossal opportunities, but also threats that are difficult to predict. Whoever becomes the leader in this sphere will become the ruler of the world."
– Vladimir Putin

AI has become a revolutionary national security technology and it permeates all systems, including finance, healthcare, supply chain, and even military surveillance, reconnaissance, and weapon systems. Cyberattacks in the new era of the "Internet of Everything" are massive, stealthier, complex, growing rapidly and becoming more impactful. The cyber threat landscape has expanded exponentially as a result. AI is fast becoming a necessity in strategically managing the defensive posture of all systems as they are more effective, smarter than standard systems and faster than cybersecurity professionals can keep up. AI is underpinning a powerful human-machine partnership and is driving cybersecurity in a manner that seems greater than the sum of its parts. This chapter discusses the growing challenges and threats of cyberattacks, and how AI is augmenting humans and the existing cybersecurity infrastructure in charting the changing cybersecurity landscape.

The Threat of Cyberattacks

There are an estimated 30 billion connected devices, and they are growing exponentially as millions are being added on a weekly basis. By 2030 or sooner, each household in developed countries will have 50 active connected devices. These range from smartwatches to voice assistants, refrigerators, cars, aircraft, spacecraft, pacemakers and other products which are shaping our lives. According to the Ericsson Mobility Report, 5G cellular network subscription is expected to reach 4.4 billion globally by the end of 2027. The growth of data is exploding and will remain unstoppable. According to Seed Scientific, the world is currently estimated to generate 1,000 petabytes of data per day. By 2025, the amount of data generated each day is expected to reach 463 exabytes globally. With this unrelenting penetration of connected devices, the number of security flaws and vulnerabilities is also exploding. Current security technologies put businesses and nations at risk.

Cybercriminals are taking advantage of AI, and the notably higher speed of 5G networks is a potent mix for cyberattacks and new risks. Governments and organisations face increased risk as cyberattacks become more sophisticated in the virtual world. Also, cyberattacks are becoming faster and smarter with each success and failure, making it difficult to predict or neutralise them. According to the 2022 Cyber Threat Report by internet cybersecurity company SonicWall, governments worldwide saw a 1,885% increase in ransomware attacks in 2021. And during the same period, the world experienced a staggering 105% surge in ransomware attacks. The specific causes are yet to be determined, but one factor is surely the increase in remote working during the pandemic.

Undoubtedly, the attacks are increasing in variety, volume and viciousness, causing financial losses, lost productivity, supply chain disruptions and reputational damage. Hackers may make a tidy sum; political parties and nations may also influence voters, public opinion and ideologies or even engage in cyber-warfare and espionage. According to the Allianz Risk Barometer, cyberattacks and data breaches have become the most important business risk since 2020. Gartner forecasted the global information security market to grow at a compound annual growth rate (CAGR) of 12.4% and exceed $150 billion in 2021, reflecting the growing demand.

AI is revolutionising every industry, including cybersecurity, and changing the game. There are predominantly two types of cyberattacks.

One of them attacks individual accounts and organisations, which has been going on since the first ransomware in 1989 (PS Cyborg) and the first phishing attacks in the mid-1990s. The other type, which is far more dangerous and impactful, involves attacking anything that is considered critical infrastructure for the economy and society, such as supply chains, power grids, nuclear facilities, water supplies and gas supplies.

It is over 30 years since the first cyberattack set the stage for modern cybersecurity threats and challenges. In November 1988, a graduate student at Cornell University, Thomas Tappan Morris, developed an application as he wanted to know how big the internet was. He developed a program, now known as Morris Worm, that would travel from computer to computer via the internet and send a message to the control server, which would keep count. The program travelled so fast around the globe, clogging up the internet, even Morris's attempts to warn the system administrators couldn't get through.

This was the first "distributed denial of service" (DDoS), where a system shuts down because of overwhelmingly heavy traffic or the network is blocked. This event set the stage for modern cyberattacks, which are much more frequent, damaging and crippling. Another notorious attack was by a Canadian high-schooler who launched a DDoS attack on several commercial sites in 2000, including big players like CNN, eBay, and Amazon. The hacks resulted in an estimated $1.2 billion of damage.

The first reported cyber-warfare began in 2010 with Stuxnet, which destroyed 20% of the centrifuges Iran used to create as part of its nuclear arsenal. Another allegedly state-sponsored cyberattack was on 24 November 2014. Hackers broke into the IT infrastructure of Sony Pictures and stole a massive trove of confidential documents, and posted them online in the subsequent days. This exposed Sony and its employees to everyone, from potential fraudsters to journalists.

In the interconnected world, speed kills. Within the span of a few minutes, a skilled hacker can break into the network of a business and exfiltrate sensitive and vital datasets (data theft). It is fast becoming a challenge for a security analyst to identify malicious activities given the increasing volume, variety and velocity of Big Data. This is further complicated by the complexity and the fast-changing landscape of persistent attacks.

Data breaches happen to many businesses every day, and everyone is at risk. The world has pivoted online, and the e-commerce market is valued to be worth nearly $10 trillion (2021) and growing at a CAGR of 14.7%. Undoubtedly this is drawing flocks of cyber-bandits and fraudsters to the web. Personal information such as names, national IDs, emails, passwords, credit card numbers and other sensitive information is being sold and bought on the dark web. Because of the growing complexity and frequency of modern cyberattacks, it is difficult for cybersecurity analysts to keep up with them. Until recently, most cyber threat detection was performed by a technique known as "signature-based detection". There is no doubt that signature-based detection has been a critical component of the security arsenal since the first antivirus was introduced, but the cyberattack landscape isn't static. It is evolving rapidly and newer attack techniques are entering the fray every day.

Security That Thinks

What is AI security? It is a set of tools and techniques that leverages AI to autonomously identify any malicious behaviour and takes action to defend against potential cyber-threats based on similar or previous activity. AI has fast become an integral part of cybersecurity. AI can compute and analyse a trove of data and predict, identify patterns of malicious activities, indicate potential threats, send alerts, and automate countermeasures to defend and neutralise the attacks. Because of AI's capabilities in being able to quickly process a voluminous amount of information, it can locate, quarantine, and remediate cyberattacks more efficiently than humans.

As cybersecurity specialists are overwhelmed with alerts, of which many are false positives, they may miss the real problems and miss the advanced attacks. AI can step up and proactively take care of security incidents and event management as the AI algorithms are good at pattern analysis. AI can provide much-needed insight, predictive analysis and threat intelligence in real-time to enhance the security of the system. It can also alert security analysts about any potential attack because of its ability to detect any anomalous behaviour and speed up the understanding of the threat.

In addition, AI can assist antivirus software in identifying malicious files and new forms of malware that traditional antivirus software may not be able to detect. ML and DL algorithms learn the network's behaviour over time and use that information to improve security in the future. In essence, AI cybersecurity behaves much like its human counterpart except with much more speed and efficiency, hence augmenting some of the work done by security analysts.

Leveraging AI, organisations need to build a "zero trust" architecture. AI-enabled authentication can ensure that only authorised individuals have access to sensitive information. Zero-trust AI systems leverage multiple data points and perform multi-factor authentication in real-time. ML-based security algorithms analyse information such as device ID, working hours, geographical location, facial recognition, behavioural data, including typing or scrolling patterns on the devices, and other assigned criteria to calculate a risk factor before granting or denying access. The stakes are too high to be complacent about the growing presence of cyber-threats. AI is an indispensable technology in dealing with the ever-growing volume and variety of cyberattacks. AI will play a vitally crucial role in cybersecurity!

As discussed in the chapter on AI and ethics, the trust between AI and humans can be improved with Explainable Artificial Intelligence (XAI). XAI enhances the ability of the cybersecurity team to understand the AI black box and the complex security technologies, rather than AI merely sending alerts of a potential breach or uncommon system behaviour.

Anomaly Detection

Both supervised and unsupervised ML algorithms can be applied for fraud detection such as in credit card scams. Classification and anomaly detection algorithms can identify events that do not conform to an expected pattern or other information in a dataset. This is one of the areas where AI tools are contributing to the effectiveness of cybersecurity and have shown remarkable results in identifying and classifying complex scams.

In real-time, anomaly detection algorithms can help determine whether a transaction has any unusual patterns, such as date and time or location of purchase.

Different AI algorithms can be used to detect fraud and each of them has its pros and cons. Some AI models are complex (neural networks) and require much bigger datasets, but they have remarkable accuracy. In contrast, others are simpler classification models – such as logistic regression, Naive Bayes, SVM and decision trees – which can be easily interpreted and visualised. Classification algorithms are linear and generally applied for spamming and phishing-related malicious activities. Clustering techniques are used for forensic analysis as they can provide information on the type of cyberattack and what was compromised. And generative models can be used for complex problems to check for system vulnerabilities by performing penetration testing of the system. Detecting any attempts to penetrate the system is key to securing an organisation's network.

ML algorithms can also better manage other time-consuming tasks such as malware analysis, network traffic analysis, triaging intelligence, network risk scoring and vulnerability assessment. AI-based fraud detection and analytics dashboards provide comprehensive information about the security breach for the security analyst to investigate and take necessary countermeasures with or without the use of AI. With auto ML, the network can be self-diagnosing, self-provisioning, and self-healing.

AI and DDoS

Distributed Denial of Service (DDoS) is one of the major methods of cyberattacks and one of the most potent hacking techniques; it has become an everyday occurrence for most organisations. The average enterprise receives more than 10,000 alerts per day, and according to *American Banker*, more than 37% of banks receive north of 200,000 alerts per day. According to AV-TEST, there are a staggering 12 million new variants per month, and the institute registers over 390,000 new malicious programs every day. These threats underscore the growing need for advanced tools and technologies to bolster cybersecurity to stem cybercrimes.

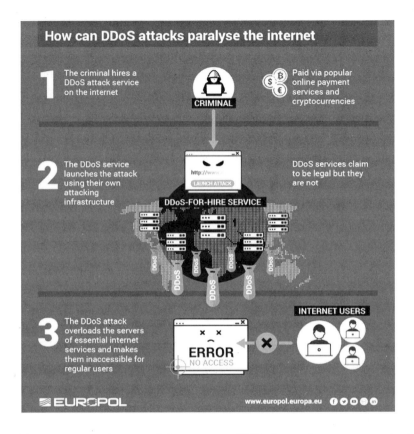

The growing volume and frequency of DDoS attacks can cause significant loss and damage to governments and businesses. The base weapon that hackers use during DDoS is to take down or crash websites, email servers, databases or any other connected system – not just the website, as this is a general misconception. With the pervasiveness of technologies such as cloud computing, attackers can launch a massive volume of vicious DDoS attacks at lower cost, from anywhere, from any device, and more frequently. DDoS are furthermore hard to detect and prevent. These attacks disrupt and damage the system with criminal intent for ransom. There are two primary types of DDoS attacks: (a) spoofing attacks, where cybercriminals impersonate; and (b) flooding attacks, where they send a flood of packet requests to disrupt the availability of services.

Traditional approaches of firewalls and hardware-based Intrusion Detection Systems (IDS) aren't capable of handling modern and sophisticated cyberattacks. Firewalls and IDS devices use a set of rules to determine which outside connections to allow and which to block. Today's cyberattacks are capable of creating a sudden and exponential increase in network traffic in the order of 10,000x in split seconds. Hence, traditional approaches may not be able to cope with the surge in pings. DDoS attacks can come in different varieties depending on the methods used. Networking Layer or Protocol attacks and Volume-based Traffic attacks are the most common ones. The growing onslaught and penetration of connected IoT devices will lead to more intense attacks in scope and size. Cybercriminals also leverage the vast internet bandwidth to target their victims with increasing speed, frequency and ferocity from multiple launch points simultaneously.

According to an annual survey conducted by Cloudflare, "ransom-motivated DDoS attacks increased 29% year-on-year and 175% between Q3 2021 and Q4 2022". According to reports, in the first three months of 2021 alone, there were more attacks of over 50 Gbps than in all of 2019. Attacks of this scale can bring down any website or system.

In late 2018, the FBI took down a dozen DDoS-for-hire marketplaces, and Europol shut down Webstresser, the world's largest marketplace for buying DDoS attacks. At the time of shutting down, Webstresser had over 130,000 registered users and was responsible for 4 million attacks in 2018. These attacks were targeted at critical online services offered by financial institutions, government agencies and security forces, as well as victims in the gaming industry. Obviously, cybercrime is on the rise as this is a profitable business for the bad actors of society, and there is a growing need to step up innovative security measures to counter "smart cyberattacks".

AI and ML algorithms are predominantly used for two purposes: to detect and to prevent DDoS. This is generally achieved by attack prevention, attack detection, and attack reaction. It is challenging to detect DDoS attacks because it is hard to differentiate the cyberattack traffic and regular traffic. ML classification algorithms can be used to differentiate the good and bad requests. Requests that are classified as DDoS attacks will be terminated. Some of the metrics used to detect cyberattacks include the number of request packets, average request packet size, time interval variance, request packet size variance, number of bytes, request rate and bit rate.

Firstly, we need to monitor the traffic to spot anomalies. The AI models will constantly monitor the system traffic for the origin of any uncommon behaviour and analyse any potential attack by using specific metrics to determine whether a response is needed. As soon as the AI model starts seeing abnormalities through behavioural analytics, it will take countermeasures to neutralise the requests, generally by terminating the requests while undertaking other measures to avoid compromising the bandwidth and to maintain acceptable levels of latency of the system, either by redirecting the network, filtering the requests or even terminating the requests. The log will be analysed and used to continue training the model. AI models can automatically detect and learn from both historical data and real-time data. However, the performance of AI models will depend on the quality of data.

AI vs AI: Cybersecurity Arms Race

AI is neither good nor bad; it really depends on how humans use it. Nothing is immune to attacks, and the same is true with AI. ML algorithms are being used for sophisticated cyberattacks, which can be more destructive than traditional attacks and are expanding the cyber-threat landscape by introducing new kinds of attacks or altering existing characteristics of cyberattacks. They can use AI to uncover system vulnerabilities of the target network. Cyberattackers can also design fresh attacks based on insights gathered from previous attacks by leveraging ML. As enterprises continue to leverage AI technology for business and strategic purposes, bad actors and cyber-criminals will modify their penetration strategies to avoid or circumvent detection and increase the speed of their attacks.

Before, phishing attackers manually collected information about their targets and sent messages through email or social media using social engineering techniques such as spoofing. But today, cyberattackers can use ML algorithms to scrape the target's profile from any social media or other digital platforms to launch a phishing and spear-phishing attack, which are far more effective than human-created phishing attacks. Such attacks are much faster than traditional phishing and can reach out to much bigger targets. Moreover, cyberattackers can personalise target information, thus making it more convincing and credible.

Brute force attacks are becoming more sophisticated and complex as hackers are using ML to automatically generate valid password lists of targets. There are a multitude of applications across industries where fraudsters can cause significant damage and chaos. For instance, while ML plays a pivotal role in developing autonomous vehicles, it is equally important to consider the security implications of hard-to-detect criminal acts such as hijacking and crashing an autonomous vehicle, which can be done remotely and would be difficult to trace.

As AI requires massive quantities and diverse types of digital data, it presents new complexities not found in traditional systems and is vulnerable to data breaches. Another emerging advanced cyberattack technique is to compromise the integrity of AI's decision-making capabilities. These attacks are designed to make ML algorithms make wrong predictions by "feeding" malicious and unverified input or training data such as fake news or doctored videos, or through data poisoning. These attacks can be catastrophic and long-lasting. Hence, it is critical to ensure that the training data used comes from trusted sources. This will also require a robust data ingestion process so that any anomalies can be identified. And if there is any breach, data versioning should be activated for the ML model to roll back to the pre-attack version.

We also need to ensure that both data and algorithms are secured and only accessed by authorised individuals. In addition, it is also important for security professionals to be alert for any suspicious activity or unanticipated behaviour of AI. Through constant monitoring, we can prevent these attacks from taking place or at least greatly minimise the damage and losses sustained.

There are also other advanced ML-based techniques including using only encrypted input data and encrypted models. Hence, training data and model algorithms will be fully secured and protected against potential threats. The other side of the coin is to engage AI to manage these potential cyberattacks. ML models can be trained to evaluate threats and to take countermeasures to defend against a threat. DL models learn and evolve over time so they can pre-emptively identify and defend against new threats that they have not seen before. In short, the only way to tackle this is to use AI against these malicious activities.

AI-driven Fraud

According to a Nilson Report, credit card fraud is projected to cost the industry $408.5 billion in losses over the next decade. Globally, there are nearly 3 billion credit cards in use. This number will only continue to grow as we move towards cashless transactions. The Covid-19 pandemic has fuelled an explosive growth of cybercrimes, as digital purchases have dramatically increased in volume during this period. Cybercriminals are weaponising AI by leveraging it to design and execute cyberattacks. They use AI to learn about the target victim and use online robots to make copies of their online behaviour and actions. They replicate the same playbook that retail businesses use to gather insights about their customers.

There are various forms of identity theft, including synthetic theft (where a fraudster creates a new identity by combining natural and artificial information); actual name theft (which takes place by phishing); and account take-over or account compromise (where a cybercriminal gains control of a legitimate account).

Credit card fraud can happen online, over the phone, by text, or in person. You can be scammed by fake emails, or have your information stolen in a data breach by hackers gaining access to your bank or credit card accounts. The fraudster then intercepts communication about the account to keep the victim blind to any breach. These are just a few of the many possibilities. Amongst them, web shell is a common technique. It is an interface (a piece of code) that is maliciously loaded onto a website in order for the fraudsters to remotely access and steal data or take control of the root directory of the server. This serves as a backdoor to the server for exfiltrating and harvesting sensitive information and credentials. Data breaches and identity thefts are a growing problem and a form of cybercrime that can have serious outcomes, such as losing all the funds in your bank account. With growing online penetration, it is just a mouse click away for cybercriminals to buy and sell criminal services online on the dark web.

Intelligent Warfare

AI technology is already transforming the future of warfare and is fast becoming the most important factor in determining the effectiveness of a country's military might. AI is being used for information warfare, cyber-attacks, satellite imagery, and simulators. AI algorithms have demonstrated that they can match the skills of veteran human pilots in gruelling "dog-fights". Maryland-based Heron Systems has reportedly beaten an F-16 Fighting Falcon pilot. AI is no longer just beating humans in chess, bridge and Jeopardy, but on the battlefields as well. Intelligent cyberattacks could be the first line of warfare by knocking out all communications, includ-ing satellites, thus crippling the entire network, bringing everything that is connected to a grinding halt, including aircraft in the sky, autonomous vehicles, hospital systems, power grids and nuclear plants, and life will be thrown into utter chaos.

The war between Armenia and Azerbaijan in 2020, while the world was consumed with the pandemic, is an excellent case study of the future of warfare: man vs machine. It showed how a small military could punch above their weight and win wars by leveraging technology. Azerbaijan won the war decisively, decimated the Armenian defence forces, and avoided being bogged down in a lengthy war of human casualties. The military strategy was simple but ingenious. Azerbaijan deployed autonomously operating Harop munitions (now nicknamed "kamikaze drones"), which loiter in the sky for hours until they find their target – typically the ene-my's defence radar systems – before destroying it by crashing into it. It was reported that the Armenians converted vintage Soviet-built Antonov An-2 biplanes into remote-controlled decoys, which were deployed to fool the Armenian air force into activating their radars, which were then destroyed by the Harop drones. This made a real difference on the battlefield. With a weakened air force capability, the Armenian ground forces were attacked with more Harop drone strikes. Azerbaijan achieved this incredible suc-cess because of its technological edge over its enemy by leveraging auton-omous drones; most importantly, this resulted in fewer casualties. This is none other than the modernisation of warfare with AI and autonomous technologies!

The US Defense Advanced Research Project Agency's (DARPA) Target Recognition and Adaption in Contested Environments (TRACE) is another such defence system based on an ML program that is capable of real-time long-range targeting for airborne surveillance and strike capabilities. Drone swarms have also drawn the attention of militaries around the world. These "suicide drones" can be launched from remote locations, rain down and cause collateral damage to the enemy, and unleash destruction. Currently, swarming is one of the state-of-the-art areas of autonomous weapons devel-opment as they are highly effective and can be lethal and change the course of war.

This new paradigm of intelligent warfare started only recently, and there are many areas where military capability will be enhanced using AI. One of them is logistics. During the ongoing Russian-Ukraine war, the Rus-sians could have avoided significant setbacks faced in their logistics had they used AI. An efficient logistics system is critical for success on the bat-tlefield to ensure that weapons, food, medicine, troops, and other essential items get to the intended destinations on time. The future of the battlefield will be increasingly autonomous, driven by AI.

China and Russia have been leveraging AI to design and build new engines for hypersonic missiles without any human intervention. Hyper-sonic flights generally travel beyond Mach 5 or 1.6 kilometres per second, meaning five times faster than the speed of sound. However, recent hyper-sonic engines being built by AI can travel at Mach 8. The technology involved in building these engines is complex, as engineers have to analyse and scrutinise tens of thousands of images and a voluminous amount of technical data, which AI now handles.

As we have recently witnessed in the Russian-Ukraine war, hypersonic missiles are difficult to intercept and defend as they fly five times the speed of sound. Though slower than Intercontinental Ballistic Missiles (ICBM), hypersonic missiles do not travel on a fixed parabolic trajectory. Hence they are challenging to track. Russia became the first country in history to use this hypersonic missile, billed as "unstoppable", in combat. China's People's Liberation Army (PLA) recently announced (as part of their modernisation plans) a three-pronged integrated approach: "mechanisation, informatisation, and intelligentisation". This is an incredible paradigm shift in modern warfare.

These missile technologies also present other challenges as satellites in space will remain highly vulnerable, particularly those in Low Earth Orbit (LEO). They are located at altitudes that are within reach of these missiles. This is just an example, and the world may not fully appreciate the significance of this today, but AI technology is advancing faster than we might imagine. In March 2022, King's College London and Collaborations Pharmaceuticals, Inc. reported that it took just six hours for a drug-seeking AI system to generate 40,000 potentially lethal chemical modules. Like any technology, humans will use technology for good and evil purposes to achieve their own monetary or nationalistic endeavours. These AI technologies falling into the hands of the immoral and malevolent remains a looming danger for possible territorial or even global catastrophes.

As AI and Big Data advance and become more sophisticated, they will alter tomorrow's weapons of war and change the face of war. Human bravery on the battlefields now has an additional dimension: digitised warfare. AI is the new generation of military weaponry for defence forces to train, operate and fight on the battlefield. Superiority in AI can provide deep strategic real-time insights and predictive analytics and potentially reduce human casualties. AI will greatly influence the race for global dominance, including in economics and politics. It is not all doom and gloom, though, as it is ultimately about using AI and technology for the betterment of humanity through safeguards, collaboration and investment in the right places.

Conclusion

With growing digitisation, the looming threat of cybercrime is also increasing and the threat landscape is constantly changing. Humans and standard cybersecurity tools can no longer scale to adequately secure against the growing onslaught of cyberattacks without the support of AI. The cybercrime industry has been growing and even becoming an (illicit) economic model for some while it remains increasingly difficult to identify the perpetrators. The dark web is full of "dark online businesses" for illegal activities, including the selling of computer viruses, tools and services for hacking, zero-day attacks, ransomware and bitcoin services, amongst other fraudulent activities. Bitcoin is one of the leading cryptocurrencies used in dark web marketplaces due to its relative anonymity as a currency. Fraudulent cyber-activity on social media, emails and other social engineering activities can be significantly enhanced by leveraging AI and ML. Also, as discussed in the chapter on AI ethics, deepfakes can propagate misinformation.

Because of their technical superiority, AI and ML are now part of the cybersecurity arms race. AI has emerged as the cornerstone of cybersecurity, but adversaries are trying to use AI to compromise target systems. There are several benefits of using AI for cybersecurity. With AI and ML, cybersecurity tasks can be made more robust and efficient in activities such as threat detection, system behaviour analytics, and accurately identifying attacks and automatically remediating them. Also, AI and ML models can reduce human error and oversight, reduce the workload of cybersecurity professionals and be customised for specific organisational needs. In short, the real benefits of AI in cybersecurity are about *speed* in identifying and *intelligence* in establishing the context of the threat.

AI is a powerful and critical technology for cybersecurity, but it is not the panacea for all human ills and clandestine behaviour. Also, it is only as good as the skills of the security analyst using it. The industry needs more AI and ML skilled security experts and analysts, and there is a growing demand for such skills. Organisations must also continuously upgrade their systems as technology advances, as the cost of outdated systems may constitute a far greater threat as cyberattacks become more advanced and sinister. Regulatory guidelines, policies and laws must be periodically updated at a faster pace to protect data privacy. AI capabilities are deeply alluring for cybersecurity, even for military intelligence, surveillance, reconnaissance and national security. AI will be an integral part of the overall cybersecurity ecosystem of businesses and governments. This chapter has only touched on some of the critical issues of this complex and evolving technology of great significance. Going forward, AI will critically impact the new age of cyber-defence. In sum, perhaps only AI can neutralise AI.

References

Bruijn, H., Warnier, M., Janssen, M. (2021, December 30). The perils and pitfalls of explainable AI: Strategies for explaining algorithmic decision-making. *Government Information Quarterly*, 39(2). DOI:101666. https://doi.org/10.1016/j.giq.2021.101666.

Charan, H. (2019, March 31). Use of ML and AI in BlackHat Hacking. HackerNoon. Available at: https://medium.com/hackernoon/use-of-ml-and-ai-in-blackhat-hacking-737a621e4694.

SeedScientific. (2021, October 28). How Much Data Is Created Every Day? 27 Staggering Stats. SeedScientific. Available at: https://seedscientific.com/how-much-data-is-created-every-day?utm_source=privacy-hub-foleon&utm_medium=referral.

SonicWall. (2022, February 17). 2022 SonicWall: Cyber Treat Report. SonicWall. https://www.infopoint-security.de/media/2022-sonicwall-cyber-threat-report.pdf.

Zhang, B., Zhang, T., Yu, Z. (2018, March 26). DDoS detection and prevention based on artificial intelligence techniques. *IEEE*, 1276–1280. DOI:10.1109/Comp-Comm.2017.8322748. https://ieeexplore.ieee.org/document/8322748.

CHAPTER 5

AI and Law

Law touches every citizen and every aspect of the business world, virtually everything companies do. Everyone needs legal help and access to justice. AI for the legal profession is no longer a futuristic or abstract concept. So, what good can AI do for law firms and clients? Will AI bring about much-needed innovation for the legal industry and transform or revitalise the profession? This chapter will examine how AI has been transforming the legal profession from a practice perspective and delivering legal services to businesses and the man on the street. It will examine the current state of the legal tech industry, drivers for change, challenges and limitations for adoption and the future of AI for all the key segments of the legal sector, including the judiciary, law firms, in-house counsels and clients.

Introduction

There is growing inequality, and to some extent, the poorer quarters of society are being excluded from legal advice and access to justice. Some call it a "crisis of unmet legal need". AI and online legal services are beginning to address some of this much-needed access to legal support and justice. The adoption of technology in the legal industry seems to lag behind others, and the impact of technology is generally perceived to be slow and incremental in the legal profession. However, it is gaining momentum, driven by exponential internet penetration, Big Data, and demand-based cloud computing services worldwide. Many leading law firms have already deployed AI tools. According to a report in *The Times* of London (2021), most of the

UK's top 100 law firms are either already using AI technologies or are in the process of evaluating AI tools. Leading global law firms such as Baker & McKenzie, Freshfields, Latham & Watkins are some of the early adopters. Dentons, Rodyk & Davidson and Rajah & Tann have been the frontrunners in Singapore.

Barriers to Innovation and Adoption

While technologies such as AI have become the drivers of innovation and are the cornerstone for the transformation of other industries, it is important to acknowledge that long-established practices and norms remain inhibitors for adopting new technologies in the legal profession, which stifles innovation. The primary inhibitor for the adoption of new technologies, hence transformation, is the business culture and the traditional practices in the legal profession dating back decades, if not centuries. The legal profession is a highly regulated industry, unlike many other industries; businesses are owned and managed by licensed lawyers, who have typically not been responsive to change. Innovation has never been a priority or on the agenda of law firms partly because of the conservatism of lawyers, resistance to change, a risk-averse mindset and culture, the complexity of the law, and to some extent, the unique nature of each legal matter. In more ways than one, the legal profession has been largely reactive to adopting technology and business transformation, unlike other industries.

Over the last few decades, other industries have swiftly embraced and deployed the latest technologies such as Big Data and AI or Machine Learning to become competitive, which has transformed those industries. However, for the longest time, the legal profession has leveraged technology only in a limited fashion for some non-core areas and support functions – emails, calendaring, and document management systems. This is largely because the legal profession has been traditionally dependent on the experience and expertise of individual lawyers (human resources) for legal research and the preparation of substantive legal solutions for the legal matter at hand. This is time-consuming, labour-intensive, inefficient, and not scalable.

Another key concern in the legal industry is the privacy and security of data, as lawyers hold confidential client information where trust is a key component of the lawyer-client relationship. Any breach can have both tangible damage such as hefty fines as well as intangible fallout such as reputational damage. These issues and other challenges are discussed later in this chapter.

Drivers for Change

"Creativity is intelligence having fun." — Albert Einstein

Unlike industries such as finance and manufacturing, the legal industry has been traditionally conservative and is a laggard in embracing technology. Many might argue that this is one profession where technology has been under-utilised except in large global law firms. From a demand perspective, in today's data-driven society, the legal industry faces pressures to leverage AI to innovate and transform the delivery of legal services. The industry is at the threshold of disruption like other industries that have already embraced AI to re-engineer their business processes and service delivery models. The old and traditional model of delivering legal services may not survive for long. The legal industry has undergone several developments unique to its traditional and conservative culture and practice in the recent past. This includes allowing non-lawyers to be involved in law firms as board members, CEOs, COOs and CFOs, and accepting investments from external parties and individuals. These developments and the growing pervasiveness of technology have led to Alternative Legal Service Providers (ALSPs) and introduced fresh new perspectives for the legal industry.

With the proliferation of digital technology at all levels of society and the successful adoption and delivery of online services across other industries, there is an ever-growing demand and willingness by consumers to engage in anything that is virtual. This has now begun to spill over into the legal industry, and these developments are beginning to disrupt the traditional business models of law firms. Obviously, this disruption in the legal industry is gaining traction because of technological advances, in tandem with market forces. This augurs well for the future of the legal tech industry. Ron Dolin, a senior research fellow at Harvard Law School's Center for the

Legal Profession, states, "Artificial Intelligence software can do the contract review work of first-year law associates at a speed and scale that no human could – or should – be asked to do" (as cited in Rosenbaum, 2016). "And as AI systems become more commonplace, it becomes more problematic for law firms not to follow that trend. This is not reversible."

Technology-enabled legal services are virtual, agile, and not constrained by time or location. Hence, they can be on an "on-demand basis" for those who need the services. Besides, and more importantly, it can also be cost-effective because of economies of scale. Based on these drivers and benefits, the adoption is no longer a question of *whether* to deploy but *when and how* to deploy as AI is bound to become a mainstay in the legal industry in the coming years. To successfully deploy and leverage AI, there are certain non-technical elements that every organisation must focus on. The following are four key areas:

1. Process and procedures of the firm
2. Culture and structure of the firm
3. Skillsets and appreciation of the technology by members of the firm and their ability to leverage technology to deliver services
4. User experience of the legal services delivered online

To enable a comprehensive discussion in this chapter, I have divided the legal industry broadly into four main categories:

1. Judiciary – judges, judicial staff, prosecution lawyers
2. Law firms – lawyers, legal assistants, legal secretaries
3. In-house general/legal counsels
4. End users/clients

Judiciary

"As computational technology and artificial intelligence mature, more people will be able to have better access to justice."
— Monica Bay, Fellow, Stanford Law School CodeX

In many countries, there is a significant backlog of cases. Justice delayed is justice denied, as the cliché goes. AI technology that facilitates different processes such as data mining, legal research, projecting case progress and outcomes can assist in judicial tasks and administrative functions, improving efficiency and productivity. AI tools can also support judges with legal research, analysis of factual propositions, and determining the appropriateness of relevant legal provisions and other similar areas, expediting justice delivery.

AI tools are already assisting judges in arriving at decisions in cases such as motor vehicle accidents and compensation claims, where the judge's role is limited and seldom involves complex legal arguments and interpretation. AI technology-based tools can also aid judges in cataloguing legal and claims documents and glean the relevant information that will facilitate the determination of matters such as whether compensation is due, who is the party that is liable to pay, and the quantum of compensation.

In recent years, various Big Data and AI-driven technological applications have been already successfully introduced in the administration of justice in several countries, and the list is growing. These range from predictive analytics to automated divorce proceedings and automated decisions in small claims cases. The People's Republic of China stands at the vanguard of this development. Its judiciary has embraced the power of technology to promote judicial reform and "to build a judicial mechanism that is open, dynamic, transparent, and convenient and improve public understanding, trust, and supervision of the judiciary" (The Supreme People's Court, 26 February 2015).

China's first digital court based in Hangzhou launched a comprehensive online litigation platform in 2017 for internet-related civil and administrative cases. Since then, there have been initiatives supported by The Supreme People's Court to build "smart courts" in China, and many courts across China have digitised court proceedings. Jiangxi's High Court's "Judge e-assistant" tool uses image and text recognition technologies and semantic analysis to scan, analyse, index, and organise litigation material and generate relevant legal documents. The system can also recommend laws, relevant precedents and verdicts to guide judges.

In India, it is common knowledge that there is only one judge for every 50,000 citizens, while there is one police officer for 858 people. In 2019, the Supreme Court of India introduced a translation tool called SUVAAS. This tool can translate judicial documents from English to nine Indian vernacular languages, which has often been the bane of India's economic growth and, in this context, even their legal system. Another AI-based project called SUPACE (Supreme Court Portal for Assistance in Court Efficiency) has also been launched, aimed at data mining, tracking the progress of cases, and legal research to ensure timely delivery of justice by judges.

Across the United States, courts, corrections departments, and prisons have been using AI tools to determine the accused's risk based on the probability of a bailee appearing for his or her court date, and to assess the probability of an ex-offender committing another crime. These tools assist in making decisions about bail amount, sentencing as well as the likely duration of parole.

Although these AI tools can complement the judiciary in the decision-making process and facilitate better management of limited resources in the judiciary, these AI-assisted court verdicts have been challenged. There are several instances where the defendant challenged the ruling, and Wisconsin v. Loomis is one such case. The Wisconsin Department of Corrections leverages a risk assessment tool (COMPAS), and the trial judge sentenced Eric Loomis based on the "high risk" score allocated by COMPAS. Loomis appealed the verdict on the basis that he was not allowed to access the algorithm of COMPAS. Wisconsin's Supreme Court ruled against Loomis on the grounds that the risk assessment capabilities were acceptable and that there was an adequate level of transparency. This is not the first instance of challenge to the use of AI at sentencing. The plaintiffs in DeHoyos v. Allstate Corp. brought a class action suit on the basis that algorithms used by Allstate Corp for credit rating discriminated against minorities in violation of civil rights and federal law. The case was settled, and Allstate Corp agreed to reengineer the algorithm to make their credit scoring formula transparent and publicly available.

As this book focuses on different industries and verticals with respect to AI and its impact, I have kept the examples to a select few. But there is growing evidence that AI tools are gradually becoming pervasive across various jurisdictions and territories. Arguably, the justice of the future will be complemented by AI.

While AI is not magic or a silver bullet for all challenges, it has begun to significantly improve the judiciary by removing roadblocks and unclogging inefficiencies while challenging and even improving fundamental views on civil rights, due process and even fairness.

What Can AI Do for Lawyers?
And How Does AI Impact Law Firms?

"Computers are going to take over certain legal tasks – the practice of law will focus more on advice."
— Ricardo Anzaldua, Executive Vice President and General Counsel, Metlife

These are central questions confronting law firms and lawyers with respect to AI. The delivery of legal services has been undergoing changes over the past 5–10 years. The dreadful impact of the Covid-19 pandemic has accelerated the pace of these changes and has been a catalyst for innovation facilitated by IT, including AI. It is important to define what AI represents in the legal profession in order to fully appreciate its impact and the value proposition for the industry. Because of the rapid advances in AI technology, the adoption of AI solutions is slowly beginning to grow in law firms. However, two critical issues need to be addressed for greater adoption of AI:

(a) The fuzziness and confusion of what is "true AI" – there is a lack of comprehension about the term AI amongst the legal fraternity, its capabilities, and what AI can do for the legal profession. Also, the fear that AI could replace lawyers has posed even bigger challenges. This can only be addressed by greater awareness of the technology and its value proposition.

(b) Because of the upfront financial investments required to implement AI and the fear of expected disruption to existing customs and traditions of law firms and the industry, it remains out of reach for some, hence the low adoption rate. AI products complement lawyers by intelligently automating many of their tasks, but AI cannot automate lawyers. Hence, AI is unlikely to replace lawyers anytime in the near future but has been replacing some routine tasks undertaken by legal secretaries and paralegals, as evidenced (by way of example) in the banking industry, where technology has significantly reduced the number of human bank tellers by deploying ATMs. Broadly speaking, there are three key areas where AI is already impacting the legal profession.

1. eDiscovery/eResearch
2. eContract Review, Analysis and Due Diligence
3. ePrediction

eDiscovery

This is the first and most widely used AI application in the legal industry and is becoming even more ubiquitous over time. Wikipedia defines eDiscovery as "discovery in legal proceedings such as litigation, government investigations, or Freedom of Information Act requests, where the information sought is in electronic format (often referred to as electronically stored information or ESI)".

Several vendors offer eDiscovery solutions – Catalyst, Concordance, Eclipse, Kroll Ontrack, Relativity, and Summation are just some of the options. These eDiscovery solutions are offered either as a desktop version, which can be purchased for a one-time fee and downloaded onto your computer, or a web version hosted on the cloud. Cloud-based eDiscovery applications are hosted and managed by the vendor and can be used on a pay-per-use basis or on a monthly or annual subscription basis. The advantage of this model is that the law firm does not have to purchase the licence, install and maintain the eDiscovery application and does not need in-house technical support.

How do eDiscovery applications work? In a nutshell, they capture documents' metadata and image, allowing users to search based on the metadata or images. Leveraging Natural Language Processing (NLP) capabilities, eDiscovery solutions allow lawyers and paralegals to scan volumes of documents in split seconds. This frees up lawyers' time in order to focus on more strategic legal work and glean more relevant information from these documents. This also translates into saving clients' and customers' money. Advanced functionality under this category includes legal research, contract/document analysis and review. This reduces manual review time by 30–90% while also increasing accuracy and relevancy. Analyse 50+ documents in less than a minute and minimise the risk of missing key information – sounds good, doesn't it?

There are a growing number of online databases of case law, precedents, statutes, judgments, rules and regulations from global jurisdictions offered by commercial entities such as Westlaw and Lexis. They provide software applications that extend features and functions to research online, which are multiple times faster than traditional research by lawyers. These searches are not only faster but evidently extend cost savings (lawyers' time and resources) and potentially achieve more accuracy. The Commonwealth Legal Information Institute offers an online legal library where you can search for free. LawNet, managed by the Singapore Academy of Law (SAL), is a Singapore repository for online legal research. However, it does not have AI features and is essentially still very much a search engine/discovery tool.

Organisations and firms have begun to set up internal IT departments or are partnering with IT organisations to develop eDiscovery and legal research solutions. JP Morgan, a pioneer in this space, has reportedly developed an AI-based software termed COiN (Contract Intelligence), which performs legal research in seconds for what would usually take 360,000 hours of lawyers' time. This is a phenomenal amount of time and cost savings for such users. It frees up resources which can be dedicated to more strategic and complex legal matters to serve clients better. Companies have hundreds of thousands of documents, contracts, and agreements to be reviewed periodically. Such AI solutions will gradually be adopted by both law firms and in-house legal departments to increase productivity.

In the near future, AI tools will be able to go a step further and generate complex legal contracts without the need for a lawyer and with little margin of error. There are already solutions in the market, such as LISA, which can construct agreements requiring minimal human intervention.

eDue Diligence, Contract Analysis and Review

Due diligence is generally very labour-intensive and mainly consists of repetitive tasks where lawyers are involved in examining and advising clients about operating the framework of a business from a legal perspective and identifying financial risks and exposures. This includes going through a myriad of agreements and contracts of the company. Unlike financial due diligence, where the information examined is structured and mostly available in a spreadsheet, legal due diligence involves going through multitudinous contracts and agreements to investigate and study contractual risks.

According to Gartner (2019) research, the average time taken to finalise an M&A or acquisition has increased by 30% during the last decade. Gartner attributes this to several factors, including growing global compliance and regulatory requirements, complex structures of the deals, and the demands of investors. As mentioned previously in this chapter, AI tools can read hundreds of pages in split seconds, making them more suited for reviewing contracts and agreements. AI tools can be used to search for variations in the agreements efficiently, thus allowing lawyers to focus on more strategic tasks such as analysing and examining the impact of these variations and structuring the deal to the client's advantage.

There are several AI tools for contract review and analysis in the market, including Kiara Systems, SmartLaw Pte Ltd, ThoughtRiver and Luminance. These solutions are transforming the contract analysis and review process. These tools can read, understand, compare, contrast, identify anomalies in contracts and agreements in split seconds and, most importantly, without a lawyer's intervention. AI will play a key role in accelerating the legal due diligence process and delivering performance and cost savings which will be transformative for legal practices involved in due diligence for M&A and related activities. The time-consuming and laborious tasks of reviewing thousands of pages of documents can now be assigned to an AI tool. The lawyers can focus on performing analysis and providing valuable insights to clients on other aspects.

Though AI tools for due diligence, contract analysis and review will improve productivity and efficiency, they cannot provide comprehensive risk assessment. Hence, AI tools are complementary and cannot, at this time, replace lawyers and in-house legal counsels.

ePrediction

Generally, clients expect their lawyers to have a crystal ball with respect to the outcome of their specific cases. Secondly, they struggle with the decision as to whether to settle the case or to continue with trial and appeals. Though senior lawyers can tap on their years of practice and experience, no single lawyer can ever be replete with all relevant information and data. AI driven by Big Data can process voluminous up-to-date information and, by leveraging advanced statistical modelling techniques, predict outcomes with a high level of probability.

For example, legal tech startup SmartLaw Pte Ltd's Predictor module, when fine-tuned, will be able to predict sentencing outcomes for criminal offences, medical negligence, and divorce for a start, by leveraging an AI-trained neural brain. This may assist clients in deciding whether to engage a lawyer, go for trial, appeal, or try to arrive at a settlement on the matter without resorting to litigation.

Toronto-based Blue J uses ML-based algorithms to predict tax law-related outcomes. Ravel Law, which was acquired by LexisNexis and is now known as Context, has developed an AI tool that can aid lawyers in understanding how a judge (based on his/her reasoning in numerous decisions) is likely to rule on a specific case.

These tools are especially useful for lawyers preparing their litigation strategy based on how individual judges arrive at their decisions. Another such tool for ePrediction is Lex Machina (another LexisNexis company). It has developed an engine that mines and processes voluminous litigation data to uncover insights about judges, lawyers, parties, and the subjects of the cases themselves. Premonition, which reportedly has the world's largest litigation database, has developed tools to predict a lawyer's success by analysing his/her win rate.

AI and the Evolving Role of In-house Legal Counsels

With increasing regulatory and compliance requirements coupled with the explosion of enterprise and personal data, the responsibilities of in-house legal counsels continue to grow significantly. Big Data has rendered manual review of documents by both lawyers and in-house counsels unsustainable, and this challenge will only intensify going forward.

According to reports, in the UK, the number of in-house counsels more than doubled in a span of 15 years (between 2002 and 2017), growing from 13,000 to 28,000. Legal and compliance teams have rarely been front-runners of automation and digitisation. For long, there has been hesitation by in-house legal counsels because of the perception that AI will replace their jobs, and many of them fail to recognise that AI will only complement their work and not replace them, hence saving time, while improving efficiency and productivity.

"The pandemic has flattened staffing budgets and increased legal workloads; technology is the most obvious solution for many legal departments," says Zack Hutto, Director of Advisory, Gartner (as cited in Meulen, 2022). The Covid-19 pandemic has been a catalyst for technological adoption and innovation as working remotely is the default operating mode.

As discussed, AI technology can dramatically increase speed and productivity, including for in-house legal counsels working from home or the office. Thus, legal teams can act quickly and decisively on time-sensitive matters. In-house legal counsels are now beginning to recognise that they can handle some of their more complex legal matters internally and act quickly and decisively as AI technology frees up their time, thus reducing costs for outsourcing legal work. The key development with respect to the evolution of the role of in-house lawyers is their growing contribution to the growth of the business as business enablers. The most successful in-house counsels are those who embrace technology to reduce costs and handle more legal work internally rather than outsourcing it.

Thus, AI is already playing a significant role in transforming in-house legal departments of the companies who have deployed these AI solutions by impacting the delivery of their in-house legal services by automating routine tasks such as legal research, document review and analysis, due diligence, and even drafting simple or initial versions of contracts, thus empowering in-house legal counsels for more business-related focus. Some of the key areas where we can see the most impact are in repetitive tasks, for streamlining of workflows, undertaking laborious number-crunching activities and even simple decision-making tasks. As such, in-house lawyers can now begin to shift their focus to strategic areas of the business where AI technology will not compete with them.

This transformation has already begun; fully stacked law libraries have been replaced with online digital libraries such as LexisNexis, Westlaw and Singapore's LawNet, which can be accessed from any digital device from anywhere and anytime. Studies indicate that AI tools can reduce the time consumed for contract review and analysis by almost 90%. Tools like Luminance, Kiara and SmartLaw Pte Ltd promote AI-based solutions that can read hundreds of pages of contracts in split seconds.

The following is a list of functions where AI is contributing to the increased productivity of in-house legal departments:

- AI bots as legal secretaries
- AI bots for managing appointments
- Analysing trends and predicting outcomes
- Legal research and eDiscovery
- Drafting of simple and non-complex agreements
- Finding and spotting legal clauses in the process of due diligence
- Contract analysis and review
- Reviewing invoices and making decisions on external counsel legal costs

End-users/Clients

As former law professor and President of Harvard Derek Bok famously remarked, "there is far too much law for those who can afford it and far too little for those who cannot". Justice is about timely and fair legal solutions and should not be about access to lawyers and affordability.

The good news is that law and justice are no longer about lawyers and judges as technology has become pivotal in this transformation. This disruption is good for business and society. Access to justice is not only for a privileged few wealthy enough to hire lawyers, but is a fundamental human right.

The man on the street often cannot afford legal representation when confronted with a legal predicament. Pro bono lawyers and civil societies provide a benevolent service to citizens. But studies indicate that the demand for legal support outstrips the supply of pro bono legal aid services available. Although inroads made into permitting contingency fees and third-party funding in the UK and Singapore in recent times may alleviate such inadequacies, these take time to roll out. AI can support and complement such efforts to an even greater extent.

Financial challenges should not be a hurdle to justice. Legal, technological solutions are gradually addressing the economic inequality equation for informed decision-making, seeking legal assistance, and timely justice.

Online divorce portals such as SmartLaw and HelloDivorce will allow contesting parties to evaluate the initially expected outcome in a divorce matter without having to consult a lawyer. This preliminary online service not only provides an opportunity for legal advice at a fraction of the usual costs in the convenience of home or on the go (as these are also available on mobile phones) but also provides an avenue for couples to decide whether to engage a lawyer to contest or to come to an amicable settlement, and even performs court filing online given that therapeutic family justice is now all the rage.

Similarly, for criminal offences, the defendant (accused) can use predictive AI to predict the expected outcome of the alleged violation without consulting a criminal lawyer for a fraction of the costs. This will allow the defendant to decide whether to defend the case or plead guilty without consulting a lawyer.

UK-based Justpoint and SmartLaw Pte Ltd are two companies that offer a similar feature for disputes concerning medical negligence. The module can be used both by lawyers and clients to evaluate the potential outcome in split seconds and not depend on a particular lawyer's experience and expertise for a legal opinion that differs from that of another lawyer. The AI tool leverages a vast repository of previous judgements and verdicts to predict outcomes in split seconds. Such AI tools and user-friendly government websites (such as in Singapore) can be used to further enable access to justice for all.

Robot lawyer LISA, an AI platform with its flagship product NDA AI app, has been disrupting the legal profession by making everyday basic legal services accessible and affordable online anytime, for anyone from anywhere. These are still early days and we have only scratched the surface of what AI can do to transform the profession.

Legal tech and Alternative Legal Service Provider (ALSP) companies such as LegalZoom, Hello, DoNotPay and SmartLaw Pte Ltd offer services to both individuals and businesses which lawyers and law firms traditionally handled as bespoke services. Online solution DoNotPay is an AI-driven chatbot that allows users to contest parking tickets in London and New York City. It was reported that in its first 21 months of operations, DoNotPay handled 250,000 cases and won more than 160,000 of them, reportedly saving some $4 million worth of fines for its users. Below is a list of services offered by legal tech firms:

For Individuals
- Last will and testament
- Divorce
- Deed poll
- Probate
- Deputyship
- Power of Attorney
- Lasting Power of Attorney
- Drafting agreements
- Review of contracts
- Prediction of sentencing outcomes
- Traffic summons and fines
- Protection from harassment

For Businesses
- Contract review
- Contract analysis
- Drafting agreements
- Intellectual property agreements
- Company formation

Common Challenges Faced in Adopting AI Technology Across the Legal Profession and Legal Industry

The key challenge is data security, privacy and confidentiality of the data that law firms and in-house legal departments possess. Lawyers sit on a mountain of confidential information belonging to their clients; trust is a crucial component of the relationship between the law firm and the client.

Any breach of data can lead to both financial losses as well as loss of reputation for the law firm. These breaches can also lead to fines, suspensions and penalties from regulatory authorities, including being struck off. The recent spate of cybercrimes such as ransomware attacks and phishing may have further delayed the adoption of AI technology in the legal industry.

Another issue is the quality of data fed into AI. AI solutions are data-hungry. The amount, quality, and accuracy of the data input directly impact the quality of the output from the system. Law firms are wary of being exposed to negligence due to poor-quality output from AI solutions that may have poor-quality data. Also, arbitration cases, being confidential in nature, limit the amount of such data that can be fed into AI.

Many AI solutions, like other IT applications, are hosted in the cloud. While the cloud offers several benefits such as pay per use, on-demand services, no upfront investments in IT infrastructure and IT resources, the biggest bottleneck is the apprehension of storing client information in the cloud, potentially exposing it to data breaches. However, this issue can be addressed by adopting AI solutions deployed in the private cloud.

With respect to the challenges of AI in the courts and for judges, some have highlighted the concern that the AI tool may perpetuate biases unintentionally as they depend on large datasets to infer their knowledge from. The accuracy and quality of the decisions made by AI will be predicated on the availability and quality of well-labelled datasets.

Given the vast caseload and backlogs, AI tools in the judiciary will be valuable in unclogging the process that slows down justice, improving the judiciary's efficiency, leading to improving the judicial decision-making process and adjudication generally. It must be emphasised that it is not about replacing the experience and expertise of judges but complementing their expertise.

Lack of understanding of AI technology has made some lawyers and in-house counsels worry warts for various reasons. In addition to education, a change of mindset and organisational culture is required to encourage adoption. This can only be achieved when there is a change management strategy and a champion within the legal department. Another impediment in the adoption of AI is ethical considerations, the "audit-ability" of AI decisions, and reliability. Can a machine be held liable? Who carries the liability and costs?

Another key concern with respect to AI adoption is budgetary constraints, particularly for smaller law firms and for small and medium-sized companies as opposed to large law firms and corporations with sizeable in-house legal departments and budgets.

There are also concerns about requiring in-house IT support for the deployment and maintenance of AI applications. With many of the AI solutions now being offered in the cloud, both the issues of cost and technical support/maintenance have been addressed. The cloud-based model allows access to AI solutions on a need-and-demand basis, eliminating the need for upfront investments and in-house technical support. The benefits outweigh many of the concerns, and in-house counsels will soon realise that whether they agree or not, AI is already here to stay.

Studies indicate that the primary reason for resistance to the adoption of AI is the fear of reducing the importance of their role or even being replaced in their role. Law firms and in-house counsels who are complacent, not fully appreciating the benefits of AI solutions and their disruptive nature, are likely to face the "Kodak moment". Both in private practice and in-house, lawyers need to appreciate how AI technology can augment their roles, and not replace them.

The legal profession should advance in tandem with the advances in AI technology to offer next-generation legal services. As Chay Brooks, Christian Gherhes and Tim Vorley (Brooks, 2020) state, "while the pressures for transformation are rooted in technological developments, the challenges to transformation and adaptation are largely social in nature". Various studies have proven that enterprises that embrace innovation outperform their competition.

Lastly, fear of change is a common impediment in adopting new technologies and innovation. Many studies across industries have indicated that education, training, and a better appreciation of AI are primary tools to overcome conservatism, lack of skills and fear. The level of acceptance of new technology increases if professionals are made to understand the benefits of technology and their potential to lighten their workload and not replace them altogether. Early adopters of AI in the legal industry have created new roles that did not exist a few years ago, such as legal engineer, legal technologist and legal analyst, amongst others. Studies also resoundingly indicate that the legal industry is ready for transformation driven by AI.

According to Caroline Hill (2016) of Deloitte, it is estimated that AI algorithms will replace 100,000 legal roles by 2036. The study also found that it's not all about job loss but about creating more and better-paying jobs such as legal technology managers and legal analysts than the jobs lost such as legal secretaries. This also means law firms need to embrace an AI-readiness culture and educate their internal teams to leverage technology as this would assist in the "transfer of skills" more swiftly and readily.

Advances in AI technology are both an opportunity as new jobs are created, and a challenge as some of the traditional job scope becomes obsolete, requiring job redesign. Studies predict that we are nearing a tipping point where the legal industry will need fewer traditional lawyers, and a new mix of skills will be required. If this transition is managed judiciously, technology will not replace human expertise and jobs but complement and enhance outcomes.

Conclusion

The technological advances and the penetration of AI solutions in the legal industry will continue to grow unabated and become smarter and more ubiquitous over time. I foresee that more and more self-help applications and DIY online legal solutions driven by AI will become mainstream, and clients will have more offerings to choose from. The legal profession needs to embrace this shift through a greater appreciation of AI technology and be ready for the subsequent changes in delivering legal services. Roll back 20 years to before Google and smartphones, imagine where the world was. Correspondingly, roll forward ten years from now, and the legal profession will be different, as many tasks will be managed by AI solutions. While there are challenges, the benefits of AI applications for law firms, in-house counsels, judiciary, and clients are compelling. Somewhat like in other industries, the adoption of AI technology will lead to the transformation of the legal industry, but the shift may not be as swift within the legal industry as it is with other sectors which have seen a sea change. Studies indicate that the legal profession is also reaching an inflection point, and law firms relying on old models will face the inevitable or extinction.

In summary, there are three key elements as to how AI is already contributing to the legal profession and the legal industry:

- From a business perspective, AI has improved workflow, office automation and business process management, hence improving overall efficiency, speed, and productivity.

- From a legal practice perspective, AI technology has already begun to undertake tasks that lawyers, in-house counsels and judges previously handled. This includes AI solutions in areas such as basic research, eDiscovery, due diligence, prediction, contract review and contract analysis. This will free up much-needed time for legal professionals to focus on more strategic legal work, such as preparing their briefs and defence. All this will eventually reduce costs, minimise risks, improve productivity and better deliver legal services to clients and customers. For the foreseeable future, AI is not a complete replacement tool for lawyers and judges but will add significant enhancements to their expertise. It will likely create new jobs that do not exist today and the legal profession will become multidisciplinary and no longer solely about lawyers and judges.

- From a client and consumer perspective, AI provides more options for seeking legal advice and legal remedies for disputes through online offerings. With AI tools in play, lawyers will no longer be able to dictate the terms of engagement. Clients will have alternatives to look to, such as online access to legal services that do not necessarily involve the current full-blown lawyer engagement.

It will no longer be about the "lawyers know-and-do-all model" where lawyers bill for numerous hours of discovery and preparation of legal documents. Now it is about integrating the legal expertise of a lawyer by leveraging AI tools to solve legal issues – cost-effectively, transparently, and without delay to justice. The profound impact of AI on the legal industry is also for mass use by end-users, thus making legal services universally more pervasive, accessible and affordable. While AI can automate many tasks which judges, lawyers and in-house counsels do, it cannot yet fully automate what judges and lawyers do. While it's impossible to predict the future 5–10 years from now, AI will inevitably perform many of the tasks being performed in the legal profession.

Future lawyers will need to have a good grasp of the nuances of AI and adopt new models of delivering legal services. Numerous studies also report that remote work will continue to increase and become more common both for law firms and in-house counsels. Some companies have moved to working from home (WFH) completely, facilitated by technology and accelerated by Covid-19. This saves overhead costs and travel time. With further advances in technology, we will continue to see changes in the years ahead, and some of them will remain unpredictable. But it is becoming increasingly evident that the legal profession will no longer be solely about lawyers and an insular and monolithic job but a multi-disciplinary profession where lawyers, data scientists, AI developers and other auxiliary professionals will work side by side to deliver supreme legal services. The fate of the legal profession in the time of AI? The only fait accompli is to change!

References

Brooks, C., Gherhes, C., Vorley, T. (2020, January 27). Artificial intelligence in the legal sector: pressures and challenges of transformation. *Cambridge Journal of Regions, Economy and Society*, 13(1), 135–152. DOI:10.1093/cjres/rsz026. https://doi.org/10.1093/cjres/rsz026.

Hill, C. (2016, March 16). Deloitte Insight: Over 100,000 legal roles to be automated. Legal IT Insider. Available at: https://legaltechnology.com/2016/03/16/deloitte-insight-over-100000-legal-roles-to-be-automated/.

Lavelle, J. (2019, October 15). Gartner Says the Average Time to Close an M&A Deal Has Risen More Than 30 Percent in the Last Decade. Gartner. Available at: https://www.gartner.com/en/newsroom/press-releases/2018-10-15-gartner-says-the-average-time-to-close-an-manda-deal-has-risen-more-than-30-percent-in-the-last-decade.

Meulen, R. van der (2022, February 24). 5 Legal Technology Trends Changing In-House Legal Departments. Gartner. Available at: https://www.gartner.com/smarterwithgartner/5-legal-technology-trends-changing-in-house-legal-departments.

Rosenbaum, E. (2016, November 17). Can elite law firms survive the rise of artificial intelligence? The jury is still out. CNBC. Available at: https://www.cnbc.com/2016/11/17/can-cash-cow-of-elite-legal-firms-survive-ai-the-jury-is-still-out.html.

CHAPTER 6

AI and Healthcare

Why does AI matter for healthcare? Will AI be able to warn us of a future pandemic so that the world can be better prepared and avoid another paralysing crisis? How will AI impact the future of healthcare? Will we consult an AI doctor in our lifetime?

Healthcare is one of the significant achievements of this century, and advances in medical sciences and pharmaceuticals have raised the quality of life and life expectancy globally. At the same time, there is an unprecedented and unmet demand for healthcare services because of the increase in longevity, growing geriatric populations, changing patient lifestyles and expectations, growing demand for better patient care, growing rate of chronic diseases, and new pandemics.

Amongst these mounting pressures, the fast-ageing population looms large. According to a report, by 2050, the world's population of persons 60 years and older will double to 2.1 billion. The number of persons aged 80 years or older is expected to triple between 2020 and 2050 to reach 426 million. In the last five decades, average life expectancy has increased from just over 77 years to above 84 years for women and from just over 72 years to nearly 81 years for men. The number of people living past 100 years of age is also increasing, and based on statistical modelling, a life span of 130 years is a possibility by 2100. This means that managing senior citizens will require healthcare systems to evolve from the traditional "episodic-care-based" systems to more proactive systems driven by early diagnosis and preventive care.

But healthcare spending in most countries has not been keeping up with the growing demands for better healthcare for its citizens. Globally, healthcare systems are overburdened, and there is a disconnect between what they *can* deliver and what they *need to* deliver. According to the World Health Organization, the global economy is likely to create 40 million healthcare jobs by 2030. Still, the projected shortfall is about 9.9 million doctors, nurses, medical technicians, and midwives for the same period.

Healthcare lags behind some industries in terms of the adoption of AI. Unlike sectors such as retail, hospitality, and manufacturing, which are easy to transition from the traditional brick-and-mortar to the digital realm, healthcare presents far more complex moral, ethical, and legal considerations in the discourse of provision of such services. Nonetheless, AI presents unprecedented benefits for healthcare and is already revolutionising the industry. These are still early days, and the future is ripe with immense possibilities.

This chapter discusses recent AI applications, use cases, and how AI is transforming the healthcare industry. It also theorises AI's future impact on healthcare and society, a future that is more focused on early diagnosis, preventive care and potentially personalised medicine. Finally, it presents the potential challenges and risks of using AI, including ethical issues.

Why AI Matters for the Future of Healthcare

Will AI usage become widespread, and what are the ramifications for the healthcare industry?

AI and robots have been in use in healthcare for a few decades now. But AI has become increasingly sophisticated in recent years and is transforming many aspects of the healthcare industry, including patient care, hospital administrative processes, drug discovery, and pharmaceutical manufacturing.

AI can address many of the challenges being faced today by the healthcare industry and patients. This is because AI can be trained ("learn") faster than human clinicians and other healthcare professionals. AI can search through voluminous amounts of real-time data in different formats, including images, and provide insights on a real-time basis. It can perform tasks with much more precision than a surgeon or physician, function without burnout, and has no emotions. AI can predict and flag notoriously difficult-to-diagnose illnesses such as Alzheimer's Disease years before they happen or become noticeable. AI can develop novel drugs and vaccines much faster than conventional development approaches and can prescribe personalised treatment. These are some of the many benefits of AI in healthcare, which can help us to be prepared for future medical conditions. From a business perspective, companies involved in the intersection of AI and healthcare will have significant potential as AI-based algorithms present novel approaches and innovative solutions.

The world is now into the third year of the Covid-19 pandemic, and healthcare is continuing to face unprecedented challenges. We witnessed horrifying news updates in real-time worldwide where healthcare infrastructure was stretched beyond capacity to treat Covid-19 patients and was frequently running short of medical equipment, including oxygen ventilators, and overwhelmed by the demand for hospital emergency beds. Computing technology and AI tools have played a pivotal role in alleviating some of these burdens on the healthcare system during the pandemic in many ways, from contact tracing to vaccine development.

Contact tracing was a critical strategy in trying to contain the spread by ring-fencing the spread of the virus. Technology was instrumental in identifying patient whereabouts and infected clusters, performing remote outpatient reviews, tracking and updating the bed status in hospitals, seamlessly integrating various organs of a hospital such as an emergency department, laboratory, radiology, and pharmacy on a real-time basis, if not at least on near real-time. Several studies during the pandemic indicate that AI and ML have shown great promise in improving collaboration amongst policymakers, healthcare organisations, clinicians and pharmaceutical manufacturers, to ultimately deliver improved patient experience.

AI and ML: Disruptor of Healthcare

AI is fast becoming the disruptor of healthcare, and it is driving the ongoing shift in the patient care continuum by supporting all stakeholders in the value chain. AI tools can be the bedrock for enhanced healthcare in areas such as preventive medicine and treatment, early diagnosis, more accurate diagnoses, robotic surgery resulting in more precise clinical care and medication, personalised patient care planning, new-generation tools for radiology, advanced medical imaging, to name a few. This will lead to improved public healthcare delivery, optimisation in the day-to-day management of hospitals and nursing homes, healthcare innovations, and even the creation of new job roles at the intersection of the medical profession and AI. Therefore, it is not surprising that 62% of healthcare organisations plan to invest in AI in the near future, and 72% of companies believe that AI will be crucial to businesses.

Telemedicine: An Equaliser

The healthcare system is overburdened and underserved. Top doctors are drawn to leading hospitals and treat the patients who can afford to pay top dollar for treatment. The rising cost of medical care has created a divide even for primary medical care for many. The cost of treating chronic illness grows in tandem with the growing ageing population, which is a double whammy. Digital technology and AI have also been a great equaliser and democratiser across many industries, including healthcare. Because of digitisation, barriers have been broken with respect to geographical proximity, time, and cost by providing access to consumers across all industries and services, and healthcare is no different. Perhaps one of the most significant impacts of technology in healthcare is its capacity to reach out to those who were denied healthcare because of lack of access to hospitals and physicians.

Advances in AI are beginning to reinvent doctor-patient interactions as patients take more control of their healthcare decisions and transition from clinic-based treatment to home-based treatment. By leveraging smartwatches, sensors and AI, many of these home-based devices can collect a lot of the needed information such as blood tests for diabetes, cholesterol, urine analysis and even DNA tests without the patient having to visit the clinic or hospital. There are significant benefits for patient care as this data can be collected daily and not by way of periodic or routine tests.

Technology has empowered the average healthcare consumer with information and has brought medical care closer to the patient. Healthcare providers no longer have a monopoly on information. The patient-doctor relationship is fast becoming equitable as patients become more knowledgeable and empowered to make informed healthcare decisions and make choices for their treatments. We witnessed this unfolding when many Omicron patients could use self-testing kits to test and recover.

Telemedicine (also known as telehealth) is already providing healthcare to the most remote, inaccessible, and rural places in the world today. It is greatly enhancing accessibility and inclusivity to those underserved and most vulnerable, thus enabling delivery of specialist care and targeted treatments while lowering costs. Drones are being used to deliver lifesaving equipment and medication to remote areas where there is no other mode of transportation and for those who have been denied healthcare access for so long. AI tools are also being used to improve efficiencies and enable alternative care delivery models such as remote patient monitoring (RPM), leading to improvement in timely patient care. According to studies, RPM can help reduce readmissions by 38%, emergency room visits by 25%, improve patient satisfaction by 25%, and cost savings by 17% for patient care. Digitisation has also resulted in instant access to information through sources such as WebMD, CareZone, Open mHealth, Drugs.com, and Mayo Clinic. This has empowered digital natives to make informed decisions when seeking treatment from medical professionals and practise self-care.

The world's most valued companies, including Google, Apple, Amazon, and IBM, have not stopped with the finance, manufacturing, and retail sectors, but are actively getting involved in the healthcare industry with innovative business models. In the US, healthcare accounts for about 20% of the GDP, and in most Western countries, it is between 12% and 18%. IBM's Watson Health, Google Health, and Amazon Care are three amongst several other initiatives disrupting the industry through health-care innovation. They are in their nascent stages, but these companies have significant financial backing and consequently access to talent. Though Google has struggled with its initiative on healthcare at the initial stages, the tech giant is still betting on AI for health. However, in January 2022, IBM divested part of Watson and sold its "healthcare data and analytics asset" to Francisco Partners. This reflects the challenges tech giants face in the healthcare industry even as AI has made rapid inroads into other sectors.

A Paradigm Shift in Healthcare

Historically, healthcare has been based on a fee-for-service model where patients pay for the services of the healthcare provider. But with advances in technology, this is beginning to shift towards value-based care. This paradigm shift will require healthcare providers to engage the patients proactively and reduce any risk of poor health outcomes. Previous predictive models could only predict, as the name suggests, and were based on historical data. They are generally unable to provide any additional guidance to the healthcare provider on the risk profile of the patient. AI-based prescriptive models not only improve on the degree of accuracy in predicting but can also examine the patient's history and identify the risk factors more holistically by studying an unlimited amount of data, including behavioural, lifestyle, environmental, and other health-related determinants. Therefore, AI is adding significant value towards the development of value-based care as it can have a compound effect on both increasing health outcomes and reducing costs. This also steers treatment to focus on patients' medical conditions rather than physicians' specialities.

Smartwatches such as the Apple Watch and biosensors are helping the population to monitor vital signs, diagnose diseases early, and improve health outcomes. Adobe's contact sensors can keep track and notify family members if medicine was taken, when it was taken and how often. There is growing interest in deploying AI and ML applications to intervene along the last mile of the patient care continuum. Sending message alerts and relevant targeted content to patients to initiate actions at critical moments will save lives. The same applications can also send messages to nurses, pharmacists, or other healthcare coordinators, particularly for elderly or vulnerable individuals without family support. The more connected physicians, healthcare providers and patients are, the more robust healthcare systems will be in treating illnesses holistically rather than merely treating symptoms when they surface.

Amazon's Alexa has revolutionised how patients in hospitals keep in touch with their families, connect with hospital staff, and access information. Patients from the hospital bed can ask Alexa for things they need. Leveraging AI, Alexa can interpret patient intentions and send the message to the relevant hospital staff using existing hospital communication systems. Helpsy, a Boston-based startup, has developed a virtual nurse platform that provides dynamic patient support and empowers patients. SAN (Symptom management And Navigation) is the world's first AI nurse (chatbot). A research team at Flinders University in South Australia has developed a new vaccine believed to be the first in the world to be designed entirely by AI. While other drugs were designed and developed using computers in the past, this flu vaccine was independently created by an AI algorithm called SAM (Search Algorithm for Ligands). The vaccine has been tested on animals successfully and has outperformed existing vaccines. According to lead scientist Prof. Nikolai Petrovsky, "this potentially shortens the normal drug discovery and development process by decades and saves hundreds of millions of dollars". This also sets the stage for developing other much-needed vaccines by AI. These are just a few examples of what AI is doing to disrupt and transform healthcare. The following sections will address some specific cases and areas in detail.

Though AI did not help to warn us of the Covid-19 pandemic, it played a major role in developing the vaccines at an unprecedented speed. There are already new developments driven by AI that can potentially predict future pandemics and can warn us to be better prepared. UK-based startup MedShr Insights has developed an early warning system based on AI and ML with the aim of identifying the emergence of future outbreaks of diseases and pandemics at the earliest possible stage. MedShr enables nearly

2 million doctors in 195 countries to securely share and discuss clinical cases using mobile phones. Such applications allow us to identify outbreaks, support disease surveillance and share novel developments and treatments in real-time globally.

Robots are also increasingly becoming part of healthcare in recent years. Driven by technologies such as object vision, robots are now used not only in the operating room but also in clinical settings to assist healthcare workers as triage assistants. During the Covid-19 pandemic, hospitals have been deploying robots for a range of tasks to help reduce human exposure to the virus. AI-enabled robots reduce the time it takes to identify and distribute medicine to patients in hospitals. It is predicted that they will soon take over some of the services delivered by physicians, surgeons, and healthcare administrators. Eventually, our existing traditional healthcare practices will give way to a human-AI hybrid system. In short, healthcare will increasingly become more integrated with intelligent systems.

AI Applications in Healthcare: A Game-changer

"We always overestimate the change that will occur in the next two years and underestimate the change that will occur in the next ten."
— Bill Gates

AI is becoming ever more sophisticated at doing what healthcare professionals do, but more precisely, efficiently, and more quickly while keeping the cost of healthcare low. There have been countless articles about the potential of AI and even at times euphoric utopian predictions that AI will replace physicians and surgeons altogether. On a balanced view, based on current developments and scientific literature, this is not going to happen in the next 5–10 years. AI's current potential is yet to be fully explored at this juncture in healthcare, and the AI of the future (AGI and ASI) remains a vision.

The following sections of this chapter discuss four key areas where AI applications are already making an impact:

1. Personalised patient care
2. Drug discovery
3. Treatment of chronic illness
4. Radiology and pathology

Personalised and Precision Medicine

Conventional medical treatments are based on a population-wide model. They are optimised to have an acceptable level of performance on an average number of people out of the target population. Clinical trials are based on statistical models and average treatment effects. As a result, the medication may not be responsive to some patients who could be "outliers" in the population. Though this approach has served us well for decades for the use of most of the medicines for most of the patients, it does not cater for individual reactions or for treatments needed for unique individual healthcare needs. It is not patient-specific!

Today, however, we are seeing the exponential growth of Big Data in healthcare, driven by an increasing number of data sources such as electronic health records (EHRs), lifestyle data from consumer devices, sensor applicators, clinical and genetic data. Leveraging this data, AI and ML algorithms can provide personalised medical care and treatment for each patient. AI applications are no longer confined to research labs and medtech startups but are increasingly used in clinical practice and patient care.

The ongoing Covid-19 pandemic has proven that medications such as Remdesivir, Corticosteroid, and Tocilizumab (Actemra) may not have the same degree of efficacy on all patients when progressing from mild to severe stage. Precision medicine is the answer to this problem as the treatment will be "customised" for individual patients to deliver the best care. Lam et al. (2021) undertook a study using ML algorithms to evaluate the efficacy of Remdesivir vs Corticosteroid on a sample size of 2,364 patients. This resulted in increased survival rates even though previous findings had reported that neither of the two drugs was associated with improved survival rates. The study concluded that by leveraging ML algorithms, personalised treatments can be administered for both Remdesivir and Corticosteroid so that the Covid-19 patients' health and survival outcomes improve.

Drug Discovery and Development

AI is already driving innovation and ushering in a new era of biotechnology. It is revolutionising the process of drug discovery, design, development, clinical trials, evaluation of drug efficacy, safety and toxicity. Drug discovery and development is a costly and lengthy process where pharmaceutical firms typically spend on average about $1 billion to introduce a drug to the market. The whole process takes about a decade, and reportedly 90% of drug candidates fail to be introduced, resulting in high costs to pharmaceutical firms. Traditionally, researchers go through numerous rounds of tests to identify a drug that has the potential to be introduced as a treatment for a disease. These activities are time-consuming and expensive processes as they must go through tests in laboratories followed by clinical trials on animals and then on humans. AI-driven applications have proven to be effective in saving time and resource costs during the whole process of drug discovery and development.

The objective of drug discovery is to develop a chemical compound (medicine) that can act beneficially with the targeted molecules in the body, usually a protein or receptor, which is involved with the illness. But one challenge is to ensure that the drug compound doesn't adversely affect non-targeted molecules of the body, which is not easy to predict. The efficacy of the proposed drug also needs to be measured, and that depends on its affinity for the target receptor, known as drug-target binding affinity (DTBA). Another element in the process of drug development is to predict its toxicity. In all these areas, AI-based applications are being used to speed up and strengthen the drug discovery process. According to Ratanghayra (2021), AI algorithms can be deployed to "predict target structure, identify and optimise hits, explore the biological activity of new ligands, design models that predict the pharmacokinetic and toxicological properties of drug candidates".

A new technique known as DeepBAR, based on ML and chemistry, was developed by Xinqiang Ding, a postdoc in MIT's Department of Chemistry, and Prof. Bin Zhang, the Pfizer-Laubach Career Development Associate Professor in Chemistry at MIT. DeepBAR calculates binding affinity 50 times faster than traditional methods. "Our method is orders of magnitude faster than before, meaning we can have drug discovery that is both efficient and reliable," says Zhang (2021). Pharmaceutical firms are employing AI algorithms to perform predictive modelling, which not only can tell whether a drug or compound will work but can also provide insights into how a molecule reacts. Many leading pharma companies, including Pfizer, Moderna, AstraZeneca, Johnson & Johnson, Roche and Sanofi, have already deployed AI technology.

Because of the severity, pathogenicity and transmissibility of the Covid-19 virus, pharmaceutical companies experienced a surge in the utilisation of AI to develop vaccines and treatment. The time-consuming traditional drug discovery processes could not be applied to develop vaccines to tackle the rapid spread of the virus globally. Never before in the history of humanity have we witnessed such a race for the development of a vaccine against a lethal virus. The pace of the discovery and development of vaccines was condensed to just about a year by harnessing the power of AI and DL.

AI and DL were employed at different stages in the development of drugs and vaccines at record-breaking timelines. According to Pfizer, by leveraging an ML application known as Smart Data Query (SDQ), the clinical trial data was reviewed in a mere 22 hours, when it generally takes a month. Dave Johnson, Chief Data and Artificial Intelligence Officer at Moderna, stated that because of AI, "we went from maybe about 30 mRNAs manually produced in a given month to a capacity of about a thousand in a month without significantly adding more resources and much better consistency in quality and so on". Savings of billions of dollars and potentially millions of lives!

British startup Exscientia, in collaboration with Japanese pharmaceutical firm Sumitomo Dainippon, has developed the world's first drug designed by AI for obsessive-compulsive disorder (OCD). This drug took only 12 months to develop, and phase one trials commenced in Japan in July 2021. The founder of Exscientia, Prof. Andrew Hopkins, said: "This year was the first to have an AI-designed drug, but by the end of the decade all new drugs could potentially be created by AI" (Hopkins, 2020, as cited in Bell, 2020). The startup has already developed AI-designed drugs to treat cancer patients and Alzheimer's Disease. Investments in AI by pharmaceutical manufacturers started more than ten years ago, but 80% of funding has come in the last three years. As AI becomes more advanced and accessible, the future of drug development and manufacturing will be AI-enabled. This will lead to the development of many other novel and safe drugs being manufactured much faster and becoming even more personalised. AI and DL will continue to reshape the future of drug discovery and manufacturing by revolutionising the whole value chain.

AI: Game-changer for Critical Illness Driven by Predictive Analytics and Image Scanning

There is a growing number of AI algorithms for many specialities of medicine, and this section will discuss AI applications in the context of cancer and Alzheimer's Disease. Making healthcare decisions about diagnosis and treatment for cancer has always been challenging because of the high cost of treatment, and there is furthermore no guarantee of curing the patient. Also, many factors can affect the prognosis, treatment, and mortality of cancer patients. But AI is beginning to become a game-changer in diagnosing, treating, and improving life outcomes for cancer patients. Several other research studies indicate that AI can perform as well as or better than humans at critical healthcare tasks.

AI for Skin Cancer

Since being first deployed to identify skin cancer (melanoma) in 2018, AI has gained traction in successfully diagnosing and treating skin cancer patients. It was reported that an AI algorithm, using Convolutional Neural Networks (CNN), diagnosed melanomas more accurately than 58 international dermatologists. Melanoma accounts for more than 70% of all skin cancer-related deaths worldwide. Until recently, physicians have relied mainly on visual inspection to identify suspicious pigmented lesions (SPLs) for skin cancer. AI algorithms can identify patterns of abnormality in cells that the human eye cannot see. Such early-stage identification of SPLs can improve melanoma prognosis, significantly reduce treatment costs, and ultimately save lives. AI algorithms have already achieved near-perfect results for spotting malignant tumours, detecting true positives, and ruling out false negatives of biopsies.

AI for Prostate Cancer

In another first for AI in cancer treatment, the FDA recently approved the first AI software to help doctors detect prostate cancer, which is expected to make a massive difference. Paige Prostate is a cloud-based program that can be accessed through a web browser from anywhere. Any risk of false positives or false negatives can be reduced as the pathologists and oncologists can review the AI findings along with other information such as the patient's family history and any additional clinical data. In a separate study, AI detected a small number of prostate cancer issues that pathologists had previously missed.

AI for Colorectal Cancer

In a recent study at Tulane University, researchers examined 13,000 images of colorectal cancer in 8,803 subjects by using AI models. The study discovered that AI could accurately detect and diagnose the disease by analysing the issues and perform on par with pathologists or even better.

AI for Breast and Lung Cancers

Google's AI has developed an ML algorithm to detect both breast and lung cancers. It was reported that it could detect breast cancer a year before a human doctor. Google AI researchers developed an AI model to detect lung cancer in another study in collaboration with Northwestern Medicine. The study found that the AI model was capable of screening tests better than human radiologists with an average of eight years of experience. As more novel models are developed, AI will be increasingly deployed for diagnosing tumours and treating the patient by leveraging predictive capabilities, leading to individualised or personalised treatment. This also means that we will soon have AI-driven tools that can predict the probability of a patient responding to therapy without having to wait for weeks to see the progress or response for the first-line treatment. This will increase the efficacy of the treatment, unlike the traditional practice of today, where clinicians have to wait for weeks to decide whether to continue the first-line therapy or to prescribe alternate treatments or drugs.

Cancer treatment includes chemotherapy, radiotherapy, surgery, and most recently, immunotherapy. The latter has been considered one of the most successful strategies for the treatment of different cancer types. Recent studies indicate AI has the potential to improve immunotherapy outcomes by forecasting the therapeutic effect. AI can be applied in the predicting of immunotherapy responses based on immune signatures, medical imaging, and histological analysis. It can provide unparalleled perspectives into tumours in a non-invasive manner.

These are a few examples that merely scratch the surface with respect to what is conceivable when AI and ML are fully leveraged to treat critical illnesses such as cancer. AI will be highly useful in the management of cancer treatment by improving diagnostic accuracy, optimising treatment planning, predicting outcomes of care and reducing human resource costs. In the not-too-distant future, we will see AI-assisted cancer immunotherapy becoming widespread.

AI and Alzheimer's Disease

Alzheimer's Disease affects millions of people each year worldwide and is expected to double every 20 years. AD is the most common form of dementia and is notoriously difficult to diagnose or cure. Currently, there are limited options to treat an Alzheimer's patient, and the best approach as of now is prevention until new drugs are developed. Since there is no medical treatment to cure or reverse the disease entirely, it is critical to diagnose AD early to manage the condition better. But early detection has been a challenge because physicians have traditionally relied on medical history, cognitive tests and brain imaging. It may be too late by the time obvious symptoms surface, as today's medical treatment cannot reverse the damage to the brain cells.

The good news, according to studies, is that AI can spot Alzheimer's six years earlier than doctors, way before symptoms become noticeable. AI algorithms are able to accurately predict cognitive decline in patients, which is likely to lead to Alzheimer's eventually. This has given patients much hope and a fighting chance against the chronic progression of this debilitating disease.

Up until now, clinicians have been largely dependent on magnetic resonance imaging (MRI) to identify areas in the brain that may be associated with the onset of AD. Analysing these MRI images to study the changes requires specific skills and can be time-consuming. Researchers at the Department of Multimedia Engineering, Faculty of Informatics, Kaunas University have developed a DL-based algorithm that can predict the possible onset of Alzheimer's Disease with over 99% accuracy. Because of its predictive functionalities, AI can provide much-needed early diagnosis leading to earlier therapy and improved outcomes for patients. In the near future, AI will be deployed, like existing routine screenings for breast and prostate cancers or diabetes, for brain imaging and screening to detect Alzheimer's Disease. This will lead to early detection and treatment of AD.

AI for Pathology and Radiology

Today, because of the advances in medicine, we can treat many more diseases. Nonetheless, even after many years in practice, medical professionals, including pathologists and radiologists, can still find it challenging to make the correct diagnosis and recommend the best course of treatment. Consequently, patients suffer, resulting in an increasing number of medical negligence lawsuits. According to Newman et al. (2019), an estimated 40,000 to

80,000 deaths occur each year in US hospitals related to misdiagnosis. And an estimated 12 million Americans suffer a diagnostic error each year in a primary care setting, 33% of which result in serious or permanent damage or death. AI has proven to be instrumental in diagnosing diseases expertly and in reading medical images far more accurately and quickly than the naked human eye.

Perhaps one of the most notable contributions of AI applications in medicine is medical imaging. Novel AI and DL models for pathology are a fascinating area of research and can help avoid mistakes by humans involved. These AI models extract information from volumes of medical images, including complex molecular and cellular structures of precise cancer lesions, determine genetic expression, identify the exact location and locate other anatomical objects and images that are difficult for the naked eye of a pathologist or radiologist to see. Studies have found that because of AI and DL algorithms, unnecessary biopsies and surgical excisions can be avoided. Because of AI applications, clinicians are now able to develop a better understanding of how tumours behave as a whole rather than basing treatment decisions on the analysis of a segment of the malignancy. Alex-Net and GoogLeNet are two such tools for medical image classification. These AI algorithms are revolutionising the understanding of cancer histology and treatment. These tools can also bring down the cost of expensive specialist treatments as they can be used by general medical practitioners "anytime, anywhere", as they become pervasive.

Challenges and Bioethical Dilemmas

As with the ubiquitous use of any new technology, the introduction and use of AI in healthcare has brought about new challenges, particularly in ethics and privacy-related issues. This will remain an issue of concern for some time as AI continues to evolve and more and more healthcare organisations deploy AI technologies. For a start, the sceptics argue that by developing AI algorithms that train machines to "think for themselves", "diagnose" our illnesses and "prescribe" treatment, we have given control of our lives to AI. As AI advances and becomes ubiquitous in healthcare, patients in the future may have to speak to an AI machine when they visit a clinic and may no longer see a physician or triage through a nurse. These developments will also have an impact on medical insurance policies as the insurers may need access to patients' medical records generated by AI. How will insurers compensate if the AI's diagnosis or treatment is wrong? Further, unlike misdiagnosis or wrong medicine by a human, a flaw in an AI system can harm thousands of patients.

Unlike other traditional IT applications, AI requires huge datasets, which increases security and privacy risks. Traditionally, healthcare professionals have always been responsible for making healthcare decisions. The use of AI to create or facilitate the diagnosis and treatment of patients raises novel ethical dimensions such as accountability, confidentiality, privacy, and transparency. Patient medical records constitute sensitive information, and access to confidential information must have consent, and any participation must be voluntary.

There is growing demand to acquire sensitive patient information, and the ability to re-identify previously anonymised data increases the risk of breach. Even if the data was previously scrubbed of all identifiers and anonymised, computational techniques could be used to re-identify them. This raises the security and privacy risks manifold. A regulatory framework is critical to ensure that there is no breach of confidentiality. Studies indicate that the healthcare industry is already facing a situation where regulations have fallen behind the technologies they govern. Patients may need to know who has access to their data and how that information is used. We have witnessed a growing number of security breaches of medical records and an increasing number of lawsuits for information leakage and fines for personal data privacy breaches.

AI and technology-based healthcare interventions will obviously lack the emphatic attention that patients are used to receiving from a physician. Suppose AI was used to perform image analysis to identify a tumour; it may not explain the diagnosis to the patient without the intervention of an oncologist or clinician.

Regardless of the exciting opportunities and far-reaching benefits of AI to healthcare, we need policies, guidelines, standards, and regulatory frameworks to safeguard the rights of all stakeholders in the healthcare system. This will ensure that AI is used safely, legally, and ethically to improve the quality of patient care delivery. Comprehensive governance frameworks must be in place for this transition, as the guidelines and policies are only as good as the regulatory framework that underpins them.

Conclusion: A New Era of Healthcare

There is growing evidence that traditional healthcare models are not sustainable in the long term as they face multiple challenges, including the ongoing pandemic, which is the perfect long storm, creating more momentum for AI, and the need for transformation in healthcare. AI is at the centre of the healthcare industry's much-needed innovation. Against this backdrop, it will have widespread benefits for the global healthcare system and revolutionise the patient care continuum.

We are already realising the ambitious visions of AI in healthcare through innovative approaches, including early detection of diseases, in some cases years in advance, more accurate diagnosis, robotic surgery, AI-assisted novel treatments, AI-enabled vaccine and drug development, personalised treatment and precision medicine. Because of AI, medical treatment is likely to move away from the traditional descriptive analytics model of *what happened* to the AI-driven prescriptive model of *what will happen* and patient-centric care. This will lead to timely intervention, preventive care, and personalised medicine delivery.

Driven by AI and technology, healthcare is fast becoming more accessible, affordable and personalised. Patients will have multiple options for their healthcare beyond the traditional brick-and-mortar setting of hospitals, physicians and healthcare workers of today. Patients are already beginning to take better control of their care, and telemedicine will lead to the transition from clinic-based to home-based treatment. Remote diagnosis, treatment and monitoring of patients will continue to gain traction. This will give patients access to physicians of their choice anywhere, without being constrained by geographical proximity, and to well-equipped hospitals.

AI is also rapidly becoming more sophisticated at doing what a physician, pathologist, radiologist, or oncologist does. AI algorithms are more efficient, accurate, unbiased, and cost less than a human medical professional. By supplementing diagnosis and treatment with AI, doctors can deliver better healthcare outcomes for their patients – a human-AI collaboration. It is also evident that AI will ease the strain on much-needed healthcare resources. This could also pivot towards re-balancing physicians' workload.

Lastly, the debate is whether AI will ultimately replace physicians, radiologists, and other stakeholders. A study by Deloitte in collaboration with the Oxford Martin Institute stated that AI could automate 35% of healthcare jobs in the UK in the next 10 to 20 years. Some studies suggest that AI is more likely to displace radiologists and pathologists than other medical professionals in the early stages. It is already augmenting physicians, clinicians, pathologists, radiologists, and other healthcare professionals in caring for patients. Hence, it is becoming more evident that new skills and job redesign will be required as AI technology matures and the healthcare industry transforms. Perhaps the only healthcare professionals AI will displace are those who are unwilling to acquire skills to work along with AI. In time to come, the AI doctor is more than a faint possibility!

References

Bell, J. (2020, February 7). Exscientia attempting to end 'prolonged crisis' in pharma industry by using AI to discover new drugs. NS Healthcare. Available at: https://www.ns-healthcare.com/analysis/exscientia-ai-drug-discovery/.

Davenport, T., & Kalakota, R. (2019, June 16). The potential for artificial intelligence in healthcare. *Future Healthcare Journal*, 6(2), 94–98. DOI: 10.7861/futurehosp.6-2-94. https://www.ncbi.nlm.nih.gov/pmc/articles/PMC6616181/pdf/futurehealth-6-2-94.pdf.

Lam, C., Siefkas, A., Zelin, N. S., Barnes, G., Dellinger, R. P., Vincent, J.-L., Braden, G., Burdick, H., Hoffman, J., Calvert, J., Mao, Q., & Das, R. (2021, March 29). Machine Learning as a Precision-Medicine Approach to Prescribing COVID-19 Pharmacotherapy with Remdesivir or Corticosteroids. *Clinical Therapeutics*, 43(5), 71–885. https://doi.org/10.1016/j.clinthera.2021.03.016.

Masige, H. & Business Insider. (2019, July 13). Australian Researchers Have Just Released The World's First AI-Developed Vaccine. ScienceAlert. Available at: https://www.

sciencealert.com/the-world-s-first-ai-developed-vaccine-could-prevent-another-horror-flu-season.

Massachusetts Institute of Technology. (2021, March 15). Faster drug discovery through machine learning. ScienceDaily. Available at: https://www.sciencedaily.com/releases/2021/03/210315132146.htm.

Mar, V.J. & Soyer, H.P. (2018, August 1). Artificial intelligence for melanoma diagnosis: how can we deliver on the promise? *Annals of Oncology*, 29(8), 1625–1628. https://doi.org/10.1093/annonc/mdy193.

Newman-Toker, D.E., Wang, Z., Zhu, Y., Nassery, N., Tehrani, A.S.S., Schaffer, A. C., Yu-Moe, C.W., Clemens, G.D., Fanai, M., Siegal, D. (2020, May 14). Rate of diagnostic errors and serious misdiagnosis-related harms for major vascular events, infections, and cancers: toward a national incidence estimate using the "Big Three". *Diagnosis*, 8(1), 67–84. https://doi.org/10.1515/dx-2019-0104.

Ransbotham, S. & Khodabandeh, S. (2021, July 13). AI and the COVID-19 Vaccine: Moderna's Dave Johnson. *MIT Sloan Management Review*. Available at: https://sloanreview.mit.edu/audio/ai-and-the-covid-19-vaccine-modernas-dave-johnson/.

Ratanghayra, N. (2021, April 16). Automating Drug Discovery With Machine Learning. Technology Networks. Available at: https://www.technologynetworks.com/drug-discovery/articles/automating-drug-discovery-with-machine-learning-347763.

World Health Organization UHL. (2020, July 7). *Global strategy on human resources for health: Workforce 2030*. World Health Organization. https://www.who.int/publications/i/item/9789241511131.

CHAPTER 7

AI and Manufacturing

Industry 4.0, Industrial Artificial Intelligence, Smart Factory, Industrial Internet of Things (IIoT), and Robotic Process Automation (RPA) are terms that have become commonplace even in daily parlance and our lives, especially for those who are involved in the manufacturing sector. Therefore, the expectations of AI and ML can be polarised, ranging from euphoric followership, hoping for all-encompassing solutions to all things related to manufacturing, to those who view AI with scepticism. As in any emerging technology, one would expect the reality to be somewhere in between until it matures. But the impact of AI has been far more significant than any other precedent technology even at this stage and is already disrupting the industry. The benefits are numerous and can lead to extraordinary advances in manufacturing, including the concepts of autonomous smart factories and mass customisation. This chapter will examine how AI and ML are adding value to transform the manufacturing industry, and present AI-based industrial solutions and use cases.

A Brief History of Manufacturing

"We cannot wait until there are massive dislocations in our society to prepare for the Fourth Industrial Revolution."
— Prof. Robert J. Shiller, Nobel Laureate, Yale University

Manufacturing has a long history of nearly three centuries. In the early 18th century, the major transformation was the Industrial Revolution, when we moved from man-made to machine-made, which mechanised the manufacturing process. Most importantly, this resulted in a dramatic shift in the marketplace and brought prosperity and progress to society. This was followed by the discovery of electricity and assembly-line production (Second Industrial Revolution), the next major shift in manufacturing, resulting in cost efficiencies. Though the assembly line was first patented in 1901 by car manufacturer Ransom E. Olds, Henry Ford is credited as the father of the assembly line and the automotive industry. He improved Olds's original assembly line production system using moving platforms and a conveyor belt system. Michigan-based Buick further enhanced this by introducing unified assembly line production, increasing production capacity while cutting manufacturing costs.

Nearly five decades later, in 1948, Toyota Motors began to focus on methodologies to improve production flow by identifying and eliminating waste, which became popularly known as Lean Manufacturing. This system became widely adopted by other sectors, including electronics, contract manufacturing, aerospace, defence, pharmaceutical, building and construction, food manufacturing, amongst others. Toyota continued to perfect the manufacturing workflow methodology of Lean Manufacturing, and nearly two decades later, it came to be known as Just-in-Time (JIT) systems. The primary objective of JIT is to maximise return on investment (ROI) by maintaining zero inventory across the organisation and its supply chain. JIT emphasises manufacturing only "what is needed when needed, and in the exact amount needed".

Fast-forward another 50 years to modern-day manufacturing driven by machines and robots that are now becoming "smarter." Robots are not new, having been introduced almost a century ago. In 1926, Westinghouse Electric Corporation developed a robot named Mr. Televox, which could respond to the human voice and perform some elementary tasks. R.J. Wensley designed the first robot to perform a meaningful task beyond trivial activities. According to the *New York Times* (2013), Wensley stated presciently in 1933, "In time to come the only work to be done by men and women will be that which requires faculties of discernment, discretion, and judgment. All other work – anything repetitive, routine, standardised – can be better done by machines."

Since then, the manufacturing industry has made rapid advances by introducing more robots into assembly lines. The first industrial robot, Unimate, designed for assembly line production, was introduced in 1961 by General Motors. This laid the foundation for today's research and the development of intelligent robots. There have been significant advances in robotics over the years, and companies such as Rethink Robotics have developed collaborative robotic solutions where robots can work next to humans. These robots have brought about dramatic efficiency improvements and have increased productivity while lowering the cost of production and improved quality.

It's been a long journey of nearly a century. We're now at an inflection point in manufacturing history where machines are becoming more intelligent, setting the stage for the next industrial revolution, driven by smart robots and smart factories. For most of the second half of the 20th century, the manufacturing industry has leveraged computers, robots, and information technology, which is known as Industry 3.0. In recent years, the transition to Industry 4.0 has been driven by a potent mix of newer technologies, including cloud computing, AI, IIoT, and Big Data, also known as Smart Manufacturing. Though both eras are about computing, automation and digitisation of the manufacturing process, Industry 4.0 has added a new dimension to manufacturing by transforming it from the current value proposition of mere *digitisation* to improved *visualisation*, and most importantly, to *intelligence.*

According to market studies, global manufacturing industry output was $41.9 trillion in 2021 despite the ongoing Covid-19 crisis. For manufacturers, operational efficiency, robustness and supply chain resilience are vital priorities, and digital transformation has become the key strategy to address these and differentiate them from competitors. In the last two years, there have been several worldwide supply chain disruptions, and manufacturers have faced unprecedented challenges in maintaining inventory and managing the workforce. AI and ML offer innovative solutions to these problems for the post-pandemic era. A McKinsey study (2019) found that AI can create up to $2 trillion of value per annum in manufacturing and supply chain management.

How Can AI and ML be Applied in Manufacturing?

The manufacturing industry worldwide has been undergoing significant transformation in recent years, driven by smart technologies and ongoing digital transformation. AI and ML have gained considerable traction in the manufacturing sector, particularly during the past five years. Since 2020, this transformation has been upended by an unprecedented level of urgency. Covid-19 has made manufacturers rethink their strategy in building resilience to deal with uncertainties and challenges regarding raw material, workforce and supply chain disruptions.

According to a report by Capgemini (2020), European manufacturers are ahead of their US and Japanese counterparts by more than 50%, followed by 30% in Japan and 28% in the US. China, however, has been the "factory of the world" for some years now. Even during Covid-19, as other economies struggled, China's manufacturing output grew from the previous year, accounting for nearly one-third of the global market. The Chinese economy was able to bounce back quickly from the pandemic and has leveraged AI solutions. Since 2014, China has been the global leader in the number of AI patent applications. It has surpassed the US in terms of the number of AI research publications and journal citations.

AI and ML algorithms and solutions are being deployed across the breadth of the manufacturing industry, and in particular, the following four key functions:

1. Design and product development
2. Quality control and assurance
3. Maintenance
4. Logistics and supply chain optimisation

Product Development and Generative Design

Generative Design (GD) is a disruptive technology driven by AI algorithms, which has elevated the current state of design engineering and product development. It is an AI tool that can generate multiple solutions at the same time, based on actual-world design specifications and product features, functions, and performance requirements. Manufacturers no longer need to rely on design engineers and be limited by their creativity, imagination or experience. Generative Design leverages AI and ML and extends the "power" to manufacturers to optimise procurement of raw materials and manufacturing methods, so design engineers can focus on innovation and increase productivity.

For example, by inputting different parameters such as materials, size, weight, strength, manufacturing methods, cost constraints, and time, GD tools can generate multiple solutions. This set of solutions can then be fed to a pre-trained Deep Learning engine that can select the optimal solution and provide insights. This can be an iterative process until the design team is comfortable with the optimal solution. This also allows designers and engineers to simultaneously explore and validate hundreds or even thousands of design options. They can then test and filter the solutions to select the outcomes that can best meet their organisational needs.

Use cases:

Japan's DENSO leveraged GD to redesign the engine control unit (ECU) to meet the global auto industry's need for improved engine performance and reduced vehicle weight. The ECU is an electronic fuel-injection control system that determines the required fuel supply for the optimal performance of an engine. DENSO's design engineers were able to modify the ECU to be lighter and smaller – able to fit in the palm of the hand – while retaining heat-dispersing capabilities and other properties.

Automaker General Motors (GM) leveraged GD to consolidate an eight-part seat bracket into a single part, and, in the process, made the new bracket 40% lighter and 20% stronger.

Quality Control and Assurance

AI is fast becoming the quality control specialist in manufacturing. It is a game-changer as it substantially reduces product and manufacturing defects, anomalies, and recalls. High-resolution smart cameras, IIoT, object vision, and related AI-enabled software are helping manufacturers to achieve improved quality checks at speeds, latency, and costs beyond human capability while providing insights into what causes the problems. These AI solutions are incredibly beneficial for automotive, airline and pharmaceutical manufacturers as they must meet stringent quality standards and regulatory requirements.

Use cases:

Automakers are leveraging AI's object vision capabilities to spot cracks, dents, scratches, perform paint surface inspection, and identify any other deviations from quality standards, and all these are being achieved in real-time.

BMW Group uses AI at several of its auto manufacturing locations. In Steyr, Austria, the BMW plant has deployed an Autonomous Machine Vision application, Inspekto S70, developed by a German-Israeli JV company. According to Harel Boren, CEO and co-founder of Inspekto, "it is self-learning, self-setting, and self-adjusting" – that is to say, it is a fully autonomous AI application. This has resulted in tangible improvements in quality and reduction of false detection. Another BMW plant, in Dingolfing, Germany, leverages automated image recognition to evaluate component images during production and compares them in milliseconds to hundreds of other images. The AI application then detects any deviations, for instance whether all necessary parts have been mounted and whether they are mounted in the right place. All this is done in real-time.

The Japanese tire manufacturer Bridgestone uses a tire assembly system known as EXAMATION, which leverages AI and sensors to measure the characteristics of each tire manufactured. The quality of the tire is based on 480 quality characteristics, thus enabling high-level precision and superior quality in manufacturing the tires. It is reported that they have achieved more than 15% improvement in uniformity compared to conventional manufacturing processes.

Smart Maintenance

Manufacturing is an asset-intensive industry, and the maintenance of machines has always been a practical dilemma. High uptime is critical to ensure ROI on equipment and machines. According to a study by Capgemini (2020), 29% of use cases of AI in manufacturing are related to maintenance, followed by 27% for quality and 20% for product development. Unlike preventive maintenance, predictive maintenance is performed only when needed, reducing labour and material costs. It analyses the historical performance of data to predict with an assigned/acceptable level of probability (generally north of 90%) as to when a machine is likely to fail and even the cause of the problem or failure.

The AI "brain" can process the data from diverse sources, including videos and audios, to identify any anomaly and prevent breakdowns and failures in the production belt, assembly line, or an aircraft en route in the sky. Some studies indicate that cost savings from predictive maintenance can be as high as 25–30% as opposed to 12–15% for preventive maintenance. A predictive maintenance schedule can be either a time-based or usage-based alert system. A time-based predictive maintenance system will perform periodic checks and alerts as and when a particular piece of equipment needs inspection or repair. At the same time, a usage-based system will trigger an alert after a specified number of activities, number of production cycles, or miles travelled by a vehicle. A McKinsey study reports that predictive maintenance reduces machine downtime by an impressive 30–50% while increasing machine lifetime by 20–40%.

Use cases:

Aircraft engine manufacturer Rolls-Royce leverages an Intelligent Engine platform to monitor engine flight and collate data on weather conditions and individual pilots' flying patterns. Based on this data, ML algorithms are applied to customise maintenance regimes for unique engines and optimise the engine's life.

According to Honeywell, airlines that deployed its Forged Connected Maintenance (FCM) application have experienced a 30–50% reduction in operational disruptions caused by the Auxiliary Power Unit (APU) and a 10–15% reduction in costly premature removals. FCM leverages AI and ML algorithms techniques to identify problems quickly and efficiently with a near-perfect 99% accuracy, thus eliminating the need for technicians to monitor and interpret data.

Food manufacturer Frito-Lay's plant in Fayetteville, Tennessee, leverages predictive maintenance, with year-to-date equipment downtime at 0.75% and unplanned downtime at 2.88%, according to Carlos Calloway, the facility's reliability engineering manager.

Supply Chain Optimisation

The supply chain is one of the key functional domains in manufacturing that has made significant progress in the last two decades, sometimes called a "digital supply chain". This would not have been possible but for the advances in IT as today's supply chains are intricate networks across different locations, different time zones, made up of thousands and thousands of parts, and delivered globally. Given the growing complexity of supply chains, manufacturers are increasingly leveraging AI and ML technologies for improved decision-making, planning, procurement, inventory optimisation, asset tracking accuracy, and logistics, amongst other critical activities. In short, AI enables real-time supply chain visibility.

Manufacturers use AI tools to forecast consumer demands, coordinate procurement, better manage inventory, and optimise production schedules. Over the years, forecasting has been based on statistical modelling that draws on historical data. But ML has introduced an additional dimension of intelligence for demand forecasting, planning, and supply chain decision-making. AI tools can examine inventory and the number of parts in stock, check for expiration dates, place orders to replenish the inventory, manage delivery schedules, thus optimising the supply chain in real-time. On-time product delivery to the customer is of primary importance in the supply chain. This is critical for the manufacturer's credibility and for winning customer trust. However, it is not always easy to predict what is ahead of the route as there can be delays due to weather conditions and traffic accidents, amongst others. We have witnessed significant supply chain disruptions globally during the Covid-19 pandemic. An AI-driven GPS tool can assist in optimising and navigating the delivery of goods by providing access to the most efficient route.

Use cases:

BASF Nutrition & Health engaged IBM to build a Replenishment Advisor tool leveraging the AI and ML capabilities of IBM Cloud and IBM Watson AI. The Replenishment Advisor can accurately predict when product stock is running low, provide timely alerts, and forecast the optimal time needed to replenish supply and significantly reduce any disruptions. This allows production planners to take timely action, assisting to avoid under- and over-stocking. The AI supports smarter inventories and efficient demand fulfilment. Most importantly, superior customer experience is derived by ensuring products are always in the right place at the right time.

Digital Twins in Manufacturing

The Digital Twin is not a new concept, but because of Big Data, AI, and IIoT, there has been a resurgence of interest and focus on this. It is a fast-evolving concept and presents significant benefits for the manufacturing industry. According to Deloitte (2022), "manufacturing is estimated to generate about 1,812 petabytes (PB) of data every year, more than communications, finance, retail, and several other industries". By leveraging digital twins, manufacturers can run "what if" experiments to explore what works and what will not in the virtual factory and discover the optimal solution, which in the past took several production cycles to perfect. This also reduces the lead-time in testing, identifies defects early, and reduces the costly recalls faced by traditional manufacturing.

Another critical area is in managing inventory levels. Raw materials are the cornerstone of manufacturing. Managing supply and inventory levels of raw materials will significantly impact any manufacturer's overall success and failure. Historically, manufacturers had to deal with the extreme volatility and the unstable price of raw materials. AI-based algorithms can forecast price volatility and required inventory more precisely than humans. Digital twins use data generated from sensors to feed into AI and ML algorithms to forecast output precisely and accurately. They have an immediate and significant impact, as real-time insights augment production and performance optimisation. Manufacturers can leverage digital twins for predictive maintenance, allowing technicians to act before failure occurs, so that businesses can minimise downtime and improve the overall efficiency of machines.

Use cases:

Porsche, the German sports car manufacturer, reported in October 2021 that it sold more Taycans than its flagship 911. The 911 has been in production for the past six decades, and is into its eighth-generation model, while the Taycan appeared in the market only in 2019. The Taycan is an electric car, and Porsche had to ensure a significant reduction in carbon emissions and resource consumption while retaining the performance levels of a sports car. It has been reported that it took only four years from initial planning to production of the first Taycan. To achieve this, Porsche took a revolutionary step by leveraging digital twins and robots, abandoning the traditional assembly line model for production, and deploying Automatic Guided Vehicle (AGV) technology. Porsche's innovative approach is a model for the future of manufacturing – the "factory of the future".

In the past, manufacturers would go through a lengthy physical process of testing and fixing (by trial and error), but digital twins can simulate virtual models to test, which significantly lowers the risks and expensive miscalculations while optimising production time. This means significant time and cost savings for the business. Digital twins can identify problems and defects which may not be visible to the naked human eye. Auto manufacturers leverage digital twins to create a virtual model of a vehicle to predict outcomes. They can simulate and analyse during the production phase and anticipate problems before the car hits the roads. They use digital twin technology to design the ideal automotive product even before production starts.

Canon uses a system known as Assisted Defect Recognition which leverages ML algorithms, predictive analytics, and object vision to examine and determine the integrity of each part. This has enabled Canon to track potential defects in advance and make improvements in areas that the naked human eye may not be able to detect.

Dark Factories

"Dark" factories, also known as "automatic" or "smart" factories, are manufacturing facilities that do not depend on human labour and are operated by robots with no need for lighting, air-conditioning, heating, or other amenities required by humans. They are environmentally friendly and present significant cost savings. These range from steel plants to mobile phone manufacturers who have leveraged smart factories to manufacture on 24/7 mode in an uninterrupted and unattended fashion.

Dark factories are not new – they have a history of nearly four decades, first appearing in Japan in the 1980s, as manufacturers took advantage of robotics and automation to better manage labour supply and cost issues.

Covid-19 has changed our world, and social distancing has become part of life and work. Many companies have embraced work-from-home or a hybrid model. Because of their high reliance on the presence of human capital at the factory, many manufacturers have faced challenges, and some have sadly ceased operations. This development has brought awareness, attention, and relevance to the concept of the dark factory.

Use cases:

Today, robots have become commonplace in factories and warehouses. Amazon leverages Amazon Robotics (previously known as Kiva Systems) in its warehouses and has two different robot models. The smaller model can carry pallets with loads up to 1,000 pounds, and the larger model can carry a pallet with loads of 3,000 pounds. These robots navigate the warehouse by following a series of computerised bar-code stickers on the floor, picking the pods, and delivering them to the target destination or a human.

Xiaomi Corporation, at its factory in Beijing, uses intelligent robots to manufacture an estimated one million phones a year. Production of each of these smartphones requires more than 200 steps, most of which are handled by these robots.

In the Netherlands, Philips is reported to produce 15 million electric razors a year in its automated factory leveraging 128 robots. The only task where humans are involved is during quality assurance, and only nine humans are employed for this task.

While smart factories deliver productivity improvements and cost savings, and are environmentally friendly, some have questioned whether replacing humans with computers and robots is good for humanity.

How to Successfully Deploy AI for Manufacturing

For successful implementation of AI, manufacturers need to take care of four key areas: business strategy as well as technical strategy; well-defined policies and processes; and AI skills and competencies.

- **Strategy:** To successfully deploy AI and to deliver on its promise, the company will require a comprehensive AI transformation strategy to be in place. More importantly, like in any solution, there is no one-size-fits-all, and AI and ML are not silver bullets. From a management perspective, business strategy for AI implementation should focus on defining business needs and targets, change management strategy, examining existing processes and operations, setting measurable objectives including ROI and Key Performance Indicators (KPIs), identifying business owners, and specifying timelines for the AI project. From a technical perspective, developing AI algorithms and successfully deploying them requires a technical AI implementation strategy that has a critical focus on data, which is the "fuel" for AI engines and the "brains" for smart manufacturing. These "AI brains" need to be trained. Hence the quality of the data is critical for successful implementation. There is a growing abundance of data (Big Data) generated by the proliferation of sensors, IIoT, and connectivity. The metadata ("data that describes other data") must be consistent, of good quality, and trustworthy. Open data movements worldwide are focusing on improving data accessibility, overall quality, and transparency.

- **Policies and Processes**: Secondly, AI implementation is not simply about technology. It is a new way of manufacturing that requires a rethinking of existing manufacturing processes. In addition, like in any project implementation, the factory must have established roles and responsibilities, organisational reporting, and communication structure for AI implementation. The manufacturer must also have specific policies in place for capturing, extracting, organising, using, storing, and securing data both from a physical and logical perspective. Leveraging quality data, AI algorithms will highlight consistent patterns and identify outliers. Thus, manufacturing can transform from traditional *digitisation* to improved *visualisation* (drawing insights), and to *optimisation* from intelligent systems.

- **AI Skills and Talent:** Successful development and deployment of AI solutions will also require skilled and talented data scientists and the involvement of process and product owners. Rolling out a successful AI project requires access to quality metadata, expertise in data science, and a thorough knowledge of the manufacturing process. There is a shrinking supply of skilled AI-savvy talent, which is one of the barriers to the adoption of AI. Companies should not implement AI and ML for technology's sake. Instead, they need to have a clear strategy to ensure that the team has the technical competency and workforce transformation readiness skills. This should include an inventory of skills the company has, as well as a plan to acquire needed external resources and skills, and upskill internal resources.

Conclusion

Where is all this headed? The future is now, as AI is fast becoming the heart of smart manufacturing and driving Industry 4.0, delivering enhanced productivity and quality while becoming increasingly environmentally friendly. AI will help manufacturers decide on the most optimal sequence of activities for achieving production goals and enable them to remotely manage in real-time. It will transform manufacturing processes from end to end, including product design, engineering, procurement, inventory management, industrial operations (including production and quality control), logistics, marketing, sales, aftersales support and predictive maintenance.

Hence, AI promises to be a game-changer at every level of the value chain and has begun to reshape the industry with new business models, including mass customisation, while giving new life to concepts such as product servitisation – selling a product outcome as a service rather than a one-off sale. Manufacturers can tap on AI's disruptive potential and make the grand vision a reality by building products to suit a customer's personal preference and exact specification. The conventional perspective of manufacturing and offering as a one-time product sale is fast changing to future revenue models based on product-as-a-platform, and AI is driving this shift.

Over the last several decades, computer automation has increasingly transformed the manufacturing industry as it has enabled machines to perform thousands of repetitive tasks effectively, efficiently, with precision, and with improved quality and profitability. But the existing production models are not geared for sudden or frequent changes to requirements and personalisation. That is where AI-based autonomous self-learning systems are beginning to transform the industry, yet again. These systems based on AI can respond in real-time to changes in requirements and individual specifications. Fully autonomous factories, also known as "lights-out manufacturing", are rising. These factories will also be environmentally friendly as there will be no need for climate control systems.

The deployment of AI and robots is particularly useful in manufacturing. They increase product innovation, cost-effectiveness, product quality, mass customisation, personalisation, production efficiency, supply chain efficiency, and overall speed. From an employment and skills perspective, the industry will need to reskill. There will also be growing demand for data scientists and machine learning engineers, amongst other technical positions with manufacturing domain knowledge. Demand for "fusion skills" such as collaborative robotics and AI specialists will similarly rise. Fusion skills in manufacturing occur when combining human and intelligent machines (working in concert) to produce superior outcomes instead of each working independently.

In recent years, there has been a significant increase in the use of Robotic Process Automation (RPA). For decades, manufacturers have leveraged physical robots to streamline the assembly line for tasks such as assembly, testing, and packaging their products. Manufacturers are now leveraging intelligent automation tools ("software robots") driven by RPA for process automation and to streamline and optimise complex back-office operations. I can foresee a time when robots and AI will undertake design, production, and delivery tasks, thus potentially leading to more significant cost savings. Robots will become self-repairing and even partially self-designing. AI will increasingly design houses and apartment buildings, and the use of prefabricated modules that robots can put together will become pervasive. AI and ML algorithms will predict the arrival and schedule the departure of the product in and out of the warehouse without human intervention. And just-in-time autonomous robot delivery vans will deliver manufactured finished products to customers. Manufacturers in China are already laying the groundwork right now, setting themselves up to be leaders in leveraging AI for smart manufacturing. Undoubtedly, the AI revolution in manufacturing is already in motion. Transformation towards a new way of manufacturing is already emerging with new roles as AI is already augmenting many human capabilities. But it will be some years before AI technology matures and the vision of the future with autonomous factories becomes universally available.

References

Brosset, P., Patsko, S., Khadikar, A., Thieullent, A., Buvat, J., Khemka, Y., Jain, A. (2019, December 12). Scaling AI in Manufacturing Operations: A Practitioners' Perspective. Capgemini. DOI:MACS_CS_ AP_ 20190718. https://www.capgemini.com/wp-content/uploads/2019/12/AI-in-manufacturing-operations.pdf.

Chui, M., Henke, N. & Miremadi, M. (2019, March 7). Most of AI's business uses will be in two areas. McKinsey. Available at: https://www.mckinsey.com/business-functions/mckinsey-analytics/our-insights/most-of-ais-business-uses-will-be-in-two-areas.

Deloitte. (2020, January 16). AI Enablement on the Way to Smart Manufacturing: Deloitte Survey on AI Adoption in Manufacturing. Deloitte. DOI:RITM0357951. https://www2.deloitte.com/content/dam/Deloitte/cn/Documents/cip/deloitte-cn-cip-ai-manufacturing-application-survey-en-200116.pdf.

Hiler, K. (2013, October 28). The Automatons of Yesteryear. *The New York Times*. Available at: https://www.nytimes.com/2013/10/29/science/the-automatons-of-yesteryear.html.

Melin, J. (2018, June 15). Moving Beyond the Hype of Predictive Maintenance. Honey-
    well. Available at: https://aerospace.honeywell.com/us/en/learn/about-us/blogs/
    moving-beyond-the-hype-of-predictive-maintenance.

Scane, S. (2020, November 13). BMW: Quality Control Through Artificial Intelligence.
    Manufacturing. Available at: https://manufacturingdigital.com/ai-and-automation/
    bmw-quality-control-through-artificial-intelligence.

CHAPTER 8

AI and Mobility

VINCENT WONG

DR. ANTON RAVINDRAN

"Mobility is the heartbeat of life" – this slogan, coined by German automotive company Continental in 2019, aptly summarises the impact of mobility in our everyday lives:

- A navigated drive on the least congested roads reduces carbon emission.
- An order via an intelligent ride-hailing app connects a driver in the shortest time.
- A journey supported by smart Advanced Driver Assistance Systems (ADAS) ensures a safer ride.

The movement of people and transportation of goods over air, land, and sea has enabled trade and commerce to grow. Countries invest heavily in airports, seaports, rails, roads, and infrastructures to promote economic growth, with the mobility of people and goods enabling them to trade and flourish. In addition, many major cities like the city-state of Singapore are currently facing manpower shortage due to their ageing populations; Singapore government agencies like the Land Transport Authority (LTA) and Infocomm Media Development Authority (IMDA) are already test-bedding AI-enabled solutions to mitigate such workforce challenges in Singapore's mobility industry.

However, mobility also brings about issues for mega cities: pollution, traffic-clogged highways, road accidents, to name a few. Yet, AI is touted as the magic panacea for these problems. Modern cities aim to use smart mobility technologies to bring convenience, safety and comfort back to their inhabitants. This chapter introduces some of the latest trends in AI-powered mobility, with discussions on case studies of (1) Mobility as a Service; (2) autonomous driving and mobile robots; (3) driver profiling and monitoring; and (4) smart fleet maintenance. Challenges encountered by the mobility industry in deploying AI will also be shared.

1. Mobility as a Service (MaaS): Multimodal mobility

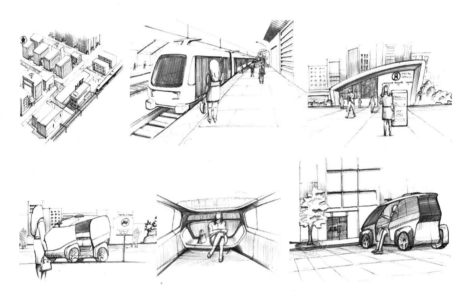

With globalisation, urbanised millennials now opt for new forms of transportation in line with the mega-trends of the sharing economy and sustainability. The concept of owning and maintaining a car has now shifted towards using green public transportation together with bike and car-sharing services. This prevalence has also been encouraged, with several cities investing heavily in smart infrastructure to enable real-time monitoring of traffic conditions and location of transportation agents within its network. A journey using multiple means of transportation modes that connect seamlessly into a single mobility service accessible on demand is now a reality. This is known as Mobility as a Service (MaaS) and is defined as "integrating various forms of transport services into a single mobility service accessible on-demand" (Manjrekar, 2020).

With the MaaS market currently at an inflection point, it is expected to expand from $4.7 billion in 2020 to a $70 billion market by 2030, at a 31.1% compound annual growth rate. A key feature of MaaS is the recommendation of end-to-end transportation modes with smart AI algorithms. This can be accessed by users via a phone app that bestows them with the certainty of connection between transportation services and arrival time. Crucially, the concept of MaaS drives the travel trends of smart city dwellers.

Societal Trends as Trigger

Societal trends and advancements in technology have led to the rise of MaaS.

The increasing usage and reliance on public transportation networks has driven cities to modernise their transportation network. This includes advancements such as sustainable transportation modes and clean energy sources in public infrastructure, especially since the encouragement of green mobility devices has taken centre stage. For example, the Ministry of Transport in Singapore takes a holistic view towards sustainable transportation by focusing on enhancing public transportation services, improving transportation resources usage, and lowering carbon emissions via a vehicle taxation system (Ministry of Transport, 2019). These initiatives encourage citizens to adopt greener forms of transport.

In various first world countries where transportation infrastructures, the sharing economy and sustainability efforts are evident, private vehicle car sales are declining. While emerging markets will continue to see growth in car ownership, developed, high-income countries will witness a trend of declining car ownership. Global car sales reached a peak in 2019 with 74.9 million units, and have declined since then (Wall, 2019).

The following figure shows light vehicle sales across various markets since 2012. Mature markets will see a decline of 5% until 2027. Commuters will migrate towards a model of MaaS instead of vehicle ownership.

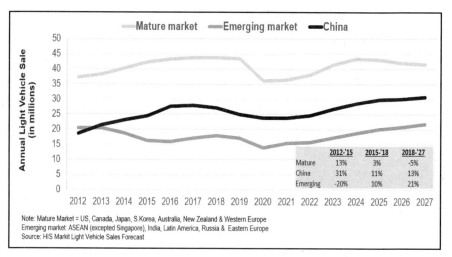

Annual Light Vehicle Sales

AI Technology for MaaS

MaaS is dubbed a technology ecosystem, which means that the presence of AI is imperative for its developments. AI technologies play a pivotal role in aggregating various forms of transportation data from the ecosystem of public and private operators, before fusing them together into travel options for the commuter. Amazingly, this can be done smoothly in a single application, which is facilitated by every aspect of this ecosystem either being steeped in data or being data-driven. Leveraging ML, DL and Big Data technologies, MaaS is the future of transport.

MaaS AI-based systems can aptly identify the best transportation option, fulfilling the two factors that all commuters look towards: time and cost. With massive amounts of data spanning across multiple transportation platforms such as public bus arrival schedules, train departure timings, road traffic conditions and personal mobility device (PMD) rental availability being fed into the system, the wonders of MaaS have ignited a transformation in the mobility world.

The table on the next page shows four companies who provide MaaS solutions.

Company	Description	Scope
REACH NOW	REACH NOW app allows commuters to search, book and pay for different modes of public transport including taxis, bikes and e-scooters. Instant cost and trip length comparison	Various cities in Germany
MaaS Global	All-in-one mobility app Whim offers a subscription service for public transportation, ridesharing, bike rentals, scooter rentals, taxis or car rentals.	Basel, Zurich, Helsinki
Beeline	Suggest, book and ride. Book a seat on buses listed by private bus operators. New routes are activated by community demand. On the day of your ride, you will be able to track the bus you booked.	Singapore
MaaStran	With strategic partnerships in place, MaaStran retails tickets for all 27 UK rail operators. Through MaaStran, all bus and tram operators can now offer integrated, multi-model tickets to their customers for longer journeys.	United Kingdom

Sources: REACH NOW, https://www.reach-now.com/; Whim, http://whimapp.com; Beeline, https://www.beeline.sg/; MaaStran, https://www.maastran.co.uk/

Moving Forward

It is important that the technology powering MaaS continues to evolve and adapt to the growing demands of a globalised world. A few key factors will determine the success of MaaS deployment in a city. Strong collaboration between transportation and city planning departments, public and private transportation providers, mobility management players, telcos and payment processing systems will allow a thoughtful and holistic integration of services. The various stakeholders also have to allow data to be accessible and exchanged via API feeds in a safe and secured manner, resulting in the creation of a journey plan that is the most efficient and accurate.

Future MaaS offerings will trend towards an integrated end-to-end version of a pay-as-you-go solution. Fares are bundled as a single trip and paid for in one click, based on the distance travelled rather than as a consolidation of à la carte transportation services. This provides huge incentives, with commuters being able to enjoy lower ridership costs as a result.

MaaS powered by AI represents the next evolution in mobility. If it's not there yet, it's coming to a city near you soon!

2. Autonomous Vehicles and Mobile Robots

Over the last few years, the race to fully autonomous vehicles has never been more intense, with companies devoting large amounts of resources and manpower towards the Research and Development (R&D) of it. An autonomous vehicle refers to one that drives itself in "autopilot" mode, requiring minimum intervention from the driver. It is equipped with a suite of exterior sensors which scan the environment continuously for obstacles, landmarks and traffic signals, creating and maintaining a map of the surroundings (Synopsys, 2022). The presence of onboard Global Positioning System (GPS) allows a vehicle to accurately locate its position on Earth, while a High Definition (HD) map containing high environmental fidelity data on roads, intersections and pedestrian crossings allows the vehicle to pinpoint itself on a street. Despite bustling traffic and swarms of pedestrians, real-time computing of the sensor inputs also enables the vehicle to avoid obstacles, moving harmoniously and safely with the traffic. All these functions combine smoothly to allow a vehicle to navigate safely, smoothly and efficiently on a planned path towards the destination entered.

However, while the term "autonomous vehicles" has been commonly thrown around, it is ultimately myopic to characterise such vehicles as monolithic entities. As such, the Society of Automotive Engineers (SAE) has developed a classification system (J3016_201806) that defines the degree of driving automation a vehicle can offer. The classification system has detailed definitions for six levels of driving automation, ranging from no driving automation (Level 0) to full driving automation in all conditions without human interaction (Level 5) (SAE International, 2018).

The introduction of AI in various parts of the software stack with improvements at the hardware level propels the rapid advancement of autonomous vehicle technologies. Three market use cases will be presented for a deeper look at AI technologies.

Markets

Overall the autonomous vehicle market is still very nascent. With the overall market being predicted to grow to a whopping ~US$1.8 trillion by 2030 (Autonomous Vehicle Market Report, 2020), it makes sense for large companies to strive towards developing the technology.

Robo-taxis

Robo-taxi, also known as self-driving taxi or driverless taxi, is arguably the service with the most hype surrounding it, as it constitutes a direct impact on the end user (the commuters). Several market drivers fuel the demand, which helps the growing popularity of ride-hailing services, increasing safety regulations, gas emission reduction, etc. The popularity of such vehicles has been recognised worldwide, with companies such as Waymo LLC, Uber Technologies, Baidu and Amazon taking steps to tackle the challenge of developing and deploying such robo-taxis. Numerous public deployment trials are also currently running or are planned to start in different cities, including Shenzhen (AutoX), Shanghai (Didi), Arizona (Waymo) and San Francisco (Cruise).

Partnering the automakers are self-driving technology providers who develop software and hardware solutions to enable a vehicle to sense, plan and act in an autonomous manner, with major companies including Nvidia, Motional, Continental and Velodyne. While it seems wondrous that vehicles are able to move independently and safely in a bustling city, one cannot ignore the large incorporations of AI that have made this possible. The domains of AI involved include: computer vision, machine learning and reinforcement learning, which are deployed in various aspects of an autonomous driving system to properly perceive a surrounding environment, plan the vehicle route and guide the vehicle around danger and obstacles.

However, despite the incorporation of modern technology, deployment in urban areas has been more difficult than anticipated. Densely populated areas come with their fair share of complexity that would challenge the AI system.

To name a few cases:

- At the navigation level:
  » pedestrians' behaviour at the zebra crossing that would defeat the decision-making part of the vehicle (when to slowly drive past the crossing and force your way in, when to wait, etc.)
  » roundabout management during peak hours
  » intersection crossing during traffic jams

- At the perception level:
  » unanticipated construction work areas that render road markings unreliable
  » unmarked or poorly marked roads
  » temporary construction traffic signs that would prevail over a regular one

With such complexity that needs to be addressed, the excessive cost of R&D that comes with urban use-case management has provided impetus for several companies to look at alternative "simpler" markets with a relatively more structured environment, and less safety risk for both drivers and pedestrians.

Self-Driving Trucks and Commercial Vehicles

Recently, autonomous trucks have also gained attention with the adoption of a point-to-point model. Some key market players include AB Volvo (Sweden), Continental AG (Germany), TuSimple (US), General Motors Company (US), Volkswagen AG (Germany), Waymo LLC (US), Ford Motor Co. (US), Robert Bosch GmbH (Germany), DENSO (Japan) and Daimler AG (Germany). This may partly be because there is less technological challenge at a higher level compared to the robo-taxi, due to the favourable conditions the trucks operate in, being able to:

- Follow fixed routes
- Drive mainly on highways, which are usually more structured, with road markings and larger lane sizes, allowing for more predictable driving conditions

Another market driver is the shortage of truck drivers in the US, due to challenging working conditions coupled with the Covid-19 pandemic (Shepardson, 2021).

Currently technology is at a test/pilot deployment phase, with, depending on the use case, a safety driver onboard the truck. For instance:

- TuSimple has completed a first round of tests of its driverless semi-truck in Arizona, lately without human intervention (no driver intervention, no teleoperation or traffic intervention) (Wiles, 2021).
- The alliance between Waymo and J.B. Hunt Transport Services is being expanded in 2022, which has resulted in the testing of self-driving truck technology on the roads between Houston and Fort Worth for cargo deliveries (Reuters, 2022).

One can expect the first commercial operations in the coming years.

Mobile Robots

With the proliferation of technology and busier working schedules, the demand for delivery of goods, parcels and food has seen a significant increase over the last several years. The pandemic has boosted this demand even further, being projected to create a market upwards of tens of billions of dollars. With an increased demand, this provides a huge opportunity and incentive for technology providers to leverage automation to delegate a portion of this delivery workflow. Using automation is no longer just a choice; it is being driven significantly by e-commerce growth and shortages in the labour market. It can be argued that with these driving factors, robotic delivery for last-mile delivery will become a thing of the norm in a not-so-distant future. State-of-the-art algorithms for environment perception, mapping, localisation, navigation and control are made possible with AI, so robots are capable of navigating fully autonomously in pedestrian spaces in an urban environment, such as footpaths, road-crossings and building lobbies.

In fact, this is already a reality, with Starship, Nuro and Kiwirobots deploying many of such robots in certain cities and campuses. In the Singapore context, this will start with implementation in the new zones demarcated as "carless" by the government, such as the Tengah and Punggol digital districts.

However, the autonomous functionality of such robots has more often than not encountered challenges of scalability and deployment efficiency due to the limited availability of computing and sensing resources.

AI Technology for Autonomy

AI has been recently introduced in several parts of the driverless software stack to address the shortcomings of classical approaches (handcrafted designs), as well as to complement it.

Perception: One of the most prominent applications of AI is within the perception module of a driverless solution. Recent state-of-the-art models have outperformed standard algorithm-based approaches, making it a more tractable choice.

Semantic segmentation using AI (how to classify what is seen by the vehicle cameras) proves to be useful in detecting navigable areas, lane markings, curbs and other static obstacles, as well as dynamic objects such as road users. Traffic signs/lights recognition also allows the vehicle to detect the state of the said traffic sign/light as it approaches.

However, perception can be badly affected by environmental conditions such as a downpour, which hamper visibility. This is where AI can play a significant role. In a recent project funded by AI Singapore, teams from Continental and the National University of Singapore (NUS) have collaborated with the aim of developing novel AI models that can be used to increase the accuracy of object detection and classification in such conditions by fusing data coming from both camera and radar sensors (Toh, 2021).

Navigation: One promising technology is reinforcement learning for navigation, or in simpler terms, learning how to navigate by making AI-based sequences of decisions that follow a set of rules and policies. The learning phase is usually done in a simulator where the system reacts to simulated data and scenarios or simulated scenarios augmented by pre-recorded real data. One of the challenges faced by such a technique is the ability of the system to "adapt" to real scenarios and data.

An alternative approach would be imitation learning: Given a set of examples of how to drive in different conditions and contexts, the AI module would imitate the behaviour when facing an analogous situation.

Localisation: AI/DL-based localisation has recently gained attention. One application is to estimate the vehicle's change of position with respect to a known initial position.

Other aspects: As with many autonomous robot technological solutions, the algorithms that underpin the software processing modules are the key focus of AI, scaling the deployment area to tens of square kilometres while being restricted by the processing capabilities. One of the main challenges to make sure AI modules operate efficiently is the presence of both processing and memory limitations. A learning-based approach that is more resistant to inherent sensor and environmental noise is useful, while a modular navigation system is one that is highly customisable and supports both safety and productivity.

Although the market is de facto non-existent today, this is expected to change dramatically, as it has been observed that legislators worldwide are creating regulatory frameworks that would allow the operation of such robots.

Moving Forward

The market hype around autonomous driving seems to have reached a peak, or Phase 2 of Gartner hype cycle. The pace of development and deployment has been slowing down recently, with consequent expected waves of consolidation across the industry. Here are three key factors:

- High overall R&D and hardware costs. Such technology is capital-intensive and there is a long way to go before reaching a Minimum Viable Product.
- The Covid-19 pandemic forced countries into lockdown, inducing a global halt in the deployment and testing of the technology, due to the inaccessibility of testing areas, less demand for ride-hailing services, etc. A disruption in the supply chain is also limiting the availability of some crucial hardware parts needed for the production of such vehicles.
- On a positive note, commercialisation and operation of such technologies have moved past the *if* question towards the *when* question – it is now a combination of the following factors to take it on the road at full scale: technical prowess, infrastructure improvement, regulations and legal framework, public acceptance of the technology.

3. Fleet Driver Profiling and Monitoring

Drivers in commercial vehicles have a higher risk of road accidents as they spend longer periods of time on the road, potentially leading to fatigue and loss of concentration. With the recent boom in the logistics industry resulting in the increase of delivery trucks on the roads, accident rates have inevitably gone up too.

Accidents, be they major or minor, bring about significant marginal societal costs (MSC), such as increasing the operational costs of the fleet operators, e.g. repair cost, insurance cost, vehicle downtime, which leads to operational losses; not to mention the indirect impacts on other commuters on the road, such as reduced productivity and increased carbon dioxide emissions of stalling cars.

Markets

Several driver behavioural monitoring systems exist in today's market, providing fleet operators with insights into their fleet drivers' driving patterns and risk factors. The monitoring system detects and reports abnormal or risky driving behaviour, such speeding, harsh turns, and even reports the state of the driver, such as whether they are sleepy or distracted. Fleet operators can then leverage such insights to implement corresponding preventive measures, thus increasing the safety of all road users.

However, most solutions in today's market only provide passive data without a deeper understanding of root causes, and do not provide proactive risk prediction as a precaution. Obviously, only reporting the detected abnormal/risky activities would not be enough to provide a comprehensive risk analysis and/or performance evaluation of the drivers.

Emerging solutions that can provide more insightful risk evaluations and explainable, accurate decision supports on risk predictions are in great demand, leading to research institutes and companies embarking on projects to develop analytical models powered by various AI techniques. An example is the research team at the Continental-NTU Corporate lab, who are developing and testing AI analytical algorithms based on:

1. Driver profiling model
2. Driver well-being monitoring model
3. Risk assessment model
4. Risk prediction model

AI Technology

Driver profiling model: Driver profiling aims to characterise drivers from their multi-dimensional behaviours through comprehensive analyses. It does not only produce objective evaluations of drivers to the fleet operators, but also provides drivers with personalised feedback on how to enhance safety as well as punctuality. Existing driver profiling models mostly produce general/high-level characteristics of drivers (e.g., aggressive, normal, conservative) (Toh, 2021), without providing more fine-grained associations such as being aggressive at high speed. The team collects comprehensive sensory data from both the vehicles and the drivers, and then develops AI analytics models to provide fine-grained driver profiles, which are more person-centric and informative. The provision of objective in-depth understanding of the drivers' behavioural patterns enables the fleet operators to have a systematically obtained unbiased summary of their drivers and allows for customised measures tailored for the individual driver, for safety enhancement.

Driver well-being model: As reported by the Singapore Police Force in 2019 (Data.gov.sg, 2019), 53.13% of road fatalities and 59.31% of road injuries in Singapore are associated with drivers' physiological and psychological factors. However, these physiological and psychological factors are not captured and analysed by most existing commercialised solutions. To capture a comprehensive spectrum of risk factors, the team uses a driver well-being model to monitor the drivers' physiological status and provide longitudinal health status trajectory analysis. Specifically, the team has devised a wearable skin patch to unobtrusively collect physiological data from the fleet drivers in real time, including blood glucose, drug residual, body temperature, etc. Complementing such physiological data with detected long-term in-cabin behaviours, such as attention, fatigue, drowsiness, etc., the team can further provide longitudinal well-being analysis using its AI analytics models; this additional dimension on tracking the well-being of the fleet drivers will significantly enhance the risk prediction model, and subsequently improve the safety performance of fleet operations.

Risk assessment model: Risk assessment is a fundamental task for reducing traffic accidents. To accurately recognise and evaluate the risks associated with the dynamic transportation system, it is essential to analyse the contextual information from multiple dimensions, including drivers, vehicles, road condition, and environmental state (Xu, 2020). Contemporary solutions adopted by fleet operators generally require a large amount of human effort to complete the risk assessment task due to the large volume and high complexity of the data. In contrast, the research solution aims towards a more efficient and comprehensive model, which focuses on data-driven risk assessment and root cause analysis of individual events using explainable AI models. With the support of its risk assessment model, fleet operators can save a considerable amount of manpower in the traditionally tedious manual processing of driver performance evaluation and root cause analysis.

Risk prediction model: As mentioned earlier, almost all existing commercialised solutions do not provide proactive risk prediction to fleet operators as a precaution. The research team develops AI models to identify low-level risky patterns, such as low blood glucose and/or frequent distractions, to subsequently provide proactive risk predictions as warnings to the fleet operators. With corresponding preventive measures in place, such risk predictions in real time will definitely reduce accidents for fleet operators.

Moving Forward

Several AI techniques were proposed here with good potential for fleet driver profiling and monitoring; what remains to be seen is their practical viability in the real world. This would require live trials with fleet drivers over a substantial period of time to validate their accuracy and usefulness in encouraging safe driving behaviour. Hopefully, research and development activities will result in solutions for safer roads for all users.

4. Smart Fleet Maintenance

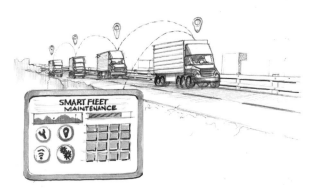

Smart fleet maintenance services are focused on improving the maintenance efficiency of a fleet of vehicles. Although this mainly benefits the fleet operator, it also enhances the quality of service for MaaS providers and commuters.

Fault detection and classification is challenging, and various techniques have been used in the past. Fault detection can be as basic as evaluation of data against known limits, analysis against patterns using deep learning or neural networks, while in fleet type operations, fault detection can be performed by assessing statistical deviation of fleet averages and statistical deviations over time.

A fleet can be a single operator but also a combination of multiple fleets by multiple operators. All these techniques have limitations. While DL and neural networks are powerful tools to analyse known faults, statistical deviations against fleet averages can pick up faults with new failure modes not yet known. While DL based on Big Data is a powerful method, it is challenging for the introduction of recent technologies and new components where data availability is a tight constraint.

Markets

Today, most fleet operators rely on dashboard solutions with basic operational statistics to ensure their fleets have high availability with timely scheduled maintenance to minimise downtime. As operators progress from conventional fleets to fully electric fleets and eventually autonomous fleets, a more intelligent approach is needed to better optimise fleet management. For example, when a conventional truck delivery fleet operator adopts electric autonomous vehicles, it needs to worry about charging optimisation and usage patterns that may reduce the lifespan of batteries as well as sensor stack maintenance and redundancy to ensure safety. Such complicated interdependent factors would require new AI models for optimisation.

AI Technology

The prevalent smart maintenance technologies are as follows:

Preventive Maintenance Optimisation: Contemporary preventive maintenance heavily relies on the scheduled maintenance of vehicles based on time or mileage. This could be significantly improved by adopting a case-based reasoning (CBR) or optimisation approach to learn from historical data and optimise fleet availability and quality, while ensuring timely upkeep and repair.

Condition-Based Maintenance: This is the Holy Grail of fleet maintenance which can be realised as digitalisation and Big Data analytics become more prevalent in the automotive industry. Preventive maintenance would inevitably incur unnecessary costs when carried out too early or too late while a condition-based approach would only carry out maintenance when there is a real need based on usage patterns and the current state of the vehicle. One could apply efficient learning techniques, including transfer learning, for forecasting maintenance issues in advance as well as to quickly develop predictive models for different vehicle brands and models in different localities and environments.

Stochastic techniques require large amounts of data to be stored on servers, often without knowing upfront if the quality of data is sufficient to perform the analysis successfully. Also important is to ensure that analysis is done on equivalent fleets. Performing analysis on fleets with diverse usage modes will significantly challenge the analysis.

Most fault classification and fault detection methodologies are based on averages, derived from fleet data. With increasing installation of Advanced Driver Assistance Systems (ADAS) as well as future autonomous driving systems, additional driving data available might be able to be used to classify operating modes and be combined real-time in the analysis of component data to perform pre-processing in the vehicle and reduce the amount of data to be transferred to the data centre. Currently, some driving data is stored as part of diagnostics, for example 10 seconds worth of driving information as part of the airbag system and some instantaneous parameters like throttle position, RPM, vehicle speed as part of engine diagnostics. However, none of this data can provide a usage profile suitable for fleet sub-selection to improve.

So, there is a need for extensive data collection and to develop smart data sharing architectures such as the federated learning-based architecture which ensures efficient data transfer, lower latency, and enhanced data privacy. There is a need to develop an analysis framework and data models based on standard analytical tools and DL techniques to identify driving modes and usage patterns of the vehicle to provide a driving/usage classification which can be used to group fleets by use and driving style to enhance fault detection quality and better identify novel failure modes linked to usage patterns.

Such a solution framework could be deployed in individual vehicles, and the results could be communicated to the cloud data centre. Within the cloud data centre, these classifiers can then be used to group vehicles for stochastic fault detection. At the cloud data centre level, a fault detection strategy can be developed based on a hybrid approach of in-vehicle pattern recognition combined with cloud-based stochastic techniques. One of the main goals of this approach is to optimise in-vehicle analysis and reduce data transfer to the cloud while increased quality of the data will in the end ensure a higher utilisation with lower costs, both in terms of cloud storage and processing costs as well as lower fleet maintenance costs.

Moving Forward

As fleets grow and evolve, it is imperative to leverage the power of AI to manage and make sense of the immense amount of diverse data. Fleet operators need to understand that traditional approaches will not be able to cope with the complex needs of new types of vehicles and should adopt AI early to prepare for their future foray into electric and autonomous vehicles.

Looking into the Future

The President of the Michigan Savings Bank once famously quipped: "The horse is here to stay but the automobile is only a novelty – a fad." He advised Horace Rackham (Henry Ford's lawyer) not to invest in the Ford Motor Company in 1903. Looking back, the automobile has definitely advanced in leaps and bounds throughout the years.

The astonishingly rapid development of technology in the area of mobility is a reminder of how much the world has changed over the past 100 years. Predictions of autonomous mobility have been around almost as long as the history of the automobile itself. However, 100 years later, are we any closer to realising this dream? Let's take a look at the crystal ball and attempt a prediction of what the world will look like in the coming years.

Metaverse, Meta-mobility: The metaverse refers to a network of virtual worlds focusing on building social connections and is considered the next generation of the Internet (Kurohi, 2022). Being present in the virtual world would attract people of all ages, in all locations. In October 2021, Hyundai Motor Company launched the Hyundai Mobility Adventure, which is a metaverse space on Roblox, an online game platform. Roblox has five themed parks dedicated to Hyundai – Festive Square, Future Mobility City, Eco-forest, Racing Park, and Smart Tech Campus – that feature not only vehicles from Hyundai but also future mobility solutions (Hyundai Motor Company, 2021). With Hyundai being able to optimise the user experience and interface in the metaverse, this allows the company to build long-lasting relationships with young consumers interested in the virtual worlds and technology. Hyundai aims to increase familiarity with its new vision, goals, and mission on future meta-mobility and to visualise future solutions. Its metaverse is a demonstration of Hyundai's concept of a crossover between two worlds, "allow[ing] smart devices to access virtual spaces, while robots will act as a medium to connect the virtual and real worlds" (Hyundai Motor Company, 2021).

Robot delivery deployed by autonomous shuttle: As mentioned above, goods and parcel delivery is a fast-growing market and the pandemic has only added to and boosted this demand. Driven by e-commerce growth and the shortage of labour, ferrying these last-mile delivery robots from logistics centres to a distribution node will soon be an autonomous shuttle. Imagine one of these autonomous shuttles dropping off a fleet of mobile robots, before seeing each robot manoeuvring automatically to household doorsteps, efficiently dropping off packages and parcels. This is the future of automated delivery powered by AI!

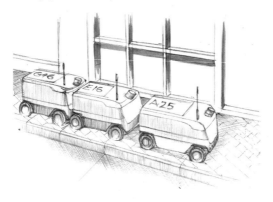

Sustainable Mobility: Crucially, the transportation of goods and people contributes approximately one-quarter of total carbon dioxide emissions (EPA 2022). With the cross-boundary/interdependent nature of climate change and the rise of environmental activism that enables individuals to make positive changes, it is everyone's responsibility to promote and be engaged in creating sustainable transportation means. Thankfully, the solution is within reach, with sustainable urban mobility likely being the solution to climate change. Instead of relying on private cars, people can – and should – now explore various modes, including electric vehicles, car sharing, and bicycles, to ensure the vivacious flow of people, goods, and services. For example, Tesla enhances its vision of clean energy by strengthening the Tesla Network and integrating car sharing in its application (Lambert, 2021). Being accessible to individuals globally, it will continue to empower zero-emissions lifestyles.

Conclusion

AI-enabled mobility has started replacing people in logistics and transportation industries. Instead of fearing for job security, it is important to view this from the perspective that AI-enabled mobility opens up new modes of transportation and logistics solutions, which in turn creates new roles and exciting opportunities. AI-enabled mobility will bring about greater convenience and safer roads for commuters. Zero emissions and zero accidents may be a reality in the near future, enabled by AI!

Acknowledgements

The authors would like to express their deepest gratitude to the following contributors for this chapter:
- Continental: Avalpreet Brar, Brandon Chen, Eric Juliani, Dr. Boris Lorenz, Rahul Singh, Dr. David Woon and Eun Bin Hong
- Nanyang Technological University (NTU): Dr. Shengfei Lyu, Ying Shu, Dr. Di Wang and Xuehao Yang

References

Goodall, W., Fishman, T., Bornstein, J., & Bonthron, B. (2017, February 24). *The rise of mobility as a service: Reshaping how urbanites get around.* Deloitte, 20, 112–128. https://www2.deloitte.com/content/dam/Deloitte/nl/Documents/consumer-business/deloitte-nl-cb-ths-rise-of-mobility-as-a-service.pdf.

Kurohi, R. (2022, January 5). Hyundai envisions a metaverse that lets you send physical robots to any location. *The Straits Times.* Available at: https://www.straitstimes.com/tech/tech-news/hyundai-envisions-a-metaverse-that-lets-you-send-physical-robots-to-any-location.

Manjrekar, S. (2020, September 14). Why AI-Based MaaS is Poised to be the Future of Transportation. Forbes. Available at: https://www.forbes.com/sites/forbestech-council/2020/09/14/why-ai-based-maas-is-poised-to-be-the-future-of-transportation/?sh=78c4c8987797.

Ministry of Home Affairs – Singapore Police Force. (2015, May 20). Causes of Road Accidents – Causes of Accidents by Severity of Injury Sustained. Data.gov.sg. https://data.gov.sg/dataset/causes-of-road-accidents-causes-of-accidents-by-severity-of-injury-sustained.

MOT Singapore – Gain new perspectives on land, sea & air transport. (2019). Retrieved February 6, 2022, from Mot.gov.sg website: https://www.mot.gov.sg/what-we-do/green-transport

Reuters. (2022, January 14). Waymo, J.B. Hunt expand tie-up to commercialize autonomous trucking technology. Reuters. Available at: https://www.reuters.com/technology/waymo-jb-hunt-expand-tie-up-commercialize-autonomous-trucking-technology-2022-01-14/.

SAE International. (2018, June 15). Taxonomy and Definitions for Terms Related to Driving Automation Systems for On-Road Motor Vehicles. *SAE International.* J3016_201806. https://doi.org/10.4271/J3016_201806.

Shepardson, D. (2021, December 16). White House looks to boost U.S. trucking industry. Reuters. Available at: https://www.reuters.com/business/autos-transportation/white-house-looks-boost-us-trucking-industry-2021-12-16/.

Singh, H., & Kathuria, A. (2021, August 16). Profiling drivers to assess safe and eco-driving behavior: A systematic review of naturalistic driving studies. *Accident Analysis and Prevention*, 161. DOI:106349. https://doi.org/10.1016/j.aap.2021.106349.

StartUs Insights. (2021, June 27). 5 Top Multimodal Mobility Solutions. StartUs Insights. Available at: https://www.startus-insights.com/innovators-guide/5-top-multimodal-mobility-solutions.

Synopsys. (2019, June 10). What is an Autonomous Car? Synopsys. Available at: https://www.synopsys.com/automotive/what-is-autonomous-car.html.

Toh, A. (2021, September 8). Continental Automotive Singapore Partners AISG to Develop Real-Time AI Solutions to Monitor Driver Heart Conditions and Intelligent

Mobility Solutions to Boost Autonomous Vehicle Safety. AI Singapore. https://aisingapore.org/2021/09/continental-automotive-singapore-partners-ai-singapore-to-develop-real-time-ai-solutions-to-monitor-driver-heart-conditions-and-intelligent-mobility-solutions-to-boost-autonomous-vehicle-safety/.

United Nations. (2022). Sustainable transport. United Nations. Available at: https://sdgs.un.org/topics/sustainable-transport.

Wall, M. (2019, February 21). Automotive Industry Outlook: Managing Volatility and Leveraging Opportunities in a Dynamic Market Environment. IHS Markit. https://www.cargroup.org/wp-content/uploads/2019/02/Wall.pdf.

Wang, J., Huang, H., Li, Y., Zhou, H., Liu, J., Xu, Q. (2020, July 21). Driving risk assessment based on naturalistic driving study and driver attitude questionnaire analysis. *Accident Analysis and Prevention*, 145. DOI:10.1016/j.aap.2020.105680. https://doi.org/10.1016/j.aap.2020.105680.

Wiles, R. (2021, December 29). California company tests driverless big-rig truck between Tucson and Phoenix. azcentral. Available at: https://www.azcentral.com/story/money/business/tech/2021/12/29/tusimple-completes-driverless-big-rig-truck-test-arizona/9044260002/.

* * *

Vincent Wong is the Director of R&D for Continental Automotive Singapore. He heads the Research & Advanced Engineering group in Singapore, where research and innovation activities in the areas of autonomous driving, artificial intelligence, robotics, and cybersecurity are carried out. Vincent holds a Bachelor of Engineering (B.Eng) from Nanyang Technological University. He has been in the automotive industry for more than 20 years, driving collaborations with public agencies, academia, corporates and startups.

CHAPTER 9

AI for Government: To Do Good, Better

SHAWN HUANG

We have a real chance at this opportunity to enable AI technology to help us serve others, to do good better for our future generations.

The Singapore government continues to accelerate AI adoption and enhance its value as it aims to become one of the global platforms where AI capabilities can be developed, tested, and thereafter implemented, unlocking the potential to transform the city-state. The launch of the National AI strategy aims to create a conducive environment to spur this acceleration to further anchor Singapore's position as a global and regional economic centre, as well as enhance the lives and livelihoods of its citizens.

Workforce and Talent: Integral to AI Strategy

"The nature of jobs will also evolve more quickly and it is therefore not a matter of if, but when, the skills we possess today will no longer be relevant."
— Chan Chun Sing, Minister for Education, Singapore

The Singapore National AI strategy has identified Singapore's key focus areas with a goal to be a leader in developing and deploying scalable and impactful AI solutions in key verticals. We need to build trust on the use of AI by raising awareness on the benefits and impact of AI. Stakeholders such as government agencies, businesses, NGOs, and researchers will also need to collaborate across domains and within the verticals to ensure that AI delivers the desired outcomes such as privacy and diversity inclusion. However, this can only be achieved with a credible and capable workforce. As such, Singapore's workforce must have the necessary skills and capabilities in the areas of research and engineering, ethics and governance to support an AI-driven economy for Singapore, the region and the global markets.

Singapore will face disruptive challenges in its continuous evolution of the economy and job landscape. The McKinsey Global Institute highlighted that about one-third of the American workforce will need to switch occupations by 2030, especially for those workers in data-intensive industries such as finance, legal support, sales and IT. Such disruption will affect Singapore due to its relatively small population and professional service-oriented economy. However, there are opportunities in this disruption as new industries emerge to replace the old.

The World Economic Forum suggests that the AI economy will yield a net increase of 58 million jobs globally. However, during this transition, there will be a substantial skills gap as the talent supply lags behind the explosive growth, exacerbated by rising demands across all industries and sectors. As such, Singapore will need to build up its AI talent capabilities quickly. Singapore will need to leverage on its education and training sectors to build its capabilities within the formal and continuously adaptable education systems.

This requires two key approaches. First, we must be able to quickly upskill and reskill existing workers from various industry sectors with relevant AI skills and knowledge. They must have the ability to apply AI in their respective job roles to a desired level of expertise. Second, we will need to build up a core group of professionals with deep ICT and AI skills and further develop them to have the ability to apply their skills across multiple domains.

Much progress has been made through SkillsFuture Singapore (SSG), a statutory board under the Ministry of Education (MOE), which aims to nurture a nation of lifelong learners and a society that values skills mastery. SSG has introduced a series of AI talent development initiatives. Some initiatives include the SkillsFuture Series, SkillsFuture for Digital Workplace (SFDW) and Digital Learner Beginner Workshop (DLBW) to help build up AI awareness whilst the wider training and formal education systems continue to build the core deep AI talent in Singapore. With this, Singapore aims to build a core of 12,000 AI-skilled professionals to support the AI ecosystem in Singapore.

AI Ecosystem: Strategy and Jumpstart Execution

AI Singapore (AISG), the national AI programme office, was established with the aim of anchoring deep national capabilities in AI and better develop the Singapore AI ecosystem. This work to build the AI ecosystem started several decades ago as smaller building blocks of capabilities via a strong education system and continued investments in research and innovation. The national AI strategy outlines key enablers such as investing in deep capabilities in AI research, promoting the development and use of AI technologies, catalysing AI innovations in the industry, building local AI talent capabilities and maintaining a progressive but robust AI governance environment to build a vibrant and sustainable AI ecosystem for Singapore. The government has identified five national projects to jumpstart the ecosystem. These five national projects are focused on solving key industry challenges where AI could substantially transform the industry and bring collective value to accelerate growth. This includes intelligent freight planning in transportation and logistics, predictive capabilities to detect chronic illnesses, healthcare management as well as homeland safety and security.

> "The national AI strategy is a key step in our smart nation journey. It spells out our plans to deepen our use of AI technologies to transform our economy, going beyond just adopting technology,

to fundamentally rethinking business models and making deep changes to reap productivity gains and create new areas of growth. As a small country, Singapore lacks the scale of large markets and R&D ecosystems, but we can make up for this by building up AI research, and working together cohesively across government, industry, and research, to develop and deploy AI solutions in key sectors. At the same time, we must also antici-pate the social challenges that AI will create by maintaining public trust and building capabilities to manage and govern AI technol-ogies, and guarding against cybersecurity attacks and breaches to data privacy."

— Singapore Prime Minister Lee Hsien Loong

Data: A Symbiotic Relationship for AI Collaboration

In order to accelerate and advance AI, researchers will need access to vast amounts of data to train and test new models. The access to data as well as computing power will continue to be the limiting factors of AI develop-ment. However, one continued concern is the sensitivity of the data and its collective value. In-depth assessments and analysis of the collective data could unravel hidden insights into government and societal vulnerabili-ties. As such, it is important to have a robust and secure data architecture that promotes responsible use and sharing of data. With access to datasets, collaborations between public and private entities can promote the develop-ment, testing and implementation of AI technologies. Singapore continues to be progressive in its data sharing and since 2011 has shared data from over 70 ministries and agencies. However, to further open up data for AI and machine learning, the segregation of large data pools into different tiers of trusted zones is essential.

In a varied controlled environment, it can help to build mutual trust and accountability over time whilst enabling sufficient accessibility to spearhead AI innovation and development. Singapore has been taking active steps to catalyse data sharing to support AI and data innovation by establishing sandboxes where companies can push the boundaries and build new applications and services. These sandboxes will enable the public sector and companies to collaborate as well as provide a marketplace to enable data providers to collaborate and share data with data consumers. With this, data can be safely shared as an asset in a safe and responsible manner to promote AI innovation.

AI for Government: Unlocking Opportunities

"Ultimately, citizens must feel these initiatives are focused on delivering welfare benefits for them and ensured their data will be protected and afforded due confidentiality."
— S Iswaran, Former Minister for Communications and Information, Singapore

Governments are poised to unlock unrealised potential by integrating AI into government services and functions. Governments can leverage on AI techniques such as machine learning, deep learning, robotics, computer vision, and speech recognition to further enhance the efficiency of government services, resource allocation and more predictive decision-making processes.

The implementation of AI in government will require time to build up as it requires a convergence of several factors to ensure sufficient readiness in each aspect before progressing to deeper AI implementation. There are two baseline areas where governments can jumpstart their AI efforts. One area is to reduce routine and repetitive tasks. The second area is to enhance the maintenance of mission critical tasks through better predictive engineering, technical and supply chain capabilities. The aggregate impact of reducing time spent on repetitive and manual tasks within a large government organisation will be substantial. Mission critical tasks will be optimised for higher performance, reliability as well as substantial cost savings.

There is much more potential where AI can enable governments to better serve its citizens through greater precision in policymaking, exceptional efficiency and engagement. AI would be able to better assess information on consumption trends, health and employment. It can help provide predictive assessments and extrapolate emerging issues that require early intervention. It can better segment issues, geographical and hyperlocal mapping, explore more accurate correlationships and identify trigger events where policies can be developed to provide targeted assistance, intervention or course of action. This will most certainly provide critical signposts for government leaders to develop relevant, cost-effective and efficient policies for citizens.

Within a multitude of policies and government services, AI can quickly automate service delivery upon a trigger event. A government AI capability would be able to better detect a vulnerable citizen who has experienced a job loss and would automatically trigger customised government assistance based on a myriad of factors to buffer the family during a crisis and assist in job placement or upskill for another job in a fast-growing sector.

However, there are intangible costs to more efficient and effective services to the citizenry. Governments will need to consider important aspects of privacy, data protection, and inclusive implementation. Citizens will need to trust that the government is using the information responsibly and for public interest. This requires a strong trusted relationship between the government and its citizenry that is centred around transparency and convincing positive outcomes for its citizens.

AI Public-Private Collaboration: Harnessing Collective Strengths for Healthcare

"Technology is now transforming healthcare in ways that were unimaginable as recently as a decade ago. We must ride on this digital healthcare revolution by going digital intelligently, using data effectively and disrupting meaningfully. In embarking on our journey, we will need to take on some coordinated large-scale initiatives as well as support ground-up efforts."
— Gan Kim Yong, Former Minister for Health, Singapore

AI has the potential to overcome challenges and improve outcomes, in particular, in healthcare. By establishing deep public-private collaborations between government and industry experts, there are opportunities to harness collective strengths within the domain to deliver targeted and meaningful solutions.

For the visually impaired, what once seemed an impossibility is now reality, as AI is able to facilitate new ways to navigate the world. Computer vision enables identification of objects, text and even handwriting, translated through the spoken word with the use of smartphone apps and other devices. While there may be disparities in how this technology is distributed to those in need, it is a monumental step forward in helping the visually impaired experience their surroundings.

In pursuit of better healthcare outcomes, SingHealth, a Singapore healthcare organisation, and Singapore Innovate, have recently collaborated to develop AI technologies for diagnostics, treatment and healthcare delivery. SingHealth has extensive healthcare data, clinical research capabilities and operational experience, whilst Singapore Innovate has expertise in AI technology and a strong AI network. By coupling core strengths from both entities, there is an opportunity to develop accretive AI technologies that would deliver better healthcare outcomes.

AI is disrupting healthcare diagnostics. One example is Selena, an AI technology developed by a local Singapore startup EyRIS, which can identify patients with different types of eye disease such as diabetic retinopathy, glaucoma and age-related macular degeneration. With their AI technology, retinal images can be analysed and graded automatically with more than 90% accuracy within minutes, hence it can improve healthcare and diagnostic outcomes significantly. These capabilities are also used for breast cancer detection at Tan Tock Seng Hospital in Singapore, where AI plays a significant role in the interpretation and assessment of X-ray imagery and breast ultrasound. These have contributed substantially as a second line of defence and have shown to reduce miss-rates.

AI Opportunities for Industry

"We will need credible and reliable partners to achieve common goals. They include other governments, businesses, researchers

and think-tanks. Each plays a useful role in creating a safer digital environment. On our part, we will continue to strengthen the global digital ecosystem by adopting a banded, collaborative and interoperable approach."
— Josephine Teo, Minister for Communications and Information, Singapore

With the high-impact potential, AI can help companies accelerate growth, reduce costs and stretch value differentiation. Several industries such as agriculture, hospitality and manufacturing are poised to benefit substantially from AI technology. With the advent of Industry 4.0 technologies in advanced manufacturing, AI would be able to improve operational efficiency and further supply chain capabilities. By using machine learning, computer vision and manufacturing data, companies drive exceptional efficiency and improve ESG outcomes by optimising the use of raw materials, reduce wastage, implement predictive maintenance and improve quality control.

In hospitality, the access to high-quality consumer and market data enables companies to implement AI capability to quickly sense-make market conditions. By analysing competition, availability, pricing trends, historical consumption trends and macro factors, companies can formulate better revenue strategies such as competitive pricing models, deepened networks for cross and up-selling and predictive capabilities to lead product differentiation. AI can also improve customer experiences as it could be highly personalised and streamlined. It also enables service providers to cater to just-in-time services to reduce waiting times and improve crowd control, an important aspect in Covid-19.

For agriculture, AI can be coupled with agricultural sciences to further improve resource efficiency, reduce cost and enhance plant growth. Through intelligent management systems and optimal crop type selections, the use of pesticides can be reduced, and fertiliser formulations can be optimised. Low-productivity and labour-intensive agriculture can be transformed to highly productive and sustainable agriculture. This is particularly critical for Singapore as it imports 90% of its food from other countries. One vegetable farm in Singapore is using AI to enhance plant growth through better lighting and climate control without the use of pesticides in urban spaces.

Investing and Institutionalising AI for Trusted Ecosystems

"AI is one such technology that can generate new solutions by harnessing data well. But AI is not easily understood or applied. Many countries have developed national AI strategies to develop the ecosystem and deploy the technology more widely. Critical to any national strategy around step-change technology is the ability for all stakeholders to work together. This is a common thread that runs through our National AI Strategy, as we seek to apply AI widely and invest systemically."

— Heng Swee Keat, Deputy Prime Minister and Coordinating Minister for Economic Policies, Singapore

Investing in a strong governance and values framework will help to accelerate institutional adoption of AI within trusted ecosystems. This is critical for the global financial ecosystem as there is substantial risk and impact of AI within these well-established networks. Singapore, a global financial centre, has taken active steps to establish a framework and mechanism to ensure the responsible adoption and implementation of AI amongst the financial institutions in Singapore. One example is Veritas, an initiative by the Monetary Authority of Singapore, which has a range of open-source tools that can enable financial institutions to better assess their AI applications for fairness, ethics, accountability and transparency. By focusing on customer marketing, risk scoring, and fraud detection, both regulators, technologist and institutions can gradually build up trust and readiness to adopt wider and deeper AI capabilities.

One other example is NoVA!, an AI capability that assists financial institutions to assess companies' environmental impact, identify emerging environmental risks, as well as check against greenwashing. By collaborating with Singapore-based banks and local FinTech firms, it aims to achieve better climate change financing and investment objectives. These are important initiatives as the values of transparency, inclusion, fairness and reliability are all cornerstones to establish a conducive and sustainable AI ecosystem for the future.

Conclusion

Singapore has strong institutional fundamentals, a capable and highly adaptive talent pool, a collaborative public-private culture as well as a progressive and forward-looking government that is capable of undertaking long-term projects. This is a confluence of essential attributes for a highly transformative nation that is ready to unlock the fullest potential of AI. With rapid evolution and the emerging Web 4.0, democratisation of knowledge and information, stressors on consumption and climate change, there is a real opportunity to rapidly develop and accelerate our ability to do good, do right and do our best for our community and the world at large.

* * *

Shawn Huang is a Member of Parliament and a member of the Government Parliamentary Committee for Finance, Trade & Industry as well as for Education. He was an F-16 fighter pilot with the Republic of Singapore Airforce and has held various appointments in Strategy, Operations and Intelligence. He is currently a Director in the Enterprise Development Group in Temasek International, with a focus on advanced manufacturing, materials and technology. He was a Distinguished Graduate in Aeronautical Engineering and the Top Graduate for Military Performance from the United States Air Force Academy in 2006. Shawn is the founding director of Tasek Jurong, a charity focused on uplifting disadvantaged individuals and families. He is also the founding director of GreenSG, a charity focused on accelerating green and sustainability programmes in Singapore. Shawn is an advocate of AI and has published on the International Joint Conference on Neural Networks (IJCNN) in 2005.

CHAPTER 10

AI for Next Generation Satellite Systems

PROF. ANDY KORONIOS

AI has been described as a technological revolution which will usher into our world "God-like technologies" that our brains will have difficulty in matching. At the same time, there is another technological revolution. The miniaturisation of electronics, the breathtaking increase in computational power and the explosion in small satellite technologies are bringing gales of innovation and spawning new industries. In this chapter, we will explore the merging of these two technological revolutions, describe the technologies, examine their causes and impacts, and peek at the future directions for understanding how space will be transformed through these game-changing technologies, and in turn, how smart, autonomous, and cooperative constellations of satellites will change our economies and daily lives.

Introduction

Like in most sectors of the economy, AI is increasingly playing a key role in space. Computer programming and software engineering ushered in the computer revolution as early as the Second World War, and the Enigma machine and computers were developed to perform mostly arithmetic and mathematical operations. Indeed, the first computers were used to decipher military communications codes, calculate artillery trajectories and test the feasibility of thermonuclear weapons. Computers have always depended on humans to program them in very precise ways and to feed them step-by-step instructions. If a step was wrong or missed, the computer would stop or give an erroneous answer. Since John McCarthy coined the term "Artificial Intelligence" in 1956, computer scientists have had dreams of making computers more intelligent and building "thinking machines". The complexity of this task (owing to the lack of computation power and memory of the human scale), however, made this an unachievable goal in the short term and the AI field experienced what is now referred to as the "AI winter", a lack of interest to advance the field. The miniaturisation of electronics and rapid advances in processing power and storage, as well as new technologies to generate enormous volumes of data at speed, resulted in a renaissance in AI, with renewed hopes of developing thinking machines. There has been stunning success in AI techniques applied to activities such as identifying and classifying images, human speech recognition, natural language processing, and in robotics, identifying anomalies and detecting changes. AI, robotics, and Big Data are now transforming a highly conservative industry, the space industry, in a revolution that has been dubbed "New Space". Like the computer revolution, it is driven by extreme miniaturisation of electronics and unimaginable computational power and storage.

In this chapter, we will focus on opportunities and the role that AI plays now and in the future for enabling New Space activities and particularly its impact on satellite technologies. AI will no doubt transform the entire space lifecycle – from designing and building to the launch and operation of satellite systems – as well as provide automated analysis of the massive amounts of data collected by advanced remote sensing technologies with ever-increasing resolutions, providing great insights to help in areas such as precision agriculture, remote mining, urban development, and smart cities, as well as managing our environment and natural resources more effectively. We will first discuss the uses of AI in space exploration, followed by applications closer to home, understanding the revolution of small satellites in the service of humanity. And finally we will discuss the future challenges and opportunities of the use of AI and its impact on the space enterprise.

The Use of AI in Space Exploration

The global space industry has experienced rapid growth over recent years, leading to increased investment in many national and commercial space programmes around the world. Several nations, including the US, Russia, India, Japan, China and Europe, have identified returning to space exploration and lunar operations as a key priority. This common interest has led to a renewed focus on international collaboration and partnerships, particularly in AI, robotics and automation.

NASA and other space agencies as well as global space companies have for many years used intelligent software for all sorts of activities, such as navigation, spacecraft health monitoring and analysis of the huge data volumes that spacecraft generate and capture with their advanced sensors.

The exponential growth in robotics, machine learning, deep learning, genetic algorithms, neuromorphic computing and other AI techniques is fast augmenting most aspects of space exploration and the use of space technologies to improve life here on Earth. The dramatic reduction in size, weight and power requirements of the hardware that drives these technologies has meant that even small satellites can now utilise such techniques in space. Such technologies are game-changing in extending human ingenuity and physical capability for space exploration, where the challenges of the harsh environment, the journey times and the risk of failure are extremely great. Even before a spacecraft is launched and sets off to explore new worlds, designers and builders of the missions need to solve many problems and prepare for all sorts of unexpected events, anticipating situations that may challenge or even terminate the mission. Astronauts travelling to other worlds will no doubt face many challenges where AI systems will provide invaluable assistance. A glimpse of these capabilities is discussed below.

AI in Spacecraft and Satellite Design, Manufacturing and Operations

Satellite manufacturers are now applying AI in many aspects of the product lifecycle, including design, manufacturing, testing, integration and operation. ML techniques are used to analyse the huge volumes of data that are generated and identify anomalous results from test data. These may be identified faster and more reliably than by human inspectors. Such analytics speed up the process and thus save time and money, ensuring that schedules are met.

In the design and manufacturing of space systems and satellites, the past practice has been for the designer to develop Computer-Aided Design (CAD) models that were sent, often via email on PDF files, to the manufacturing plant to be built in the same way as an architect prepares house plans for a builder to build you a house. AI systems enable designers to develop an entire digital model of the system, and to use this AI-enabled virtual system to test and optimise the design, which is used in the production and operation of the system, thus the birth of the concept of Digital Twins (DT). This journey for the digitalisation of space has begun and the concept of digital twins is now gaining a lot of attention in the space industry.

The application of Industry 4.0 digital technologies and processes will drive a new revolution in the space industry, one that has already been dubbed Space 4.0. The design and manufacturing of rockets and satellites are very specialised activities. The government agencies and typically large companies that build them have traditionally been very conservative and risk-averse as a single design fault can spell disaster. With the commercialisation of space, an emphasis on low cost and flexibility is now required by the end users. Digitalisation and the introduction of digital twins for the space industry will be able to achieve cost reductions and give agility in reducing time to market as well as adapting designs to meet new requirements or innovation opportunities. AI will play a pivotal role in spacecraft digital twins, which will integrate ultra-high-fidelity multiphysics simulation of the "as-built" spacecraft system using the best available physical models and will be integrated with the spacecraft's onboard vehicle health management system. Such an intelligent virtual spacecraft on the ground will need to be fully integrated, multiphysics, multiscale and have all the spacecraft onboard Integrated Vehicle Health Management (IVHM) system data, maintenance history, flight data and performance, and would mirror its flying twin in space. Such AI-driven systems will enable us to reproduce entire systems and study thermal, mechanical, acoustical and radiation effects on the structural materials as well as the systems of the entire spacecraft in the laboratory via computational simulation of the entire mission system, identifying and quantifying the operational limits of such systems.

In the area of space operations, there exists significant potential for the application of AI technologies to improve monitoring, operations and health management of the spacecraft and satellites. Some areas of opportunity include the monitoring of multiple satellites and satellite constellations, analysing telemetry data of the health monitoring of satellites, positioning, navigation and management of satellites after their operational life when they are no longer useful and can become space "junk", as well as space debris and collision avoidance.

One of the most critical responsibilities of satellite operations involves the management of the satellite whilst in orbit. Satellites orbit from the lower edge of space 200–2,000 km all the way to 35,000 km for the Geostationary satellites (GEO), and anywhere in between at Medium Earth Orbit (MEO).

Satellites have traditionally been large and complex, taking many years to build and launch. Until recently, only a few hundred satellites were in orbit, yet today there are more than 5,000 satellites in orbit around the Earth. Many of these are small satellites, only tens of kilograms in weight. The number of these small satellites is set to grow exponentially with many companies planning to put hundreds of thousands of satellites in space. For example, Elon Musk's Starlink will have constellations of more than 40,000 satellites in the near future. As satellites proliferate, the management of these objects moving at speeds as high as 24,000 km/h will be a critical activity. Collisions can have catastrophic consequences. Therefore, humans need to be supported via advanced technologies in performing the traffic management task.

Automated systems are already in operation to aid in this critical activity and will become increasingly important as the number of satellites increases. Controlled by AI-based orbit prediction algorithms, they will be able to help humans manage satellite traffic and avoid collisions. The European Space Agency (ESA), as well as several private companies, is developing such AI-enabled collision avoidance systems. Furthermore, in the future, satellites will adopt technologies developed for autonomous vehicles on Earth to make them more autonomous in changing their orbits to avoid collisions.

Space Robotics and AI Applications

Robotics capabilities emerged during the late industrial era and were initially constrained to the factory floor. They were driven by advanced procedural software which allowed them to perform very tedious but very well-defined tasks. More advanced algorithms and recent AI techniques have catapulted robots to another level, providing them with significant autonomy as long as they operate in narrow domains such as driving a car. This in-built intelligence has allowed us to put robots to work completing human tasks that may be hazardous, strenuous or boring for humans. We have also begun to personify them and give them human-like features and form.

All these capabilities will be useful in space exploration. Robots are comfortable with procedural tasks without missing a single step, and unlike humans, do not stumble through brain lapses and forget or miss important actions. In an environment where a missed step could spell disaster, such intelligent support will be invaluable.

Robotics and automation have played a role in space since as early as the 1980s with the development of the International Space Station (ISS) and have continued ever since, conducted by all space-capable nations such as the US, Russia, Japan and China. For example, Japan's advances in robotics for industrial applications were applied to the development of a logistics cargo transfer vehicle with robotics capabilities to autonomously dock on to the Japanese module of the ISS called Kibo.

With the huge growth in AI, this will provide opportunities for spacecraft and satellite autonomy and more automated decision-making in space applications. This was followed by an autonomous rendezvous between Japan's Hayabusa and Itokawa. More recently, exploration of Mars has continued to advance with AI technologies enabling autonomy in the Mars rovers. Canada's robotic arm on the space shuttle was an early visible example of that country's focus in space automation. This Special Purpose Dexterous Manipulator (Dextre) now allows automated replacement of battery boxes and other maintenance on the outside of the ISS. Two Canadian companies, MDA and Optech, have developed a LiDAR-based system with vision-based capability that can detect and track space objects from 3 km away in all light conditions, providing proximity manoeuvres for spacecraft. The Canadian Space Agency is investing in LiDAR sensor technologies for autonomous landing systems as well as drilling for In-Situ Resource Utilisation technologies. These will extend Canada's strengths in mining automation for terrestrial applications applied to collect regolith on the lunar surface and to extract oxygen out of it.

Other countries and companies are developing capabilities in the extraction of sample collection smart sensors to collect material and return it to Earth. Organisations such as JAXA have for many years been developing more and more advanced orbital robotics as well as other exploration robots for Moon, Mars and asteroid exploration. These will become even more important, given the renewed interest in space exploration. Finally, the US has had significant developments through their space exploration rovers such as the Mars exploration rovers, the latest of which was Perseverance. Perseverance uses AI to look for ancient life and identify past environments that could support life as well as testing the viability of oxygen production on Mars.

The importance of AI for space has prompted major space agencies such as NASA to establish AI-dedicated research groups and labs to exploit the opportunities of AI for space. They are exploring applications of AI in most areas of space mission design, launch, spacecraft autonomous navigation, space robotics, ground operations and advanced communications.

NASA's Frontier Development Lab has developed neural networks to sift through the huge volumes of data that NASA collects from its space missions and analyse them to identify interesting patterns and insights. In 2017 it collaborated with Google to create a program that creates 3D models of asteroids to measure their size, shape, and spin so that it can catalogue, map and track potential asteroids and develop technology that may deflect the asteroids if they are in orbit and may be hazardous to Earth. Such AI algorithms have reduced the work of scientists from months to mere days.

NASA's Exominer is a neural network that parses the huge volumes of data collected by the Kepler Mission in its quest to observe more than 200,000 stars and detect signals of planets orbiting their parent stars. To date, this Deep Learning method has added more than 300 planets to its tally of over 4,000 planets orbiting very distant stars. Other high-profile uses of AI in space include the recent mission to Mars of the Perseverance rover which is not only driven by very complex robotics technology and has an advanced navigation and landing system, but also uses an AI-powered instrument to search for traces of microscopic life on Mars even if this was billions of years old.

AI Humanoid Robotic Assistants in Space

Humanoid robots provide services like the way humans move, interact and communicate. The most common early version of such robotic service assistants for interaction on Earth are Google Assist, Amazon's Alexa, Hound, Siri and others. The movies *Star Wars* and *Interstellar* illustrated how such intelligent robots could be used in space exploration to support astronauts. C-3PO and R2-D2 in *Star Wars* and TARS in *Interstellar* were great previews of what is likely to happen very soon with AI-enhanced robotic assistants. Such robots will not only provide physical support and information on any topic that astronauts need but will also serve as companions, providing mental support in potentially lonely

journeys to far planets, such as assisting in the 7-month journey to Mars. As we move to colonise our nearby planets, these AI-enabled assistants will become indispensable. Such assistants are now being developed and deployed for space applications.

The most well-known humanoid robot is CIMON, a 5 kg, 32 cm diameter humanoid with Siri-like voice activation capabilities and constructed

so that it can hover at eye-level with the astronauts. It can answer questions in the same way as those applications on our smart devices. CIMON is used to perform tasks such as access information and read out procedures for scientific experiments. CIMON was built by Airbus on behalf of the German Aerospace Centre (DLR). Its conversational core AI system is IBM Watson, but it uses supervised learning techniques with humans actively training its model. It also has an autonomous navigation system and can rotate to where the commands or conversation from humans comes from and nod its head, and can follow the astronauts as they move through the ISS. The latest version of CIMON, CIMON 2, also uses empathic computing to assess astronauts' emotions, having been trained by experts in stress management and immunology to provide support to astronauts at times of high workload. Other space agencies are now developing similar assistants, such as Japan's Kiboro Int-Ball.

AI in Satellite Communications

Satellites are an extremely important link in providing communications and connectivity throughout the globe. Terrestrial communications (cable, fibre, and mobile networks) provide good connectivity across the land, particularly in areas of high population density, but can never cover the entire globe, the land and oceans. Satellites will fill the demand and the geographic gaps in connectivity, particularly in the areas underserviced by terrestrial communications systems or following natural disasters such as large volcanic eruptions.

AI technologies can help in several areas of satellite communications, particularly in network optimisation, data traffic management and the use of machine learning techniques to identify anomalies in traffic, including identifying undesirable network events or security breaches. Communications networks are progressively being virtualised and this generates huge amounts of data which are collected by the system. The data generated through this virtualisation of the communication networks will provide the fuel for machine learning and deep learning to be developed that will be used to identify patterns or to detect anomalies in the system. Such system intelligence will lead to the eventual automation of the whole communications system. In such a system, decisions will be made automatically based on the communications terminals operational environment. Such intelligence will offer communications network resiliency and reliability.

AI-enabled satellites will make automated decisions in routing signals through inter-satellite communications links, selecting the optimal link. The progressively virtualised networks and more software-based communications (Software Defined Radio) will allow the use of AI techniques to optimise all aspects of satellite communications. Cognitive radio allows us to intelligently detect which parts of the communications channel are not in use at any instant and automatically move the data through that channel, thus optimising the data carrying capacity of a communications channel. Cognitive radio is an extremely useful AI technique in communications. The electromagnetic spectrum that allows us to communicate wirelessly is governed by the various agencies in each country. In the US, for example, it is governed by the Federal Communications Commission (FCC). It allocates portions of the spectrum (frequencies) for several uses such as Wi-Fi transmission, satellite radio transmission, emergency services communications, civil and military aviation communications, and so on. This allocation means that some bands are overused, and others remain idle at different times. The concept of software-defined radio and cognitive radio is to use software and AI to optimise the spectrum that is not used at any given time and allocate it in a dynamic way to whatever application requires it at the specific time. It does this in a dynamic and automated way so that humans are not involved in this process. Such a concept and technology allows us to use all the spectrum at any given time and thus substantially improve communications capacity. They also automate the process and provide communications resiliency and reliability. In space communications where space weather could be a problem, cognitive radio can provide mitigation of these interruptions through such events and make the communication system more reliable. NASA and space organisations are also experimenting and developing such intelligent communication systems that are responsive to space weather events and pre-emptively, temporarily shut down the communication system to avoid damaging the sensitive equipment and algorithms on an impending space weather event. NASA's Space Communications & Navigation (SCaN) testbed onboard the ISS has been used to develop and test a number of such software-defined and cognitive radio algorithms, communications antennas and related technologies.

Vignette: Autonomy in Space
Contributed by Prof. Tat-Jun Chin,
Australian Institute of Machine Learning (AIML)

Established in 2018, the AIML is Australia's first dedicated machine learning research institute. The AIML conducts globally competitive research and development in machine learning, AI, computer vision and deep learning across six themes: machine learning, robotic vision, medical machine learning, trusted autonomous systems, surveillance and tracking, and photogrammetry and 3D modelling.

As the global space sector continues to develop around the New Space concept, which espouses more cost-effective, agile, and commercially driven space missions, the complexity and breadth of missions are also increasing. Overall, more emphasis will be placed on doing "useful things" in space, as opposed to using space mainly as a strategic vantage point for data collection. This calls for spacecraft that possess a high degree of autonomy. Supported by advances in space-based computers, novel sensing paradigms and communication technologies, it is now realistic to envision autonomous spacecraft enabled by AI and ML algorithms.

Areas that stand to gain from greater autonomy in space include on-orbit servicing (OOS) and intelligent satellite constellations. More specific applications include debris capture and removal, satellite lifetime extension, collaborative missions, and in-space maintenance and construction. Many of the above applications involve delicate manoeuvres, real-time decision-making, and multi-agent collaborations – tasks that will be difficult to execute by ground-based remote control alone. On-the-fly processing of incoming sensorial data (e.g., from optical sensors, LiDAR, radar) to extract high-level insights that inform human decision-making, if not enable outright automation, will be essential to realise the applications. The figure below illustrates an "agent-based" view of an autonomous spacecraft.

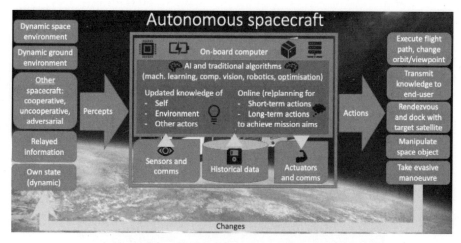

Agent-based view of an autonomous spacecraft.

Specific examples of space-based AI and ML capabilities that contribute towards autonomy in space and OOS are given in the figures on the following page. The capabilities were developed in a collaboration between the AIML and the SmartSat Cooperative Research Centre (CRC).

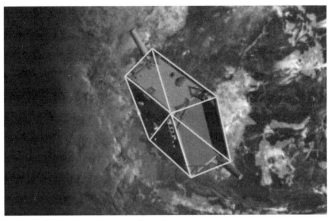

Estimating the pose (position and orientation) of a target satellite for OOS applications. The estimated pose here – indicated by the wire-frame – was produced by an ML model that processes the input image.

(Figure from Bo Chen et al., Satellite pose estimation with deep landmark regression and nonlinear pose refinement. In ICCV Workshop on Recovering 6D, 2019. The original image was from S. Sharma and S. D'Amico. Pose estimation for noncooperative rendez-vous using neural networks. In AAS/AIAA Astrodynamics Specialist Conference, 2019.)

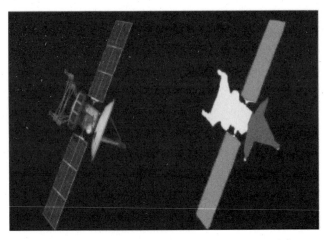

Segmenting the parts of a target satellite into meaningful components using an ML algorithm. Such a result is useful for OOS in uncoopera-tive settings, e.g., identifying and capturing defunct satellites.

(Figure from Dung Anh Hoang et al., A Spacecraft Dataset for Detection, Segmentation and Parts Recognition, In CVPR Workshop on AI for Space, 2020.)

AI for Satellites in the Service of Our Planet

Space exploration and spacecraft innovation have huge benefits for humans here on Earth. Many of the technologies developed during space exploration have found secondary uses in our daily lives. Experiments that take place in space can, for example, help us solve health problems or improve our safety. Applications include baby formula and vacuum-dried food, tiny mobile phone cameras, air purifiers, cordless vacuum cleaners, the cardiac pump, invisible dental braces, and many more.

The development of satellite technologies has been one of the most important contributions of space to our world. Satellites provide us with significant benefits and have transformed how we communicate, navigate and manage our natural resources. AI is now turbo-charging these applications in communications, position, navigation and timing (PNT), and in Earth observation and remote sensing.

Intelligent Earth Observation and Remote Sensing Analytics

This decade has been termed "The Golden Age of Earth Observation". The proliferation of satellites, particularly small satellites orbiting close to Earth at Low Earth Orbit (LEO), 200–2,000 km above Earth, has resulted in thousands of sensors, collecting data in the visible spectrum as well as other bands such as infrared, thermal infrared and radar. These high-fidelity sensors generate huge amounts of data – Big Data. This data is the fuel for ML algorithms to create intelligence applied to a wide range of applications in just about every sector of the economy, benefiting every industry and making our lives easier.

This new source of knowledge of our planet has resulted in unbridled innovation and spawned dozens of startup companies in "downstream analytics". Two notable companies, Planet Labs and Mapbox, use AI to map our changing planet daily. Planet Labs is a private US company based in San Francisco, California. Its goal is to image the entire Earth daily, to monitor changes and pinpoint trends. To date, it has successfully deployed 462 satellites and has a current fleet of 21 satellites capturing imagery at a 50 cm resolution, and 120 capturing imagery at approximately 3 metre resolution. Such high resolution can spawn a new generation of applications in many sectors. For example, Planet Labs uses ML methods to identify objects and monitor assets from space. It can count the number of cars in a shopping mall or count shipping containers stored in a shipping port and detect the change of these on a daily basis, thus inferring the productivity and economic activity of a nation. Planet Labs has developed algorithms that are analysing all the data to identify anomalies and detect changes. On that basis, it tasks a higher-resolution satellite to zoom in on anything that has changed, such as environmental changes, natural disasters, conflict zones, new developments and new constructions. It could be providing information on where people are parking, or it could be looking for new wells for oil or gas, or identifying illegal mining activity. Councils might wish to see who is installing a new addition to their house or a new swimming pool without council approval; the applications are endless.

Planet Lab Earth Observation Applications

1. **Detection of buildings**
   - Monitor infrastructure and construction/urban development
   - Update maps and charts
   - Urban development planning
   - Assess impact of natural disasters

2. **Detection of road networks**
   - Update maps and charts
   - Improve routing for fleets/resources

3. **Detection of vessels**
   - Monitor patterns/anomalies
   - Track/identify vessels for law/policy purposes
   - Enhance defence and intelligence operations

4. **Aircraft identification**
   - Monitor departure and arrival of aircraft
   - Quantify number of aircrafts
   - Monitor economic activity
   - Enhance defence and intelligence operations

5. **Monitoring of forests**
   - Monitor land use and land cover to track deforestation
   - Insights for enforcing sustainable land practices

AI Onboard the Satellites

Up until now, satellites have used an architecture called "bent pipe". This means that they simply receive information from a source and bounce it to another location. In the case of communications, they receive data from a ground station in one part of the planet and retransmit it down to another ground station in another part of the planet. In the case of Earth observation, they capture an image from the ground and then transmit it down to the ground station for processing and analysis.

If, however, it was possible for some processing to take place onboard the satellite, it would offer significant advantages. Firstly, many applications require real-time or near real-time decisions, for example in disaster detection and response, maritime monitoring and defence and national security applications. Secondly, in applications where the data needs to be secured from eavesdropping, it is safer and more efficient to process the huge data captured on "the edge" and encrypt the insights and alerts, which would be much smaller in size rather than having to encrypt the entire dataset. Finally, downloading all the images is highly inefficient in cases where the majority of the images are clouds, water or desert sand.

Until recently, it has been difficult to integrate ML models on the satellite platforms due to their significant power requirements to process the data onboard the satellite. In addition to minimising the size and weight of hardware on the satellites, power is a very limited resource and thus makes it difficult to upload machine learning models for analysis. Recent improvements in Central Processing Unit (CPU) and Graphics Processing Unit (GPU) capability have made it possible to put AI onto satellites, ushering in a new era of autonomous and intelligent satellites serving humankind.

Earth observation satellites capture more and more images of our planet with higher and higher resolutions. It is estimated that as much as 150 TB (terabytes) of data could be downloaded each day. Such amounts of data require a ground station to receive it. Many ground station installations exist around the world as satellites have a short time window to download the data as they need to serve hundreds of satellites. The exponential increase of satellite ground stations can become bottlenecks to bringing the data to Earth.

Typically, satellites pass overhead of a ground station and download the data that they collect in orbit. As the satellite passes over the ground station, it may or may not have the time to complete the download of all the data. It therefore aborts the download and waits until the next available ground station comes within range for the continuation of the download. Terrestrial communication systems are then used to bring together all of the data into the typically cloud-based data centre.

This challenge will become more problematic as the number of satellites increase and the images increase in size due to the development of higher-resolution sensors on the satellites collecting higher-fidelity images of greater size.

Onboard processing with payloads of AI can upload ML models to perform many tasks that manage the data from the time that it is captured. ML generic techniques such as image classification (classifying imagery into object classes such as clouds or land cover), object detection (identifying objects in the image such as buildings, roads, ships, etc.) and semantic segmentation (grouping together similar parts of an image) can be used to process Earth observation images onboard the satellite and generate instant insights.

For example, instead of the satellite capturing high-resolution images all the time, it may capture lower-resolution images (which may therefore use lower power) and analyse this data onboard the satellite. If the image is of no interest, it would simply delete it or store it for downloading at another time. If it is a high-quality image of interest, it would then be sent down. This would minimise resource utilisation and download only images that are useful. For example, sending images of clouds is typically not useful, in the same way that sending images of sand from the desert and water from the ocean could be wasted resources.

In a maritime monitoring system, the satellite may, at a low resolution, scan the oceans and detect an object of interest and send the images of the ship along with its position coordinates and an alert for further investigation. It would then trigger a higher-resolution capture of that object by another satellite with image processing capability to identify the object as a ship. It would then check if the vessel's Automatic Identification System (AIS) transponder is turned on and identify the ship. Given that shipping regulations require all vessels of 300 tonnes gross or above to have their AIS transponder turned on, if the detected ship does not have its AIS turned on it could mean that it is illegal shipping activity and an alert could be sent to the authorities, triggering further investigation.

AI-enabled satellites will be able to send actionable insights and alerts rather than sending the raw data files of images that then require much processing before they become useful. Such "smart sats" will require advanced chipsets to store their ML models. Most processing chips that can be bought "off-the-shelf" are not suitable for space applications due to the harsh environment of space. High levels of radiation as well as extreme temperatures can cause processing errors or even result in these processors catching fire. Such chips need to be "hardened" for the space environment. For this reason, until recently, much of the circuitry onboard satellites has been lagging that of the processors used on Earth.

Another major disadvantage of onboard AI processing is the amount of energy required in ML model processing. Given that onboard power to run the satellite systems, sensors, communications and other onboard computer functions is at a premium, the power-hungry ML algorithms such as Convolutional Neural Networks (CNNs) would typically limit their application.

However, recent advances in ML compression have enabled highly optimised ML models to be used onboard satellite platforms. Such ML compression is made possible by reducing the typically millions of parameters used in the CNN model as well as using specially designed AI architectures and specialised hardware accelerators such as GPUs, Application Specific Integrated Circuits (ASICs) and Field Programmable Gate Arrays (FPGAs).

The recent commercialisation of space activity has opened opportunities for high-end processing onboard the satellites and increased the thirst for further technology development in this area. One of the first such applications has been the recent partnership of the European Space Agency (ESA) with the processor manufacturer Intel as well as the Irish robotics company Ubotic and the Dutch company COSINE to harden an Intel processor for use onboard a satellite. This has produced the world's first nanosatellite (CubeSat) with AI capability. This CubeSat, "PhiSat 1", has an advanced imager developed by COSINE and the Intel processor Movidius Myriad 2, which costs less than $100 and is typically found on devices such as smartphones, drones, and Virtual Reality headsets. PhiSat 1 was designed to detect polar ice caps and uses AI to assess the quality of the images that it collects before transmitting them to the ground. For example, if the imaged area was covered by cloud, the processor would detect the cloud in the image and discard that data file. Some 70% of the Earth is covered in cloud at any given time and there is a substantial amount of imagery that is providing little information and thus such images are discarded. Therefore, of the 150 TB of data that a satellite can download each day, most of this data is useless, yet it consumes significant resources in downloading, storing and analysing data. By sorting the useful data from the noise close to the capture point onboard the satellite, resources and analysis time will be substantially reduced.

ESA has already launched the next generation of the PhiSat, PhiSat 2, which is capable of detecting soil moisture, wildfires and other applications with analytics in space. The SmartSat Cooperative Research Centre, in partnership with the South Australian government, Inovor Technologies and Myriota, is building a similar satellite and developing additional AI-enabled applications such as water quality monitoring from space.

The SmartSat CRC is a consortium of universities and other research organisations, partnered with industry that has been funded by the Australian Government to develop know-how and technologies in advanced satellite telecommunications and intelligent satellite systems.

SmartSat focuses its R&D in building AI space systems for applications on earth. It comprises more than 130 partners and collaborators from industry and universities and research organisations including Australia's civilian and defence science & technology establishments.

Such applications will enhance our understanding of the environment through monitoring climate change and weather patterns, helping us manage our land, water and ocean resources more effectively. They will also help detect and respond to natural disasters such as wildfires, floods and earthquakes and monitor economic activity.

Vignette: Kanyini, South Australia's First Smart Satellite

The South Australian government has invested $6.5 million to deliver the SA Space Services Mission. In partnership with the SmartSat Cooperative Research Centre, which is managing the mission and investing several million dollars in AI for space research and development, it will work with South Australian companies Myriota and Inovor Technologies to build South Australia's first "smart" CubeSat. Myriota, a spinoff company from the University of South Australia, has revolutionised the Internet of Things (IoT) by offering disruptively low-cost and long-battery-life global

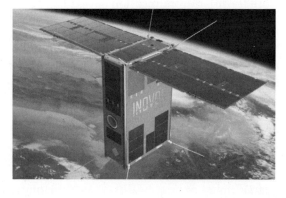

connectivity. Inovor Technologies also evolved from relationships with the University of Adelaide and the University of South Australia. Myriota will provide the IoT space services for the mission, sending data from IoT devices and sensors on Earth's surface to the satellite. The data will be securely transferred directly to the cloud and returned to Earth so it can be accessed to improve the delivery of emergency services, and environmental monitoring. For example, data will be collected on weather events, including rainfall and bushfires, which have been impacted by climate change in recent years.

The Kanyini satellite will carry two payloads: an IoT communications and an Earth observation payload. The IoT payload provides direct-to-orbit connectivity. This means that stationary or mobile devices on the ground can count on coverage without having to plan, deploy or maintain terrestrial network infrastructure. The payload supports long battery life for remotely deployed devices, which means the devices can last in the  field for years without needing to replace batteries, lowering costs and streamlining operations. Data collected from the satellite can be used for a variety of applications including informing decisions around water use, climate policy, mining, and emergency management. Once launched, the planned three-year mission in Low Earth Orbit (LEO) provides opportunities to test and develop the capability and inform future missions. The satellite will be a 6U CubeSat and at this size, will be large and powerful enough to support both the IoT communication payload and a hyperspectral imaging payload. This hyperspectral imaging payload is the Hyperscout 2, which is provided by COSINE. The imager features 45 spectral bands from 400 nm to 1,000 nm, covering the visual and near infrared ranges of the electromagnetic spectrum. This spectral range allows analysis of many characteristics of vegetation and soil that is not possible from a standard 3-band (red-green-blue) sensor. The pixel size on the ground (ground sample distance) is 75 metres in size, which allows analysis of vegetation in forested areas, crops and coastal regions that will benefit research into the understanding and management of crop health, forests, plantations and the inland water and coastal environment. The Hyperscout 2 imager also includes a three-band thermal infrared sensor that will allow new types of research and analysis of heat generators in South Australia and have potential environmental monitoring and management applications. It also features an onboard processing capability which provides the opportunity for advanced AI algorithms to conduct smart processing of the hyperspectral data directly on orbit, offering the potential to reduce the data transmission requirements and to support more rapid decision-making for time-critical applications.

Kanyini's AI module will apply ML algorithms on the data that Hyperscout 2 collects directly onboard the satellite and will prioritise which data it will send down. For example, images that are blocked by cloud will be discarded as well as low-interest images such as water. The advantage of such a system is its programmability. As more accurate prediction algorithms are developed, they can be uploaded to the satellite at any time, even after launch. Such applications will allow us to build applications that require real-time decisions, such as in wildfire detection.

AI4Space is an International Research Network whose aim is to progress the field of Artificial Intelligence as it applies to space systems and space technologies. It comprises AI researchers in academic institutions, space industry research and other government research organisations. Its mission is to bring together the impressive expertise in AI and use it to advance space exploration as well as communications and Earth observation applications through intelligent systems, sensors and algorithms. The network has begun to develop cutting-edge R&D solutions in AI to make communications, remote sensing and space systems more intelligent. Such a highly collaborative research network will amplify the AI research for space.

Some of the challenges and initiatives will include:

· The use of space systems to measure and monitor the Earth, its climate, and our impact upon it. This includes the use of space systems to support agricultural, mining, energy, defence, civil and environmental applications.

· The development of early warning detection, management and prediction systems to support our response to emergency scenarios and natural disasters.

· The development of onboard AI which can transform satellites from simple passive recorders into intelligent sensors which can automatically discover new patterns, execute analytics and enhance decision-making capabilities of humans.

The Future of AI for Space

The application of AI for space exploration as well as smarter satellites is advancing rapidly. Machine learning, deep learning, genetic algorithms, neuromorphic engineering, hardware acceleration and software-hardware optimisation will result in extremely powerful onboard processing; not only will the inferencing using already-trained models take place, but also onboard ML training in the near future. Such technologies will be game-changing for the space industry.

In the future, satellites will operate increasingly in semi-autonomous and autonomous ways and will be able to monitor their systems, predict faults and even have self-healing capabilities. Spacecraft and satellites will have extremely high levels of situational awareness with sophisticated collision avoidance systems, working independently with little or no human guidance as well as working cooperatively with other spacecraft to perform experimental and operational tasks.

In satellite swarms, the satellites will share information among themselves as they travel in formation. As one satellite identifies a particular manoeuvre as useful, it will transmit the information to the other satellites in the swarm and the manoeuvre will be replicated by the other satellites and thus the "flock" will exhibit "formation orbiting" like birds do. Such intelligence will no doubt be inspired by the advances in AI in terrestrial systems such as autonomous vehicles.

Space is a very hostile environment, and as the spacecraft leaves the security of the "mothership" Earth, the challenges become greater. The harsh environment on the Moon and other planets calls for materials that afford an extraordinary level of protection. For example, the 12 astronauts that have walked on the Moon could only survive staying on the Moon's surface for 1–2 days due to the risk that their space suits would be damaged by the harsh temperatures and radiation to the extent that they would no longer provide adequate protection. Indeed, one of the challenges causing delays to NASA's current mission to the Moon has been the nearly $1 billion development of the new-generation space suits to enable astronauts to stay on the Moon's surface beyond a few days. Furthermore, some 70% of astronauts travelling in space experience sickness due to the effects of zero gravity. Highly intelligent robots will not only be the first scouts in space exploration, but humanoid robots will in the future accompany astronauts and constantly monitor their health and behaviour and provide support and companionship to deal with the extensive challenges experienced in space.

Futurists and scientists alike are confident that at the current exponential rate of advancement of knowledge and AI, we are likely to have in a single machine, intelligence that will be superior to the intelligence of all humans combined. The most optimistic projections are that this "AI singularity" will be achieved within the next 20–30 years.

The breathtaking advances on Earth – where just about every activity and industry will be digitalised and cognitified and the basis of competition will be the level of intelligence of the AI systems – will no doubt be applied to the space sector to transform and disrupt this final frontier. We will soon shift the paradigm from the current computing model to more advanced technologies such as neuromorphic engineering and new asynchronous design architectures which, unlike the current CPUs, do not require a single clock pulse to drive the computational process. These new machines will operate like the human brain does, transferring information from neuron to neuron. Companies such as BrainChip are already advancing the field in this way. With such an architecture, we will be able to develop new neural networks (Spiking Neural Networks) and create artificial synapses in the orders of billions which can be packed into very small spaces and consume orders of magnitude less power, thus eventually making them suitable for use in space to develop highly intelligent spacecraft.

The applications of such spacecraft and satellites with intelligence that almost rivals human intelligence and being interconnected in large cognitive networks will, no doubt, be the stuff of science fiction.

As with technological advances for Earth applications, the next-order implications of such technologies in space will be seismic. We need to answer big questions such as: *Who owns space? Who yields in space? What about the security of such systems and the security of humanity? How trustworthy will these space systems be? When we have systems that can observe us from space in real-time with centimetre accuracy, how do we protect our privacy? Who will own these assets and the data that they generate by observing us and our activities?* Such questions are not different from those we are starting to ask about the applications of highly intelligent machines here on Earth and the answers are likely to be the same.

Vignette: Trusted and Ethical AI

Contributed by Dr. S. Kate Devitt,
Trusted Autonomous Systems (TAS)

Trust is critically important to the adoption, deployment, and ongoing support of autonomous systems for military and civil applications. This means trust in the technologies, as well as the methods, frameworks, and models that support legal and ethical applications. It also follows that TAS must be a trustworthy organisation to deliver this outcome. TAS achieves this through its leadership and governance; its founding by Defence, for Defence as a not-for-profit; its processes; policies; and its people who adhere to common principles. These principles are: Responsible, Trustworthy, Pragmatic and Reflective.

Responsible

TAS invests significantly in addressing ethical and legal matters regarding autonomous systems by working collaboratively with diverse stakeholders and adopting evidence-based, value-sensitive and participatory design methods (e.g., Devitt et al., 2021; Lockman, 2021). TAS has supported the Australian Government as a contributing member of the CCW (Carrying a Concealed Weapon) Group of Governmental Experts on LAWS, contributing to the "Australian Defence Force systems of control" and other key papers that have defined the responsible Australian position in international fora. TAS also has deep expertise in the regulation, accreditation and technical assurance of autonomous systems leading projects and creating methodologies, frameworks, and codes to support the assurance of autonomous systems.

1. TAS identifies ethical, legal and regulatory risks early in AI projects and ensures that they are mitigated, managed and communicated transparently.
2. TAS identifies game-changing innovation, prioritises evidence-based solutions and submits thought leadership to rigorous external review.

Trustworthy

TAS works with capable experts of high integrity across many types of institutions and work groups. TAS is receptive to diverse viewpoints and seeks authentic stakeholder engagement.

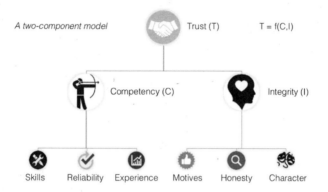

A two-component model of trust T = f(C,I),
where Trust comprises Competency and Integrity
(Connelly et al., 2015; Devitt, 2018)

TAS considers stakeholder engagement critical in establishing evidence-based best practice trust and ethics frameworks consistent with Australia's legal obligations, values, international reputation (Copeland & Sanders, 2021).

3. TAS values integrity and competence in our people, participants, partners and stakeholders.
4. TAS engages genuinely and is responsive and adaptive to diverse stakeholder priorities and needs.

Pragmatic

TAS has created three pragmatic AI ethics tools for AI project managers and evaluators: an AI Checklist; an AI Ethics Risk Matrix; and a Legal and Ethical Assurance Program Plan (LEAPP) (Devitt, et al., 2021)

5. TAS creates (or recommends) functional and high-value tools for end users.

6. TAS supports existing instruments as well as emerging best practice nationally and internationally.

Reflective

A case study on the application of ethical frameworks (Devitt, et al. 2021) to the evaluation of a tool to enable a human to manage multiple autonomous assets (Gaetjens et al., 2021) made recommendations for three stakeholder groups: developers of the technical system; defence policy teams; and stakeholders of the framework itself. Not only did the technology get reviewed, but the framework used to evaluate the tool was examined – providing two-way feedback to technologies and those in AI governance. TAS is committed to evolving frameworks and methods based on case studies and iterative feedback.

7. TAS remains humble, agile and responsive to feedback to iterate or change processes.

Acknowledgements

The author wishes to thank Ms. Emily White, Prof. Jason Scholz, Dr. Kate Devitt and Prof. Tat-Jun Chin for their contributions to writing this chapter.

References

Camps, A., Golkar, A., Gitierrez, A., Ruit-de-Azue, J., Munoz-Martin, J., & Fernadez-Capon, L. et al. (2019). FSSCat: A Cubesat-based Tandem Mission for Earth Observation of the Polar Regions. *Proceedings of the Living Planet Symposium, Milan.*

CIMON: *The Intelligent Astronaut Assistant.* German Aerospace Centre. (2021). Retrieved 5 November 2021, from https://www.dlr.de/content/en/articles/news/2018/1/20180302_cimon-the-intelligent-astronaut-assistant_26307.html-#sprungmarkeContent.

Devitt, S.K. (2018). Trustworthiness of autonomous systems. In *Foundations of Trusted Autonomy* (pp. 161–184). Springer, Cham.

Digital Twin Earth, quantum computing and AI take centre stage at ESA's Φ-week. European Space Agency. (2020). Retrieved 6 December 2021, from https://www. esa.int/Applications/Observing_the_Earth/Digital_Twin_Earth_quantum_ computing_and_AI_take_centre_stage_at_ESA_s_Ph-week.

Digital Twins: Your key to successful spacecraft design. Siemens. (2021). Retrieved 16 December 2021, from https://static.sw.cdn.siemens.com/siemens-disw-assets/ public/2LbREhST4vmvB5hag3Gu6u/en-US/Siemens-SW-Digital-twins-for-spacecraft-design-White-Paper_tcm27-101928.pdf.

Esposito, M., & Zuccaro-Marchi, A. (2018). "In-Orbit Demonstration of the first hyperspectral imager for nanosatellites. *Proceedings of the International Conference on Space Optics, Chania.*

Esposito, M., Carnicero Dominguez, B., Pastena, M., Vercruyssen, N., Silvio Conticello, S., & van Dijk, C. et al. (2019). Highly integration of hyperspectral, thermal and artificial intelligence for the ESA PhiSat-1 mission. *Proceedings of the 70th IAC (International Astronautical Congress), Washington DC.* Retrieved 16 December 2021, from https://iafastro.directory/iac/proceedings/IAC-19/IAC-19/B4/4/manuscripts/IAC-19,B4,4,4,x54611.pdf.

First Earth observation satellite with AI ready for launch. European Space Agency. (2021). Retrieved 5 November 2021, from https://www.esa.int/Applications/Observing_the_Earth/Ph-sat/First_Earth_observation_satellite_with_AI_ready_for_launch.

Foglia Manzillo, P., Babic, L., Esposito, M., Corneliu Chitu, C., Canetri, M., & Corradi, P. et al. (2018). TIRI: A Multi-Purpose Thermal Infrared Payload for Planetary Exploration. *Proceedings from the 69th IAC (International Astronautical Congress), Bremen, Germany.* Retrieved 20 November 2021, from https://iafastro.directory/ iac/proceedings/IAC-18/IAC-18/A3/4B/manuscripts/IAC-18,A3,4B,4,x47339.pdf.

Golkar, A. (2021). *Overview of the FSSCAT Optical Intersatellite Link (O-ISL) – Technology Demonstration – EPFL.* Memento. Retrieved 6 December 2021, from https:// memento.epfl.ch/event/overview-of-the-fsscat-optical-intersatellite-link/.

Intel Powers First Satellite with AI on Board | Intel Newsroom | Deutschland. Intel. (2021). Retrieved 6 December 2021, from https://newsroom.intel.de/news/intel-powers-first-satellite-with-ai-on-board/#gs.jvbakw.

Pastena, M., Carnicero Dominguez, B., Philippe Mathieu, P., da Regan, A., Esposito, M., & Conticello, S. et al. (2019). Earth Observation Directorate NewSpace Initiatives. *Proceedings from the 70th IAC (International Astronautical Congress), Washington.* Retrieved 10 December 2021, from https://digitalcommons.usu.edu/cgi/viewcontent. cgi?article=4391&context=smallsat.

Preetipadma, K. (2021). *Artificial Intelligence, IoT Sensors tech, Aboard NASA's Perseverance Rover.* Analytics Insight. Retrieved 12 November 2021, from https://www. analyticsinsight.net/artificial-intelligence-iot-sensors-tech-aboard-nasas-perseverance-rover/.

Safyan, M. (2020). *Planet's First Launch of 2020: 26 SuperDoves on a Vega.* Planet.com.

Retrieved 6 December 2021, from https://www.planet.com/pulse/planets-first-launch-of-2020-26-superdoves-on-a-vega/.

Smallsats win big prize at Copernicus Masters. European Space Agency. (2021). Retrieved 5 November 2021, from https://www.esa.int/Applications/Observing_the_Earth/Copernicus/Smallsats_win_big_prize_at_Copernicus_Masters.

Smith, C., McGuire, B., Huang, T., & Yang, G. (2006). *The History of Artificial Intelligence.* University of Washington. Retrieved 16 December 2021, from https://courses.cs.washington.edu/courses/csep590/06au/projects/history-ai.pdf.

Vega return to flight proves new rideshare service. European Space Agency. (2020). Retrieved 20 November 2021, from https://www.esa.int/Enabling_Support/Space_Transportation/Vega/Vega_return_to_flight_proves_new_rideshare_service.

With Vega, Arianespace successfully performs the first European mission to launch multiple small satellites. Arianespace. (2020). Retrieved 6 December 2021, from https://www.arianespace.com/press-release/with-vega-arianespace-successfully-performs-the-first-european-mission-to-launch-multiple-small-satellites/.

* * *

Prof. Andy Koronios is the CEO of the SmartSat CRC, a consortium of industry and research organisations developing game-changing satellite technologies to catapult Australia into the global space economy.

Andy has previously held the positions of Dean, Industry & Enterprise, and Head of the School of Information Technology & Mathematical Sciences at the University of South Australia.

Andy holds academic qualifications in Electrical Engineering, Computing and Education as well as a PhD from the University of Queensland. He has extensive experience in both commercial and academic environments and his research areas include data quality, information management and governance, data analytics and the strategic exploitation of information.

Andy has worked both as a consultant as well as a professional speaker on IT issues in Australia and Southeast Asia and has over 30 years' experience in the academic environment. He is a Fellow of the Australian Computer Society, a Founding Fellow of the International Institute of Engineering Asset Management, a Distinguished Speaker of the ACM and was conferred as an Emeritus Professor at UniSA in 2021.

CHAPTER 11

AI for Higher Education

PROF. LIZ BACON

This chapter reviews the current and potential impact of technology and AI on higher education. It discusses the current state of play, the impact of the pandemic, the typical uses of AI in education, the impact on higher education, and includes a brief discussion of the challenges of using AI technology, such as the ethical and legal issues. It reflects on the impact on key higher education stakeholders – the students, staff and senior leaders – and discusses a typical higher education digital strategy. Finally, it draws some conclusions about the future.

Introduction

AI has the potential to transform how academics teach and work, and how students learn and study, as well as how higher education institutions manage their businesses. As outlined in the JISC report (JISC, 2021), which reviews the current state of play in tertiary education, primarily in the UK, higher education institutions typically follow a well-recognised maturity model with regard to AI. This starts with understanding and experimentation, progressing through operationalising one or more AI applications, and finally to embedding AI with the aim of achieving a transformational experience for staff and students. Most education institutions across the world are in the early stages of maturity; however, many have not yet begun their journey for a variety of reasons, such as a lack of technical expertise, a lack of understanding of AI, including how it is already impacting the world, and its potential within a higher education environment.

The experience of the pandemic for most institutions has accelerated a pre-existing direction of travel, offering opportunities to reimagine higher education (Williamson and Hogan, 2021). Moving to an era of living with Covid-19, staff and students have now experienced the online world, albeit not always the best pedagogy for online, given the speed with which most institutions initially made the move to online education. Most institutions did their best to upskill staff during the pandemic to design learning materials for an online delivery using a better pedagogy than the transfer of the classroom approach to online. However, it was an environment which most academics found challenging due to a lack of prior experience, which required them to change their approach to learning design, as well as to learn new technologies at pace. The experience was further exacerbated by home circumstances for both academics and students, e.g., difficulties finding a quiet space to work/study, poor internet connection, students switching their cameras off, leaving academics talking to black boxes, wondering if students were even listening. Online learning typically requires more self-direction and motivation by students to study and many academics understandably struggled to engage students in a variety of activities including group work typically undertaken in breakout rooms, where students were often tempted to give up and leave the session. Equally, many academics and students found the experience liberating. It is clear (Lindner and Schwab, 2020) that educationally, one size does not fit all, but that no longer has to be the case as a range of technologies, including AI, can provide students with a more personalised learning experience.

Technology has supported traditional face-to-face (F2F) on-campus learning for the past 20–30 years, for example with ever more sophisticated virtual learning environments. In other words, the learning experience has been blended for a long time, but with technology very much taking a support role in the background. Going forward, higher education institutions need to take forward the best of online and the best of F2F in supporting traditional on-campus learners. It is clear that some learning experiences are best delivered online, for example simulations, educational games and videos, which can provide students with learning experiences that cannot be easily replicated in a classroom (Müller and Mildenberger, 2021). Equally, learning experiences such as role play, presentations, discussions, interactive and social learning experiences will likely be better experienced in the classroom. Regardless of what happens to the traditional lecture in the future, there is a clear message from the students during the pandemic that a recording of that lecture for them to review and reflect on has been invaluable. It makes sense that this would be the case as lectures are intense learning experiences and many students will experience cognitive overload as one pace of delivery will not suit all students (Hadie et al., 2018). The ability to work through the material at a student's own individual pace, at a time convenient to them, i.e. on demand, can only be of benefit to the students. Of course, there remains the open question of whether lectures, in their current form, will continue. This was a hot topic debated pre-pandemic and whilst some universities have made the move to eliminate them (Daly and Turner, 2021), they remain at the heart of the higher education experience across the world.

The concept of the flipped classroom (Brewer & Movahedazarhouligh, 2018), which shifts the pedagogy to a more learner-centric experience, introduces students to core content (lectures, bite-sized chunks of learning, videos, etc.) prior to class; students then practise their learning in class with their peers through problem-solving exercises, etc. This approach has been employed successfully by many for a long time but not by most academics. The pandemic has brought this model into sharp focus and escalated a change that was already slowly occurring. The challenge going forward will be to ensure technology and AI continue to support and develop the learning experience, and that academics and students do not regress to what they know. This is not a trivial task as it requires academics to change their lifelong experience of the way they teach, and students to change the way they have learned all their lives. Some will feel comfortable in this space, others will not; however, the potential of technology and AI to enhance the experience of both educators and students, through personalisation and adaptive learning experiences, cannot be ignored. Upskilling and reskilling of staff, coupled with opportunities for students to experience different and more flexible ways of learning, will be at the heart of the education transformation in the fourth Industrial Revolution (4IR).

AI Applications in Education

AI in education is undoubtedly here to support staff and students, not to replace teachers, although that is often a point of discussion and may well be the case in the distant future. However, given that the UN sustainable goals (UN, 2015) include the right to an education, until there is true equality of access across the world, AI tutoring even at a basic level could help educate those unable to access education through traditional routes, i.e. some education via an AI bot will likely be better than no education at all.

Technology/AI can impact every aspect of higher education, from the research undertaken, to how we run our campuses, etc. Perhaps one of the biggest potential gains from AI in a higher education institution is in the automation of workflow and backend services provided to staff and students. Technology has the power to innovate business processes so it is important not to simply automate current processes, designed for a different era, which may be inefficient. These are important applications of AI. However, the greatest potential for transformation is in the teaching and learning experience, which will be the focus here. Typical examples (JISC, 2021) of educational AI in higher education include:

- Providing personalised routes through learning materials at both the programme and module level, the use of which has already demonstrated substantial successes on courses with traditionally high dropout rates.

- Intelligent tutors that adapt to a student's pace and level of understanding, guiding them through different learning materials as required to achieve their goals.

- Support for marking and feedback. A number of approaches can be used varying in levels of sophistication, such as matching words from an ideal answer to those used by a student, learning from human-marked work, and using Natural Language Processing to ensure a sentiment can be expressed in a number of ways.

- AI chatbots that answer questions, provide tailored reminders, and learn through dialogue with staff and students.

- Detection of plagiarism and cheating in student work.

- Remote proctoring of examinations, using AI to monitor a student's activities on their machine and being alert to others in their room who may be assisting them. Note that this brings with it substantial privacy issues.

The use of AI in teaching and learning is under constant innovation and is being used in a variety of ways. The challenge for academics is to reflect on how AI will change their approach to teaching, learning and assessment. It intelligently creates online learning content from presentation slides (Wildfire) and with sufficient training, AI can not only mark essays (Picciano, 2019) but author them (Geller, 2021). Academics need to rethink traditional forms of assessment, and many are turning to the concept of authentic assessment. The concept has been around for some time; however, the pandemic, together with the increasing sophistication of AI and plagiarism issues, etc., has brought it to the fore. Authentic assessment can be defined as assessment which "aims to replicate the tasks and performance standards typically found in the world of work" (Villarroel et al., 2018), although there are a variety of similar definitions in the literature and in common use. The intention is to set assessments that are real and would reflect what would happen in the workplace, moving away from traditional forms of assessment such as exams, multiple-choice questions and essays, etc., and towards the application of student learning in a more realistic setting. Whilst this intuitively sounds obvious, culturally it is a huge shift for many academics to make; however, the move away from exams during the pandemic – for practical reasons such as not being able to host them physically, and not having AI proctoring set up and ready to go – has kickstarted the change. The challenge now is to continue that direction of travel and not regress to traditional modes of assessment unless required by professional bodies for accreditation. However, higher education institutions should engage with their professional bodies who also need to engage with this agenda to reimagine and redesign assessment processes suitable for the 21st century. That said, there are likely areas where traditional recall of facts will remain important and need to be tested, potentially through traditional approaches. For example, no one expects to visit a doctor and for them to use a search engine to provide a diagnosis.

In the longer term, higher education institutions should look to better reward learning whenever and wherever it occurs. The vast majority of the higher education sector, largely due to administrative and funding reasons, requires assessments to take place at specific points in time, for example the end of a semester or the end of an academic year. Reassessments will also typically have scheduled time slots. Assessment points do not always fit with an individual student's learning pattern for a variety of reasons, such as the need to work to live or the impact of caring responsibilities. If we can authenticate student learning in the classroom as it happens, or off-campus supported by AI, then in a future world, we might not feel the need to reassess at the end of a defined period of study that learning again. It is of course recognised that the act of undertaking assessments reinforces learning; however, there may be more flexible ways to approach that reinforcement in future other than traditional approaches to assessment at specific points in time, in order to reward learning whenever and wherever it occurs.

The applications of AI in learning are growing all the time. To date, there have been some impressive examples:

- Jill Watson, based on IBM Watson technology (Eicher et al., 2018), was first used with a class on knowledge-based AI in the spring of 2016 at Georgia Tech. Jill had the ability to answer routine questions sufficiently well that many students could not distinguish Jill's responses from that of a human. In a subsequent phase of the experiment, students were asked to guess which members of their teaching team were artificial and why. Most students did not guess correctly.

- The same IBM technology has also been used by Deakin University in Australia, to develop its Genie app (Bonfield et al., 2020), which provides a personalised digital assistant to students with the aim of bridging the gap between people and technology. Discussion is in natural language and aims to provide students with a digital companion that keeps learning over time. Although many universities have developed sophisticated chatbots to support students, this was among the first and most well-known.

- Yixue Squirrel AI (Hao, 2019; Cui et al., 2018), although not a higher education application, is too significant to miss due to its large-scale implementation. It provides secondary school level education in China and has been shown to be very effective for certain types of learning. Students take an assessment before they start to determine their level so the AI system can then present the most suitable learning materials to them. The algorithm adapts to individual students to keep them engaged and learning and hence ensures they are not experiencing a one-size-fits-all approach, which could mean listening to an explanation of a concept they already understand, or being completely lost if the material has been presented too fast. The company has at least 2,000 learning centres in over 200 cities in China. Human tutors help out when the AI can't answer a question. Whilst this can work well for test-focused, more factual learning, there is some way to go before it is able to support the development of creative and soft skills in students. The world is very much at the start of the AI journey within education.

Impact of AI on Higher Education Stakeholders

If higher education institutions get their digital strategy right, it will have a profound impact on their key stakeholders. This section reflects on the impact on higher education students, staff and senior leaders.

Students

The way students learn has already changed, and as reported above, the pandemic showed that some students love technology and online learning, others do not. Most reside somewhere in the middle. However, AI has the potential to provide more personalised, 24/7 support for students, for example through a digital assistant/friend/companion that can answer questions, search for learning materials, monitor student achievement and take action, etc. While there have been a few silver linings to the pandemic such as the accelerated use and understanding of technology for teaching and learning, one impact of students engaging less with their peers has been an increased dependence on staff, resulting in many students asking staff questions they could easily answer themselves with some thought, but instead asking staff because it is quicker and easier to do so, resulting in already overburdened staff feeling even more burdened. It is easy to criticise staff for giving students too much help and not pushing back where appropriate, but given that student feedback is one of the mechanisms by which staff are judged across the world, the fear of poor student feedback can be one of the drivers for staff to respond to student queries, increasing their students' "learned helplessness" (McCarter, 2013), and resulting in students thinking less and less for themselves. This will likely make their transition to the world of work more challenging than necessary. Institutions therefore have to help set standards and expectations for both staff and students to balance the support, to scaffold learning and produce creative, resilient, entrepreneurial and critical thinkers ready for both the current and the future world of work. An AI digital friend could be built to help students become independent learners and critical thinkers and not to just blindly answer all their questions.

As discussed above, many students have relished the flexibility of learning on demand and from home during the pandemic (Meulenbroeks, 2020); however, the vast majority of students want, and will benefit from, F2F education. The important of F2F should not be underestimated, but classroom experiences need to adapt. Depending on the student, their background, preparation, etc., it is difficult to state what percentage of time students will be learning in the classroom and what percentage of time it will be at home or with peers undertaking independent learning. However, what is important is that the time spent in class is put to the best use. The traditional, relatively passive lecture has been the cornerstone of higher education and one's own experience of being taught tends to lead people to repeat their own experiences when they become academics (Grunspan et al., 2018). However, as discussed above, people are questioning whether the traditional lecture is the best use of that precious F2F contact time with students.

In the UK, there has been considerable debate for many years about poor attendance in class by students, often for good reasons such as demands of their caring responsibilities or unmoveable work schedules necessary to earn an income to survive. However, not always for good reasons, sometimes students choose not to attend when they could. For example, they may judge the perceived benefit of attending a F2F session against the effort of travelling to campus. It is also well recognised that attendance doesn't mean mental engagement. Many studies have reported on distractions during lectures such as mind wandering or use of social media not connected with the current learning (Wammes, 2019). That said, surveys of what students want have indicated many are keen to return to the lecture theatres post-pandemic. It is what they know. However, their enthusiasm to return is not necessarily because that is how they learn best, but because it is the one slot where they can meet their entire cohort of peers, a concept already well-established (Petrović and Pale, 2015). Socialisation at university, growing up (for non-mature learners), and leaving home for the first time, are key drivers for students to attend campus. Learning requires quiet time for students to think, understand and reflect; however, it also requires a variety of interactive experiences such as discussion, debate, group problem-solving. The best use of a F2F on-campus experience would be for the latter. A report focused on academic staff and the workplace (Hassell, 2021) analysed how academics work and the spaces they need to be productive. It concluded that the campus is for people work/interactions. When academics needed time to think on their own to author learning materials or write a research paper, this was best done at home, or in a quiet space on campus. This conclusion easily translates to the education of students in that students also need quiet spaces on campus or at home for focused learning and thinking, keeping F2F for interactive/social learning activities.

Technology, including the use of AI, can also provide a more accessible experience for many students. For example, whilst the provision of transcripts of lectures may be useful for all students, it has the potential to transform the learning experience for those hard of hearing, or for students who are not studying in their native language, both of whom may miss information as it is spoken in class. However, in order to reap the benefits of technology, students must be able to afford appropriate equipment, with fast and reliable internet, or they may be disadvantaged by the increased use of technology. Higher education institutions need to consider this within their strategies to ensure students are not disadvantaged in their learning experiences. Over time, access to technology tends to improve and this will reduce exclusion; however, there is a long way to go to achieve equal opportunities and access, and so higher education institutions must provide sufficient technology and study spaces for students on campus, and also recognise the impact on students without technology at home, and make appropriate adjustments.

An important consideration for students and higher education institutions is how we prepare them for the future world of work. There are many predictions around automation of the workforce such as the McKinsey report (2017), which states that 50% of current work activities "could be automatable by adapting currently demonstrated technologies". Yet, the vast majority of higher education institutions focus on educating students for their first graduate job, which is perfectly reasonable given that is the world in which they start their career. However, students who start higher education at the earliest opportunity in their lives could spend more than 50 years in the workforce. Given the likely scale of job automation during that time, the prediction is that students will have multiple careers, not just multiple jobs. It is unclear how we are preparing students for the world of work they will likely live in, which might include less job security, constant upskilling/reskilling, much of which is done just-in-time (JIT), direct to the workplace. Higher education institutions need to review their syllabi and consider how students are being prepared for this uncertain future and a world where the jobs they will undertake have not yet been invented. Understanding the likely impact of automation on a student's chosen profession is important. However, at this point in time, we can only guess, so it is important to develop a wide range of skills in students, including resilience and how to care for their own mental wellbeing. The challenge for higher education institutions is how to educate for now, which often requires a focused degree teaching specific skills and knowledge, as well as to educate for the future, which will likely require a broader range of skills to support the need for multiple careers. Some institutions have considered offering degrees that cover a broader range of skills, rather than focused on one profession. However, it may not be attractive to potential students at this point in time, which is why it is important to educate potential students about the likely impact of technology and AI on their chosen profession so they can make informed decisions.

Staff

In common with students, some staff embrace technology and enjoy the online world, others can't wait to get back in the classroom, while most are somewhere in the middle. As the world moves forward and technology provides possibilities for staff to teach and students to learn in different ways, higher education institutions need to adapt and embrace new possibilities or they may become uncompetitive and be seen as an institution which does not provide a leading-edge personalised staff and student experience. This is a huge culture change for both academic and support staff and there are substantial challenges. In the teaching and learning arena, not only does technology offer up different ways to teach that were not possible before, but many academics do not feel confident with technology and the understandable instinct is to revert to pre-pandemic ways of teaching. However, as discussed above, this has its challenges, such as student on-campus attendance and engagement in class.

Technology can also provide staff with support and different ways of working, outside of the classroom. For example, staff digital assistants/friends/companions can answer staff queries, same as for students, but also provide live data on the performance of their students, their engagement, and provide reminders as needed, etc. Learner analytics are already helping academics to understand how and when students engage with their learning materials, but they have the potential to do much more. For example, ethics aside for a moment, intelligent analysis of data from eye-tracking software has already told us much about student learning patterns, such as what they read and for how long. Information on student engagement with materials in a specific course, fed back to academics, has the potential to transform the academic-student relationship and learning experience for students.

Higher Education Senior Leadership

The 4IR has to be the most challenging time in history for any leader. Higher education, with increasing global competition for students, is no exception. Civilisation has undergone a number of revolutions such as the Industrial Revolution; however, we are now in a period of change occurring at an unprecedented pace, primarily due to the impact of technology, which is becoming ever more sophisticated and intelligent over time. Business models that have stood the test of time for decades or even centuries are already being disrupted, and higher education is no different. Higher education senior leaders need to upskill and reskill themselves as well as their staff and students. However, whilst leadership teams do not need to understand how technology works, they do need to understand the potential of technology and how it can transform the education experience for both staff and students, and to translate that potential into a vision for their institution, staff and students. This includes supporting more flexible ways of teaching and learning, venturing into the space of offering learning anywhere, anytime, anyplace, on any device, at any pace, and using any data. However, offering more flexible modes of study for on-campus students will inevitably increase the workload of staff, who may have to produce learning materials in multiple formats to meet the demands of students.

Higher education institution leaders not only have to have the vision for their institution of how they will move forward in the era of the 4IR, rebalancing investment between their physical and digital estate, they also have to consider how they will take their staff and students with them, and at what pace. All the time, the abilities of technology and AI are continually changing and becoming ever more sophisticated. Given the different attitudes of staff to technology, one of the key leadership challenges will be to keep all staff moving forward at a similar pace so students experience some level of consistency across their modules. Students understandably compare experiences, and if one academic does something they like, they expect it from all staff and may have a negative view of those who don't move as fast. It may therefore be more important to focus on raising the floor (ensuring all academics achieve a baseline use of technology) as opposed to raising the ceiling (which enthusiasts will not need pushing to do as they are always keen to embrace new technology). It is important to ensure that the gap between the floor and the ceiling is not too wide.

In order to deliver on this, leaders will need substantial and regular upskilling programmes for staff and students alongside robust mechanisms for sharing best practice (and not just between enthusiasts). Upskilling programmes must convince academics of *why it is useful* to use a piece of technology, before the *how to use it* training is provided. Venturing into the unknown can be an understandably scary place for staff, fearful of the repercussions if they experiment with technology and it doesn't yield the expected outcomes. That fear of failure may paralyse experimentation with technology, inadvertently encouraging staff to continue with outdated practices no longer suitable for the 4IR era. Leaders need to support and encourage staff to experiment and provide an environment in which staff can learn from failures and not be punished for them.

Higher Education Digital Strategies

As discussed above, technology does not stand alone, and a higher education institution's strategies need to be integrated in order to provide a unified staff and student experience. As part of an environmental strategy, given the climate emergency, it does also need to be recognised that technology/AI carries its own carbon footprint, as does travel to a campus by staff and students (Dhar, 2020). However, technology also has the capacity to substantially reduce the carbon footprint in other areas, for example through the use of telepresence technology reducing the need for staff and students to physically travel to campus to participate in an activity.

A digital strategy is not just about the staff and student experience on and off campus; it has the potential to impact more widely. The figure below shows an example of a higher education digital strategy.

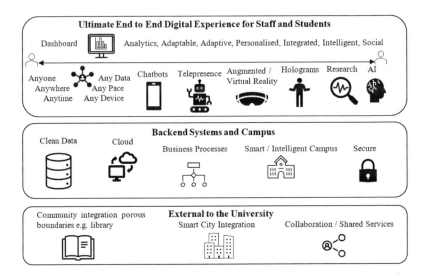

The top layer represents the key technologies and approaches required to transform user experience, which should extend beyond staff and students to applicants and alumni. Systems should be adaptable – for example, a user should be able to reconfigure the presentation of information they receive in terms of colours, position on the screen, etc. Equally, systems should intelligently adapt automatically to user needs, personalising the user experience, as well as offering socialisation features to enable interaction with others. Over time, these systems, which will likely manifest themselves as chatbots and websites, will become ever more personalised to specific users as AI learns about a specific person's preferences.

The middle layer in the figure represents what happens behind the user experience. Backend systems must contain accurate data, be available 24/7, most likely in a cloud, and secure. They should provide efficient and effective workflow management, intelligently integrating the physical campus with the digital.

The bottom layer represents the integration of systems outside the higher education institution. The extent of this will depend on the local environment. Most higher education institutions are well integrated with their local cities and are an important engine of innovation, supplying well-qualified graduates to the local community. Higher education institutions may use technology to provide more porous boundaries to, for example, help open up parts of a campus to the local community, supporting informal conversations with students in cafés and libraries; integrating Wi-Fi with the local public Wi-Fi and ensuring a seamless transition between the two; and being efficient through shared backend services such as finance and HR systems with other organisations who might be other higher education institutions. Whilst shared services can be complex to set up, the potential long-term gains can be immense, freeing up resources to invest elsewhere.

As discussed above, the impact of technology and AI on education is not just in the teaching and learning space. It will have a profound effect on the experiences of both staff and students, on and off campus, student support, our understanding of how our students learn through intelligent learning analytics, our design of smart/intelligent campuses, etc. Technology is pervasive and impacts every corner of a higher education institution, which is why any digital strategy must be integrated with other strategies such as: learning and teaching, research, estates, student support, environment, etc. Higher education institutions have tended to focus on attracting students through shiny new buildings, and past investment has typically been ten times that of investment in an institution's digital estate (JISC, 2020). However, predictions are that this needs to change and be better balanced, as the priority of the digital estate grows.

Ethical, Privacy, Moral, Legal and Security Issues

Much has been written earlier in this book about the ethical, moral and legal issues of AI, so they will not be repeated here. These challenges apply just as much in the higher education arena as in any other domain. It is therefore important for higher education leaders to understand the challenges of AI as much as they do the potential benefits. The ability of AI to find patterns in data that humans never could has the potential to transform higher education, but AI is also vulnerable to attack. It can accentuate bias buried in human decisions it has learned from, and it can also easily break down at the edge of its knowledge, potentially deducing odd answers. Coupled with ever-increasing cyberattacks, alongside a worldwide shortage of expertise in this area (Crumpler & Lewis, 2019), higher education leaders will need to assess risks and implement appropriate mitigation. Government legislation is inevitably always behind practice, so leaders need to ensure that cybersecurity is top of the list for any technology/AI developments. A basic understanding of ethical, privacy, moral, legal and security issues for higher education leaders is a must. A higher education example might come from the EU data protection law, which provides an individual with the right "not to be subject to a decision that is based solely on automated processing" (European Commission, 2018) unless explicitly consented to or based on a law, giving individuals the right to contest it. This could restrict the use of AI in marking if all students could demand a re-mark by a human. Leaders need to understand how these issues could impact their future vision, given they ultimately will be accountable for the AI they implement. They need to ensure that AI's decisions are fair, transparent (a substantial challenge given AI's difficulty in explaining how it arrives at its answers in a human-understandable form), legal, secure, and ensure individuals' rights, etc. The ethics of AI in education are under substantial scrutiny (Holmes et al., 2021) and will likely be a growing topic of discussion as applications in higher education institutions increase.

Conclusions

Higher education institutions cannot stop the 4IR. They need to embrace AI as a technology which can provide a more personalised and accessible experience for both staff and students, enabling them to compete in the marketplace for students, and offering students new ways to learn in the 21st century. AI will initially automate a lot of work that is perhaps considered the least interesting and most repetitious parts of people's jobs, freeing them up to spend more time on tasks that require higher-order thinking. However, understanding the capabilities of technology and AI, and the potential of these technologies to impact every aspect of staff and student life, including how they integrate with other institutional strategies such as estates and environment, is critical for higher education leaders in order to drive change for the better in future, and to provide flexible working for staff, and flexible learning experiences for students. Understanding the challenges AI brings with it, such as bias, privacy issues, ethical dilemmas, etc., is also vital. However, most important of all is the requirement for leaders to constantly scan the horizon and understand what is coming, so that higher education institutions can plan, adapt and continue to provide safe, secure and innovative personalised experiences for all.

References

Bonfield, C.A., Salter, M., Longmuir, A., Benson, M., & Adachi, C. (2020). Transformation or evolution?: Education 4.0, teaching and learning in the digital age. *Higher Education Pedagogies, 5*(1), 223–246.

Brewer, R., & Movahedazarhouligh, S. (2018). Successful stories and conflicts: A literature review on the effectiveness of flipped learning in higher education. *Journal of Computer Assisted Learning, 34*(4), 409–416.

Cui, W., Xue, Z., & Thai, K.P. (2018). Performance comparison of an AI-based Adaptive Learning System in China. In *2018 Chinese Automation Congress (CAC)* (pp. 3170–3175). IEEE.

Crumpler, W., & Lewis, J.A. (2019). *The cybersecurity workforce gap.* Center for Strategic and International Studies (CSIS).

Daly, G. & Turner, A. (2021). Leaving lectures behind makes sense for our university: here's why. https://www.timeshighereducation.com/opinion/leaving-lectures-behind-makes-sense-our-university-heres-why.

Dhar, P. (2020). The carbon impact of artificial intelligence. *Nature Machine Intelligence, 2*(8), 423–425.

Eicher, B., Polepeddi, L., & Goel, A. (2018, December). Jill Watson doesn't care if you're pregnant: Grounding AI ethics in empirical studies. In *Proceedings of the 2018 AAAI/ACM Conference on AI, Ethics, and Society* (pp. 88–94).

European Commission 2018. "The GDPR: new opportunities, new obligations" https:// ec.europa.eu/commission/sites/beta-political/files/data-protection-factsheet-sme- obligations_en.pdf.

Geller, A. (2021). Can AI Computers Write Essays Better Than You? https://www.forbes. com/sites/adamgeller/2021/04/05/can-ai-computers-write-essays-better-than- you/?sh=af15c58b0558.

Grunspan, D.Z., Kline, M.A., & Brownell, S.E. (2018). The lecture machine: A cultural evolutionary model of pedagogy in higher education. *CBE – Life Sciences Educa- tion, 17*(3), es6.

Hadie, S.N.H., Hassan, A., Mohd Ismail, Z.I., Ismail, H.N., Talip, S.B., & Abdul Rahim, A.F. (2018). Empowering students' minds through a cognitive load theory-based lecture model: A metacognitive approach. *Innovations in Education and Teaching International*, 55(4), 398–407.

Hao, K. (2019). China has started a grand experiment in AI education. It could reshape how the world learns. *MIT Technology Review, 123*(1).

Hassell. (2021). 'People work' on campus, 'Paper work' at home: A global view of the post-pandemic academic workplace. https://www.hassellstudio.com/uploads/RP_ PeopleWorkPaperWork_210901_single.pdf.

Holmes, W., Porayska-Pomsta, K., Holstein, K., Sutherland, E., Baker, T., Shum, S.B., ... & Koedinger, K.R. (2021). Ethics of AI in education: towards a community-wide framework. *International Journal of Artificial Intelligence in Education*, 1–23.

JISC. 2020. *Digital at the core*: A 2030 strategy framework for university leaders. https:// repository.jisc.ac.uk/8133/1/2030-strategy-framework-for-university-leaders.pdf.

JISC. 2021. *AI in Tertiary Education: A summary of the current state of play.* https:// repository.jisc.ac.uk/8360/1/ai-in-tertiary-education-report.pdf.

Lindner, K.-T. & Schwab, S. (2020). Differentiation and individualisation in inclusive education: a systematic review and narrative synthesis. *International Journal of Inclusive Education.* DOI: 10.1080/13603116.2020.1813450. https://www.tandfonline. com/doi/pdf/10.1080/13603116.2020.1813450.

McCarter, W.M. (2013). Education and learned helplessness. *Education*, 6, 1.

McKinsey. (2017). Jobs lost, jobs gained: What the future of work will mean for jobs, skills, and wages. https://www.mckinsey.com/featured-insights/future-of-work/jobs- lost-jobs-gained-what-the-future-of-work-will-mean-for-jobs-skills-and-wages.

Meulenbroeks, R. (2020). Suddenly fully online: A case study of a blended university course moving online during the Covid-19 pandemic. *Heliyon*, 6(12), e05728.

Müller, C., & Mildenberger, T. (2021). Facilitating Flexible Learning by Replacing Classroom Time With an Online Learning Environment: A Systematic Review of Blended Learning in Higher Education. *Educational Research Review*, 100394.

Petrović, J., & Pale, P. (2015). Students' perception of live lectures' inherent disadvantages. *Teaching in higher education*, 20(2), 143–157.

Picciano, A.G. (2019). Artificial Intelligence and the Academy's Loss of Purpose. *Online Learning*, 23(3), 270–284.

United Nations. (2015). 17 Goals to Transform Our World. https://www.un.org/sustainabledevelopment/.

Villarroel, V., Bloxham, S., Bruna, D., Bruna, C., & Herrera-Seda, C. (2018). Authentic assessment: Creating a blueprint for course design. *Assessment & Evaluation in Higher Education*, *43*(5), 840–854.

Wammes, J.D., Ralph, B.C., Mills, C., Bosch, N., Duncan, T.L., & Smilek, D. (2019). Disengagement during lectures: Media multitasking and mind wandering in university classrooms. *Computers & Education*, *132*, 76–89.

Wildfire Learning. n.d. http://www.wildfirelearning.co.uk/.

Williamson, B. and Hogan, A. (2021) *Pandemic Privatisation in Higher Education*: Edtech & University Reform. https://eprints.qut.edu.au/209029/1/76301373.pdf.

* * *

Professor Liz Bacon CEng, CSci, CITP, FBCS, FIScT, PFHEA, MACM is Vice-Chancellor at Abertay University and formerly Pro Vice-Chancellor at Greenwich University. She is a Trustee and Director of Bletchley Park Trust, and President of EQANIE (European Quality Assurance Network for Informatics Education). She is a past President of BCS, The Chartered Institute for IT, a past Chair of both the BCS Academy of Computing, and the CPHC (Council of Professors and Heads of Computing) national committee. She was voted the 35th "Most Influential Woman in UK IT" by *Computer Weekly* in July 2015. Liz is a National Teaching Fellow, a Professor of Computer Science and has a PhD in Artificial Intelligence. She has over 100 refereed publications and over 100 invited keynotes/talks. Her main research focus is in technology-enhanced, and immersive, learning, which involves bringing together expertise from a range of technologies in disciplines such as software engineering, AI, security and computer games, to develop novel applications in areas such as crisis management and e-health.

CHAPTER 12

AI for Law

DR. TOH SEE KIAT

Law is a rule-based discipline. It would seem therefore to be the perfect field for the deployment of AI. In fact, there are people who predict that the future has no place for lawyers. Yet there are others who believe this conclusion is exaggerated. Lawyers will never be replaced, they say. What is the truth?

Will lawyers indeed be replaced one day? What would the replacements look like? If we still need lawyers, what will be the role of lawyers and those trained in the law? What would the education of lawyers look like?

Ultimately, what will be the impact of AI on the legal systems we have, and on the practice of law?

This chapter will look at the issues from an ASEAN perspective and make suggestions for the future in this region.

AI and Lawyers: Quo Vadis?

In this chapter, I will be dealing broadly with the impact of AI on lawyers, the practice of law, legal systems and legal education. I will not deal with issues such as: how AI will be used in law (at least not at length); why lawyers are reluctant to go into technology; how AI will impact the law; or how the law should be changed to accommodate AI.

I am an impatient man and I like to cut to the chase. So to the question whether AI will ever replace lawyers, my answer is "no". Machines will never have: instinct ("gut feeling"), intuition, self-consciousness, discernment and emotions. These are the things that make humans, human. I will explain in this chapter what these are and the value of these things in law.

Now many people may think emotions are weak and should never play a part in professional legal practice. Yet, didn't the Bard say that the quality of mercy is not strained, and that mercy seasons justice?[1] Compassion, mercy, grace and generosity is what breaks the rules but what makes us human. Rule-keeping is legal, but rule-breaking is not always anarchical nor anathema. I will explain more below.

To the further question whether some legal functions or legal practices will be replaced by AI, my answer is resoundingly "yes". Why wouldn't it? Wasn't AI invented to do that? Where do I think these areas will be? I will let you in to my thinking in this chapter.

Then to the final question, how will AI change legal systems and legal practice – nay, all industries and societies with legal issues – I have no answer. I am not a seer, nor even a good "imagineer". To be honest, all my past predictions (whether on sports teams or elections or the gender of progeny) always end up being the opposite of what I predict. So don't count on my predictions of what will happen in future. But after more than four decades in the law, learning, teaching and practising it, I can venture some guesses. I will proceed to do so in this chapter. I will also try to limit my conjectures to Singapore (and by extension, perhaps ASEAN, which I am more familiar with than with any other region).

Why AI Will Never Replace Lawyers

Chapter 5 has dealt with the use of AI in the legal profession. I will not repeat the things that AI can do here. As each day passes, you can be sure that more and more proposals will be trundled out to reproduce or to augment the work of lawyers in these and numerous other areas. The two key words in my previous sentence are: "reproduce" and "augment". There are many jobs and practices in the legal profession that can be replaced by

---

1. William Shakespeare, The Merchant of Venice: Portia's speech in Act 4, Scene 1. Retrieved from http://shakespeare.mit.edu/merchant/full.html.

machines. When I started as a lawyer, my big dream was to one day have a stenographer to take down my dictation, just like my boss. Then my hands would be free and my mind could think of bigger things. Now, with voice dictation systems that can convert text to speech, who needs stenographers? Undoubtedly, AI can reproduce much of what young lawyers can do, and probably faster and with fewer mistakes. Nevertheless, isn't it better still to use AI to *augment* what lawyers can do and thus bring up the standards of legal practice to higher heights and deeper depths?

Legal research, for example, is not something just for the academics in universities. Doing legal research is one of the key things a lawyer needs to do to support his arguments and to craft opinions for clients. As a young lawyer (and cheap labour), I remember the hours of (tedious and mundane) legal research work I had to do for my seniors and my bosses. Was I glad when this work was lightened by the introduction of search engines (and merely to dig up cases using "keywords")! Now there are AI programs that dig up centuries of precedents using neural logic, natural language processing, data analytics and other magical stuff. Very soon, young lawyers would not be needed to do the research. Nor the formulation of arguments based on that research, or legal loopholes and exemptions crafted out of knowing, well and comprehensively, all the inane and arcane statutes, revisions of these statues, regulations and case precedents. AI will do all that completely – and so comprehensively that perhaps, one day soon, it would be malpractice if a law firm did not use AI for its research and instead continued to rely on mere human power. Far better though, is to subject such comprehensive legal research enhanced (and occasionally corrected) with some critical and creative oversight by a human being, even a lowly qualified legal practitioner[2] of some sort.

Young lawyers were also tasked to dig up templates and draw up draft documents for new clients and situations. Sometimes the work included synthesising the terms and appendices of different documents (especially

---

2. Here, I am deliberately vague. I leave room for future developments of new professions in the law, such as the paralegal, a legal manager or a legal technologist (much as an AI-driven hearing test machine will be overseen by a trained audio technician if not a fully qualified physician).

the "boilerplate clauses") to create a new document. This was the same whether the documents were for litigation, registration and compliance or for commercial projects. Legal expertise was of course needed for such compilation and synthesising work, but sometimes they were of such low-level (needing scant legal knowledge or knowledge of the legal processes) that it was more economically done by paralegals. Not all firms had parale-gals well-trained enough, because there was no formal school for paralegals till Temasek Polytechnic introduced such courses some two decades ago. Young lawyers were therefore used instead, and the cost passed to clients. AI can now do all the time-consuming, repetitive and boring work that paralegals and young lawyers used to do. Much faster and cheaper. If these drafting machines are used as an augmentation tool, lawyers can then be employed to carve and craft new clauses and explore new paradigms, espe-cially where dictated or required by new caselaw, statutes or other circum-stances, such as changing technology or new business practices.

A problem then arises. If young lawyers do not go through all the leg-work of knowing the documents needed in their craft and the intricacies of registration, procedure and drafting, how would they know what to do in new, unprecedented situations? How would they acquire the expertise that allows senior practitioners today to help data scientists to devise new AI systems? Further, would this mean new methods and modules, new means and measures, new courses and curricula, for legal education and continu-ing professional development? If they have no work to do, and no relevant legal experience acquired, how could junior lawyers aspire for promotions and higher positions in their careers? Will junior lawyers need to pick up non-legal skills to progress, to be "better" lawyers and to aspire to equity partnership? If so, how much law would be needed in their fundamen-tal professional skills? Would we end up with non-legal professionals with enough legal skills augmented by AI systems that we do not need "real" lawyers anymore?

In three decades of teaching in a business school, how often have I met Deans and Heads of Department in business schools telling me that legal subjects can be dispensed with or dumbed down? If we no longer need much (and expensive) "lawyering" and can just depend on AI and *Business*

Law for Dummies books (or software applications), what do we do with our law schools and law professors? As it is, AI developments are beginning to lead to business leaders asking: why are lawyers so expensive if they (that is, the businesses themselves) can use cheap (readily available) AI solutions to cut down the expensive and time-consuming, tedious and text-intensive processes for which lawyers levy immensely disproportionate invoices? I will deal with this cost issue later in this chapter.

Nevertheless, you will wonder why I am so sure that AI will never replace lawyers though I admit to not being a seer?

First of all, there is one aspect of legal practice that will never be replaced by machines. People go to lawyers not simply for the law they know. They also go to lawyers for the people they know. Sometimes, who you know is more important than what you know. In a criminal case, I, lawyer, may have a relationship with the prosecutor which allows me to have a better chance of persuading him or her to drop charges or reduce them; in a civil transaction, I may be able to persuade the other party's lawyers to consider favourably my alternatives to their clauses because I used to be their law professor and they still have deep respect for me; in a civil litigation, my reputation may be so formidable that the other party's lawyers may actually persuade the client to settle rather than face me in court. In a law practice, who I know (business leaders, prosecutors, other lawyers, etc.) also has value to my partners in the practice and gives me an edge when it comes to promotion or the generation of profits.

Secondly, in the AI-driven law firm of the future, client development and management may become more important to a law firm than expertise in law. Young lawyers will be promoted if they have better EQ (emotional quotient), more client contacts and better ability to develop new business and clients. Machines in any case will never be able to source and engage new clients and retain them.

More particularly, as a human being, I can do things that a machine cannot. I have skills and attributes that can contribute to the resolution of a legal issue which a machine does not. Here I refer to the value of instinct, intuition, self-consciousness, discernment and emotions (compassion, mercy, grace and generosity) in law and in legal systems, in theory and in practice. I will explain what these things do in general, and then the role they play in law-making and the practice of law, in the operation of judicial and legal systems, and in judicial reasoning.

Laws are made to create order in societies, to regulate human behaviour and systems. This involves predicting how humans will behave to prevent possible harmful conduct or conduct that will injure society or those who live in it. Machines will never be able to predict how a human will behave in an unprecedented situation, because in many senses, humans are unpredictable. Machines will also not be able to foresee all the ways that human systems may be misused or fail, especially with newly devised systems or technology. A good drafter of laws examines all the possible (and impossible) ways that things may go wrong and reduces the risks. Only humans will know what the human heart is capable of. The machine may be able to calculate the probabilities, not the propensities. Wasn't it a great Prophet who opined that the human heart is immeasurably deceitful and desperately wicked (Jeremiah 17:9)? Which machine would be able to predict the course and destination of a human's intentions and machinations?

Very often in my practice, I have looked at a client briefing me and concluded that I was not getting the whole truth. This was not always because the client was lying. Sometimes they did not know what was useful for me for giving good advice and thus were just simply beating around the bush with a lot of irrelevant detail. Other times, they were selectively telling me what they thought was relevant for me. Yet other times, they were simply leading me down a familiar (legal or business) path while I was looking in a different direction for what I felt would break an impasse. I would then dig for more and more information, relying on my experience, intuition and instincts to lead us to blaze a path never walked before.

Investigators unravel clues which often come as a result of "gut feeling" and connecting dots that may not seem logically connected. Prosecutors weigh all the human factors (including mercy and compassion) and not simply precedents to discern if an offence should be prosecuted or not. Judges, too, use instinct, intuition and discernment to unravel the truth to arrive at wise (not just clever) solutions and decisions. A thief might have stolen a loaf of bread to feed a hungry child, and the law mandates incarceration for the offence. I, Judge, may look at things differently from I, Robot. I may instead put the offender on probation, and find some judicial ground for that. As an appeal court judge, I may have a convicted murderer before me where all the evidence points to her, but somehow looking at the accused my judicial instinct honed by many years of judging tells me that she may not be the murderer (perhaps because she is shielding someone she loves) – and send the matter for retrial. Intuition and instinct lead us humans to decisions and conclusions that are not logical and not even explainable. How do you program machines to have such attributes?

Self-consciousness is a very human trait. They say dolphins have it too, but this is not a biological lesson, so I will not venture further on that discussion. Nevertheless, I am thoroughly certain that no machine will be self-conscious (at least not till the Terminator cyborg is created). In simple terms, self-consciousness leads a human to think: "There but for the grace of God go I". I look into a mirror and I know that I am looking at my image. I look at a criminal and I know that deep in my heart I too am capable of harbouring that evil he manifested. This leads me as a prosecutor, perhaps, to be more compassionate and empathetic in my decision on what offence to charge an accused with, or as a judge to determine the sentence. This leads me also to think of what I would need in that situation to rehabilitate or to reform the accused. I would then end up with a merciful and gracious decision that softens the harshness of the justice that I have to dispense.

It will probably never be possible for machines to have emotions. Cyborgs may – or at least the science fiction books and movies tell us. Given human ingenuity and the speed at which the metaverse of augmented reality and the merger of cybernetics, bionics and engineering develops – never say never. Nevertheless, I venture to predict that we will not see this in the next 50 years. That gives us a lot of time in which to leave lawyers be – outside of AI – because the AI legal systems we create will still need judges and lawyers to analyse, evaluate, project and apply the amalgamated knowledge of the machines. With emotions that shape what they invent and create, and priorities propelled by those same emotions. If I see an injustice, and am so impelled by it to think out a solution, I could draw on numerous strands of unrelated precedents to carve a new principle. My righteous anger will find ways and means to justify and rationalise what I create. Can a machine without emotions learn to do that?

I introduced a new concept there: projection. Using the databank of legal precedents, lawyers will have their expertise augmented. With that under their belt, lawyers will be free to project the knowledge onto a new level, a new dimension. With principles drawn (loosely) from precedent caselaw, Lord Atkin created new liabilities for negligence, and Lord Denning created new rules on estoppel. Taking a fresh perspective, this type of judicial rule-making is really rule-breaking. Lords Atkin and Denning moved down paths never traversed hitherto, all the while pretending that they were bound by precedent. I doubt that AI can perform such feats. Hence, with knowledge on the law relating to signatures, for example, we can invent new rules of engagement for biometric authentication. With knowledge on the law of electronic bills of lading, we can project that knowledge to populate legal rules and terms for blockchain documents of title. And more – much more than we can imagine.

Machines can be set to run amok to blaze chaotic and accidental but dubious new paths, but it always needs a human being to plan and plot a deliberate journey that will be productive and purposeful. Some degree of out-of-the-box, out-of-the-rules innovation and invention is always needed in such situations. Can a machine really engage in such innovation and invention, instead of merely applying old precedents and rules in new directions? An AI machine may crunch all the data fed to it in respect of all the greatest musical classics ever loved by humans, and stitch together something worthy of a human Bach-Handel. But the new music will somehow ring of familiar tunes and tones, because it is built upon those familiarities and not singularities. DeepMind's systems, which strategised to defeat a human *go* player, still needed datasets of precedent plays to learn to strategise. *Go* is still a game within boundaries and rules. What more a world needing legal rules and systems in unprecedented, boundary-less situations? Minds can project into the future unthinkable and hitherto unimaginable possibilities; machines can only forecast based on what has gone on before.

But enough of emotions. What about bias?

Humans are immensely and deeply biased. Their biases are moulded by emotions (fear, envy, anger, greed ... and so on). Even then, humans (being self-conscious) are aware that their emotions can create undesirable outcomes. They can then calibrate and modulate their decisions to consciously and deliberately remove bias. Machine decisions will be made without this self-awareness, this ability to watch out for biases. Many biased decisions could be made if there is no human supervision or monitoring. For example, an AI judge may trawl though the databank to identify criminals with high likelihood to re-offend and base its sentencing on curbing that tendency. The databank may consist of a disproportionate number of people from a certain neighbourhood in town, a certain race, a certain gender or a certain social background. The machine may then end up profiling mistaken categories without awareness that the databank's logical conclusion is deeply prejudicial and inimical to true justice. Without a human pulse, the machine may work too well and propagate unacceptable conclusions that no human would consciously produce.

Obviously, drafting of legislation will be another area that AI will not replace lawyers. Legislation is a tool to implement policies and political philosophies. What is to be prohibited or promoted by laws is never based on precedents. AI can be used to analyse words and their meanings, to track the interpretation of words and phrases by courts, and to create templates for legislation from different countries. Ultimately, because these laws come from countries with different political, cultural, socio-economic and legal systems, the wording and the desired outcomes may be very different. Human legislation experts will be needed to recommend different words and principles based on, for instance, the chosen policy or political perspective of a country. International "best practice" in certain laws can be traced and collected by an AI system, but the final legislation drafting will still depend on a human being who picks and chooses the rules (or creates new rules) based on what is desired as an outcome in a specific religious, cultural, social or legislative context.

I can imagine, too, that AI can be used to generate self-updating law textbooks or information portals, so that they become points of reference for people who need to update themselves on the law. Every time a new statute, regulation, directive, case or procedure is created, that addition is uploaded and the portal gets updated (and perhaps summarised in terms understandable by laypeople). Such a portal may perhaps be overseen by a member of the legal or related profession (employed, say, by the Attorney General's Chambers, the Ministry of Law, the Courts, Parliament or a totally new and separate government department tasked with this function[3]). The information on this portal may also be populated with commentaries, critiques, analyses, articles and notes written by academics who have studied, analysed and reviewed the law.

Up till now, we have been looking at AI replacing lawyers and have concluded that AI will not replace lawyers. What if we ask: Will there be new human professionals (hopefully charging lower fees) that will take over the functions performed by lawyers currently (as they will be amply augmented by AI)? I think that can be a possibility. First of all, we may have entrepreneurial lawyers who will create Alternative Legal Service Providers (ALSPs). These lawyers will run services thinly populated with lawyers who will draft legal documents; perform legal registrations and filings, legal reviews of transactional documents and corporate due diligence; provide legal diagnostics and analyses and other legally related services using AI technology. Initially such services may be run by lawyers in order not to fall foul of the Law Society and laws limiting the practice of law to legally qualified persons. Eventually, with the success of such practices, pressure will be put on the country's legal infrastructure and governing bodies to permit the creation of a new class of professionals who will be permitted to perform such work (whether as paralegals, legal managers or legal technologists, or whatever nomenclature we bestow on them).

The Changes That AI Will Bring to Legal Practice

Undeniably, AI promises to create great leaps and bounds for many areas of legal practice. We have already mentioned how low-level legal work can be

---

3. Here again, we see that new jobs will be created while old ones are driven extinct.

done by AI (whether through chatbots, RPA[4] or other means). This will take electronic correspondence, drafting, filing, registration, application and discovery processes out of the hands of expensive lawyers into the hands of smart machines (overseen and operated by paralegals or junior lawyers in the appropriate circumstances). Some areas of legal practice – such as corporate secretarial practice, will and contract drafting, conveyancing, trademark registration, data protection, applications for various government licences – may even go extinct as businesses do these things themselves (aided by AI programs or paralegals).

Beyond taking the mundane and tedious out of the hands of lawyers – thus freeing humans to do the value-added legal work listed above – AI's greatest contribution will be the lowering of costs all round. This will make access to justice cheaper and therefore better available to all. AI will also enable governments to put legal systems and infrastructure in place which will lift "DIY justice" to a new level. You could go to a justice centre where machines will give you general legal advice; diagnose a case for the legal issues and solutions; give advice on how to file court papers to pursue or contest claims and appeals or obtain protection and restraint orders; draft or fill in your legal forms, powers of attorney and wills; register your business or property, wills or marriages; and guide you step by step through the processes and procedures required. It would be as easy as it is to draw money from an ATM[5] today.

Lawyers will be less expensive, if they are needed. They will be used for complex and multiple-party and international registrations (e.g., intellectual property) transactions and litigation. They will be judges, law teachers, policy makers, legislation drafters, negotiators, conflict management and dispute resolution practitioners in all sorts of arbitration and adjudication contexts.

However, much more legal work (especially in the domestic arena) will be done by paralegals augmented in their skills by AI systems – which will naturally be cheaper than lawyers will be. A new profession will be created,

---

4. Robotic Process Automation.
5. An Automated Teller Machine is a bank machine that dispenses cash as a retail service.

and legal systems can be reconfigured to allow paralegals to represent clients at tribunals, mediations, adjudication centres (particularly those set up
for domestic and consumer matters) and administrative offices which can
be created to take a huge load off the courts of the land. We will no longer
need (or require) lawyers to represent us when we deal with disputes relating to landlord-tenancy, employment, insurance, consumer complaints,
harassment and neighbourhood tiffs and taunts; run-ins with municipal
and administrative agencies and authorities (in matters such as payment of
speeding and traffic tickets, parking and data protection violations, petty
offences and non-compliances; and non-payment of conservancy charges,
or taxes). The State Courts can then be released to focus on resolving and
deliberating on less ordinary, more important and more complex legal
issues and disputes.

Consequently, law firms may have to develop new billing models. Even
if no new paralegal profession is created, lawyers will no longer be able to
talk of billable hours. Clients will be more wary of firms that churn out bills
attributing hours to expensive lawyers when much of the work could (or
should) have been done by machines or paralegals. In fact, many companies
will not be sending much of their legal work to the law firms. They would
instead be using AI programs and machines (and paralegals augmenting
their knowledge with these machines) in their in-house legal departments.
They will also be deploying alternative dispute resolution models and online
dispute resolution systems (AI-enabled) to resolve their disputes. Law firms
will thus be forced to work out billing and profitability models which focus
more on making clients happy and engaged because of the intuition, empathy, creativity and discernment of the lawyers in the firm (and who they
know) – rather than their legal expertise.

AI will initially be expensive, and deployment is more likely to be by
the bigger law firms (including international law firms) with deeper pockets. On top of these, there will begin to be a proliferation of ALSPs. Would
this result in the decimation or demise of local and particularly the small
law firms? While this seems a distinct possibility, I will hazard a prediction. My instincts tell me no. As I have said, people go to lawyers for who
they know more than what they know. That will not change with AI, no

matter how pervasively used. AI-driven law practices will also not cause the demise of the specialist barrister (litigator) or arbitrator, mediator, conciliator or adjudicator (and other such experts). These are the ones pursued for their skills, experience (what they are) and knowledge (what they know). Perhaps what will change would be the way they practise in Singapore. To save costs and to obtain economies of scale, these sole practitioners or small firm practitioners could gather together and practise in a group (much like how barristers practise in chambers). I am waiting for some enterprising landlord (or lawyer[6]) who could manage[7] shared office space with legal facilities (yes, and AI-enabled equipment!) and administrative infrastructure – with a paralegal or legal manager who will help manage the shared office as a service to the lawyers.

I have said that I will not deal with how AI will impact the law. This is a huge area to consider and has been addressed in Chapter 5. Nonetheless, I will venture to make a quick and basic point. With AI becoming pervasive, one growing concern is how AI developments can be regulated and what sort of laws are needed to ensure that AI is not used wrongly. Good laws take time to draft and AI will develop too fast for the law to catch up. Legislating too early may stymie the development of AI and inhibit innovation. Legislating too late may result in the proverbial locking of the stable after the horse has bolted. The solution that Singapore has adopted is to draft a non-binding Model Framework for guiding the development and deployment of AI.[8] Much like the fictional Asimov's Three Laws of Robotics[9], these guidelines are meant to keep AI development ethically sound while encouraging innovation. Much like Asimov's Laws too, these guidelines may fail

---

6. I know one or two.

7. It does not need to be on a rental basis, or even fee-sharing basis (which is still illegal in Singapore if the fee-sharer is not a lawyer). Now, of course, I hope Singapore will change that – as has already happened in some jurisdictions.

8. The Model Framework and related documents are available on www.imda.gov.sg/AI.

9. The Three Laws are: (1) A robot may not injure a human being or, through inaction, allow a human being to come to harm. (2) A robot must obey the orders given it by human beings except where such orders would conflict with the First Law. (3) A robot must protect its own existence as long as such protection does not conflict with the First or Second Laws. See the quotation of the "Laws" in Salge (2017). Retrieved from https://www.scientificamerican.com/article/asimovs-laws-wont-stop-robots-from-harming-humans-so-weve-developed-a-better-solution/

at crucial points, in unforeseen scenarios. Furthermore, what is the use of non-binding guidelines when harm has already befallen humans?

While I accept that legislation must not be premature or excessively rigid, I do think there is room for some laws to be passed before AI proceeds too far down the wrong road. At the very least, legislation must put in place the stop signs beyond which AI must not go. I cautiously suggest that laws be passed to state the following clearly:

1. AI developments shall not harm or injure human beings, whether physically or psychologically.

2. AI shall not be used to produce criminal acts or illegal outcomes.

3. AI must not be used to deprive or deny humans of their fundamental rights, especially the right to justice.

Here we note that it is easy to draw a line where the harm done is obvious. For example, it would be obvious that a law that prohibits the weaponisation of AI (i.e. the creation of AI-operated weapons of war) is desirable. But what if a small state like Singapore needs to beat off a bigger aggressor and these weapons will ensure our survival as a nation?

To cite another example in the legal arena: No AI tool should be created with the intention of making it a tool to plan the perfect murder. How is the line to be drawn between that tool, and a tool that is manifestly designed to outsmart the perfect murderer? It has always been argued: Technology is neutral. It is the use that humans make of the tool that results in good or evil. Thus a knife is not of itself a tool to ban. Whether it is used to "cook a great meal" or "crook a great murder" is all in the hands of the user. Is it more acceptable (and easier) to state, for example, that AI shall not be used to deprive or deny humans of justice? Here the tool is not prohibited, but the way it is used is circumscribed. The tool may be developed and used, but any outcome that results in a denial of justice is invalidated.

These may all sound like motherhood statements. Considering the depravity of the human heart, they will be honoured more in the breaking than in the keeping. Nonetheless, like Singapore's oft-mocked stand on pornography, we know there are various ways to circumvent the blocks we put on pornographic portals and sites, but it serves as a symbolic statement on where we stand and what we do not accept: thus far and no farther, this much and no more. Perchance, that is all we can do. Draw faint lines in the ever-moving desert sand. Therein lies, I guess, the wisdom of the Model Framework devised by the IMDA. I shall proceed no further on this excursion.

What Should Change Look Like?

In this section of the chapter, I will set out my conclusions and recommendations on changes in the role of lawyers, and changes in the practice of law, legal systems and legal education.

The Role of Lawyers

- Lawyers should focus on multi-party, multi-jurisdictional transactions and disputes.
- Lawyers should focus on complex matters and transactions; negotiating, crafting and drafting agreements and documents for novel situations and transactions.
- Lawyers can be used to structure and devise systems, laws and policies for novel policies and legislative contexts.
- Lawyers from more advanced jurisdictions should be deployed and engaged to train lawyers and paralegals in the less developed countries in ASEAN.
- Lawyers from more advanced jurisdictions should be deployed and engaged to help lesser developed nations in ASEAN to draft legislation and develop appropriate legal infrastructure and systems for the use of future technologies.
- Lawyers will deal with more complex litigation and appeals to the higher courts; or criminal offences with penalties that affect life or liberty.

Legal Systems

- Legal systems should exclude lawyers from low-value and minor domestic, family, consumer, employment, intestacy and routine legal matters such as registrations, filings, minor disputes and low-level transactions; municipal and administrative offences, non-compliance, defaults, etc. Laypeople may be represented for such matters by paralegals and legal managers, where needed.
- A new profession of paralegal should be created and given licence to appear in tribunals and other low-level dispute resolutions for the areas mentioned in the point above. Courts (especially those in the less advanced nations) can then be relieved of the burden of handling less serious cases so that they can focus on the more complex or difficult cases.
- Mediations, adjudications should be primarily in tribunals, administrative offices and consumer-friendly dispute resolution centres such as the Financial Industry Dispute Resolution Centre in Singapore (FIDReC). These alternative dispute tribunals should be created if they are not already in existence. Appeal and supervision of these tribunals can be given to the State Courts.
- Online dispute resolution should be promoted. This is especially suitable in jurisdictions with laws permitting no-fault insurance, no-fault divorce, strict liability product liability, and for apportionment of liability and damages in courts and tribunals.
- Governments should work to make access to knowledge of the law and legal rights easier, faster and inexpensive (or free). This could be through developments of websites and portals for legal information and for registration and enforcement of rights.
- Governments will sooner or later implement AI-enabled smart registries (on distributed ledgers internationally recognised by all governments) for registration of land titles, businesses, marriages, citizenship, etc. Interaction between these registries and the populace should be via non-legal and paralegal professionals, if laypeople require assistance.

Legal Education

- Law schools should become multi-disciplinary centres of learning. Law students must be trained not only in law but leadership, negotiation, peacemaking[10], alternative dispute resolution, management skills, accounting and business skills. Political and policymaking subjects will prepare future lawyers for legislation drafting and policy rule-making.
- Law schools should focus more on research for the new environments that are fast overwhelming us.
- Schools for paralegal education should be introduced to prepare for a new generation of professionals who know how to use the technology to bring about cheaper, faster and better access to justice and the registration or protection of legal and constitutional rights. The less advanced nations thus will be able to give their citizens better access to justice without the burden of higher costs that comes about from a legal system that may not have enough lawyers or is burdened by overly taxed courts.
- Law schools and schools training paralegals should include courses on using and developing AI tools.
- Less developed nations in ASEAN can be given a leg up with scholarships (given by the more advanced nations) which will educate and train their citizens for a world where AI will dominate. This will save them the trouble and expense of having to duplicate what is already being done in the law schools of the more advanced nations.

Legal Practice

- Legal practices will employ more paralegals and AI technology for administration, office management, work processing, form-filling and

---

10. Making peace is a skill not natural or instinctive with lawyers in an adversarial legal system. Nevertheless, legal or other professionals should be trained to help disputants or potential disputants to tone down/ameliorate their disputes rather than doing things that inevitably escalate them and which then have to be resolved in a tribunal or court. Too many legal disputes could have been nipped in the bud but are allowed or encouraged to fester and explode.

filing court and other legal documents, drafting, research and engaging with the courts and the authorities.

- Legal practices should be multi-disciplinary and multi-national (or belong to multi-national networks of multi-disciplinary practices).
- Areas of legal practice that do not require much legal knowledge should be taken out of the legal profession and given to a new paralegal profession. This could include the registration of property rights, business entities, application for licences, alternative (and online) dispute resolution processes, tribunal practice, quasi-criminal offences such as parking, speeding tickets and less serious criminal offences (such as those which only incur fines, and penalties that do not affect life or liberty).
- Law firms should work on new billing models, profitability models, and training of associates with skills that cannot be acquired by machines (and promoting them on those new bases).
- There will be ALSPs and chambers of solicitors (mainly working from home – we are used to that now, thanks to Covid-19); and using shared office space when needed.

References

Bible, The. Jeremiah Chapter 17 verse 9.
Model AI Governance Framework, The. Retrieved from www.imda.gov.sg/AI.
Salge, Christoph. (2017). Asimov's laws won't stop robots from harming humans, so we've developed a better solution. *Scientific American*. Retrieved from https://www.scientificamerican.com/article/asimovs-laws-wont-stop-robots-from-harming-humans-so-weve-developed-a-better-solution/
Shakespeare, William. *The Merchant of Venice*. Retrieved from http://shakespeare.mit.edu/merchant/full.html.

* * *

Dr. Toh See Kiat is founder and Chairman of Goodwins Law Corporation; Chairman of Edition Limited (an agritech company listed on the Stock Exchange of Singapore); and Chairman of CommerceNet Singapore Limited. He has an LLB (Hons) Degree from the National University of

Singapore, an LLM from Harvard University and a PhD from the University of London.

Dr. Toh has also been active in public service, having served as a Member of Parliament in Singapore; as Chairman of the Aljunied Town Council; as a member of the National Trust Council in Singapore formed by the then Infocomm Development Authority (IDA); as President of the Consumers Association of Singapore (CASE); and as President of the Singapore Association of the Visually Handicapped. He was a Professor of business law, leadership and entrepreneurship in universities in Singapore and Canada for several decades.

Dr. Toh was admitted to the Singapore Bar in 1983. In that practice, he has acted for technology startups, multinational corporations, and for governments as a World Bank and Asian Development Bank consultant. He also helped draft legislation for several jurisdictions (including Singapore, Vietnam, Abu Dhabi and Dubai).

CHAPTER 13

AI for Financial Services: An Asian Perspective

ASSIST. PROF. ALAN MEGARGEL

PROF. VENKY SHANKARARAMAN

Artificial Intelligence technologies have provided opportunities for delivering innovative financial services to customers. Additionally, they can help to streamline and optimise business processes ranging from credit decisions to quantitative trading and financial risk management. However, the adoption and drive of such innovation is dependent on market maturity in terms of customer acceptance, innovation culture in organisations, development of appropriate regulations, and the presence of robust financial services technology infrastructure. In this chapter, we examine, from an Asian perspective, the current state of maturity of AI in the financial services industry and outline a possible plan of action by which banks and other financial services in the region may reinvent themselves by leveraging AI technologies. The chapter emphasises the need for human-centred AI systems that take into consideration four elements, namely ethics, bias, transparency, and consequences.

Current State of AI in Asia-Pacific

While still in their nascent stages, AI-enabled products and services are increasingly being introduced into both mature and emerging economies across Asia-Pac in multiple sectors, including e-commerce, healthcare, transportation, manufacturing, agriculture, and finance. According to estimates, productivity increases due to AI will contribute up to US$6.6 trillion to the global economy by 2030 (IDC, 2020). The governments of China, South Korea, and Singapore are investing heavily into regulatory frameworks, infrastructure and ecosystems which enable innovative AI-driven companies to thrive. In Malaysia, Thailand and Indonesia, many public-private sector initiatives have begun to support experimental AI projects. Beyond their national AI strategies, Singapore and China specifically are developing strong foundations with the aim of becoming regional and global AI hubs.

Financial institutions in Asia-Pac are increasing their use of AI, beyond just experimentation. AI techniques are used to profile and predict customer behaviour and to detect anomalies. For example, several insurance companies such as Ping An, Prudential Singapore, and Sompo Japan are using AI systems to learn the behaviour of their customers and adjust accordingly for a more accurate assessment of claims (IDC, 2020). AI and customer analytics are becoming the basis of client engagement. Many banks are piloting AI-enabled client advisors, where the AI engine has access to the bank's entire product catalogue, the history of past interactions with the customer, and the bank's policies and guidelines, to provide a more context-sensitive and personalised service for their customers (Courbe & Lyons, 2016). In the realm of investments, AI is being used as a key component of fund design, fund management, trading authorisation, surveillance of abnormal trading behaviour and market abuse, and driving higher yields through algorithmic triggers. In the area of financial inclusion, FinTechs are using AI to assess the creditworthiness of low-income individuals and underserved small businesses, with the aim of providing them with financial services that would be otherwise out of their reach. AI has been an enabler of financial inclusion by addressing the general problem of information asymmetry around the underserved market (Mhlanga, 2020).

A key concern for governments and companies is the pace at which AI is advancing. In Asia-Pac, advances in technology typically take place faster than policymakers and decision-makers can define and develop approaches to fully leverage them. Companies are concerned if their workers are equipped with the knowledge and skills, and confidence, to use and benefit from AI-enabled systems. Another concern is the safety and ethical use of data-driven AI. Ultimately, companies that use AI-enabled systems will need to instil trust in their customers, with assurances of data privacy. National AI strategies are addressing these concerns (IDC, 2020). Singapore and China have instituted policies designed to regulate AI deployment and to drive AI readiness. South Korea and Malaysia have included AI-related policies within their larger digital transformation initiatives. Thailand and Indonesia have launched programmes to drive public-private adoption of AI systems within strategic sectors.

AI Use Cases in Financial Services

AI use cases can be grouped in terms of a bank's front office, middle office, and back office operations (Hudson, 2018).

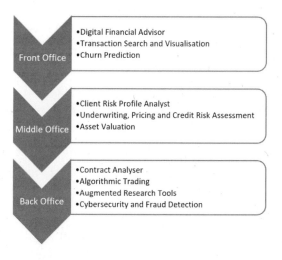

Front-office use cases include: **(a) Digital Financial Advisor,** where transactional bots enabled by Natural Language Processing (NLP) provide financial advice to customers. For example, Sun Life developed a virtual assistant, Ella, to help users stay on top of their insurance plans by sending relevant reminders that help the user adjust their plans based on new needs. Another example is Yodlee's AI Fincheck, which analyses a customer's individual account data to investigate how they're performing financially and then make recommendations on future actions to enhance financial wellbeing. **(b) Transaction Search and Visualisation,** where NLP-enabled bots assist bank client advisors in understanding the meaning of a customer request. For example, Bank of America uses a digital financial assistant bot named Erica to help clients. The bot helps with repetitive tasks such as searching for a specific transaction with a particular merchant, total amounts of credit and debit, etc. **(c) Churn Prediction,** where AI systems assist client advisors to predict churn (or attrition) rates and provide a prioritised list of customers who are likely to close their accounts. For example, the VMware Tanzu Labs Data Transformation team helped a major global bank predict corporate customer churn with a 60-day lead time.

Middle-office use cases include: **(a) Client Risk Profile Analyst**, where AI-enabled tools automate the classification of clients, from high to low, based on their risk profile. For example, Comply Advantage provides AI-driven solutions that enable suspicious clients to be identified in real-time, resulting in faster client onboarding, lower costs, and reduced risk exposure. **(b) Underwriting, Pricing and Credit Risk Assessment,** where AI-models provide a real-time assessment of a customer's credit risk so that offers can be priced accordingly. For example, Manulife is an early adopter of AI tools for its underwriting services. Another example is the Zest Automated Machine Learning (ZAML) platform, which helps companies assess borrowers with little to no credit information or history. **(c) Asset Valuation,** where AI-models provide a real-time calculation of the valuation of assets (collateral or securities) based on machine learning and assigning of the appropriate weightage to data points around the asset using historical data. For example, Refinitiv Workspace for Analysts and Portfolio Managers helps analyse and monitor portfolios and funds using AI-based algorithms

Back-office use cases include: **(a) Contract Analyser,** where repetitive human tasks can be delegated to AI-models, aided by Optical Character Recognition (OCR) for digitising hardcopy documents, and NLP to record, interpret and repair contracts. For example, JP Morgan developed an AI-based solution to help reduce employees' work effort in analysing contracts from many hours to only a few seconds. **(b) Algorithmic Trading,** where trading decisions are analysed and executed by AI models at a high level of efficiency and yield. For example, QuantRocket is a platform that offers both back-testing and live trading. **(c) Augmented Research Tools,** where AI-models increase the availability and meaning of data given trade ideas, using sentiment analysis techniques for due diligence about companies and their managers. For example, the AlphaSense platform utilises text analysis and NLP to analyse keyword searches within filings, transcripts, market research and news to discover changes and trends in financial markets. **(d) Cybersecurity and Fraud Detection,** where AI plays a key role in ensuring the security of online financial transactions. For example, the Cognito tool from Vectra automates threat detection, identification, and mitigation.

Implications of AI in Financial Services

The proliferation of AI-enabled products in the financial services industry does not come without its challenges. At the forefront are concerns around data management, data privacy and ethics, user experience and trust, and regulations for consumer protection. Competitive advantages within the digital banking landscape will be determined by how efficiently and effectively banks are able to access, process and analyse large amounts of high-quality data, while maintaining control over increasingly autonomous AI systems (Linklaters, 2019).

Banks who partner with FinTech and AI software providers will have an advantage. In recent years, AI-as-a-Service (AIaaS) providers have emerged (e.g., Google Cloud AutoML Engine) which provide a suite of easy-to-use tools for uploading and managing data, and for training common AI models using that data. There is, however, a risk of AI models being trained by invalid or flawed data, which may create the potential for discrimination or bias. Where AI-based decisions are non-transparent, there exists an accountability problem, which may result in undesirable outcomes such as: (a) data breaches which compromise data privacy/security; and (b) biased or discriminatory product eligibility or pricing, which may lead to financial exclusion. To correct this, there has been increased attention on ensuring that AI-based decision-making algorithms are transparent or "explainable".

Currently there is limited legislation regulating AI implementation by financial institutions. The prominent legislation covering AI is the General Data Protection Regulation (GDPR) developed in the European Union. The overarching principles driven by GDPR include: (a) transparency of how and where AI is being used to make decisions within the firm; (b) lawful use of data; (c) avoiding bias and discrimination; (d) accountability, to ensure firms can demonstrate compliance; and (e) data security, to ensure firms keep personal data secure. The GDPR also stresses that algorithms that set pricing must not result in anti-competitive infringement.

Over 20 countries have launched national AI programmes (Linklaters, 2019). The UK has instituted the Centre for Data Ethics and Innovation, the AI Council, and the Office of AI. The US has launched the American AI Initiative. China has launched its national Generation AI Development Plan with the aim of being the world's "premier AI innovation centre" by 2030. The Monetary Authority of Singapore (MAS) has published a set of AI principles known as Fairness, Ethics, Accountability and Transparency (FEAT) targeting the financial services sector specifically (MAS, 2018).

As the adoption of AI systems accelerates in the financial services sector, given that AI relies on robust management of data, banks need to implement stronger mitigation against execution risk. Large amounts of data must be made available securely and at scale to support millions of real-time decisions per day. For many banks, this will have implications on their legacy core systems and data warehouse infrastructure. As autonomous IT systems become more ubiquitous, banks are obliged under regulations to have in place robust and resilient systems and adequate controls to handle operational risks related to AI systems, as well as documented and tested business continuity plans in the event of AI systems failures.

Lastly, there is the challenge of user experience and trust which drives the adoption or AI-enabled financial services. Today's customers expect the same level of personalisation from their financial services provider that they have come to expect from consumer internet companies. Customers expect context-sensitive financial services and advice to be delivered to them at the right time, on the device of their choice, with each interaction building on the previous dialogue history without interruption. Research shows that improved customer experience will result in 2.4 times increase in revenue (McKinsey, 2020b). The implication for banks is that they will need to move away from a product-centric view focused on profitability to a customer-centric view focused on customer experience, using AI techniques to predict and respond to individual customer needs in real-time. However, with AI-generated recommendations comes the issue of customer trust due to a lack of "explainability" which will impact adoption rates. Besides customers, client advisors need to know how financial decisions, e.g., credit evaluation, are being made. Without an explainable model, "adoption by frontline workers is nearly impossible" (McKinsey, 2020c).

Designing Human-Centred AI for Digital Financial Services

To address the earlier discussed challenges, digital financial services that employ AI must move towards implementing systems that are human-centred (Obuchettiar, 2021). This is very important since, for example, a digital bank has to be more human-centred than a branch-based bank because it needs to "exude intuitive and intimate customer understanding through technology" (Skinner et al., 2014). The banking industry is already transforming its products and services towards self-service technologies by utilising the power of Big Data, AI, and analytics capabilities. This transformation makes customers' lives and banking operations easy, but it has gradually disconnected customers from the humans working in the industry. However, in many instances, the digital transformation has not reached a level that results in complete trustworthiness and customer satisfaction compared to performing the same operations through face-to-face interactions with a bank teller or customer care representative. Hence, there is an urgent need to bridge this gap to strengthen trust through a new mechanism of human-centred AI.

Human-centred AI can be defined as a system that uses continuous ML processes and closely interacts with humans to understand human elements such as communication, ethics, emotions, and behaviour to provide a quality service with a human touch without human assistance or interaction (Riedl, 2019). These abilities help minimise the gaps between machines and humans, so that machines perform better and enhance the users' interaction with them.

AI scientists and experts realise the importance of human-centred AI (Jordan, 2018). Stanford University, the University of California, Berkeley, and the Massachusetts Institute of Technology have established human-centred AI research institutes that emphasise that AI should combine technology and human elements in the near future without replacing humans (Xu & Corporation, 2019).

The primary advantage of shifting towards human-centred AI is that it helps AI systems to interact with humans in ways that understand their needs and emotional elements so the AI systems can respond more effectively. In parallel, the AI system continues to learn from every human who interacts with it. This learning will enhance the AI system and help it better serve users with a human touch. Studies have shown that there is a willingness to pay more to interact with humans through channels like telephones and other online chatbots (Lindberg et al., 2018). Hence, as AI technology becomes more commonly used, there is a need to enhance the existing AI algorithms by embedding them with aspects of human intelligence.

Additionally, trying to capitalise on the full power of AI does not mean that everything can be controlled without human intervention. Such a design and development approach may defeat the objective of using the power of AI, leading to failure. For example, Tesla implemented advanced autopilot features that lowered drivers' attentiveness and resulted in accidents. Such AI-related risks can be controlled by using human-centred AI. Designing any product with human-centred AI helps humans take over control in an emergency, so that fatal mistakes can be eliminated (Shneiderman, 2020).

Four elements – namely ethics, bias, consequences, and transparency – must be incorporated into AI-driven digital financial services to make them more human-centred.

The Financial Services Professional Board (FSPB) has officially published its Code of Ethics for the Financial Services Industry (The Asian

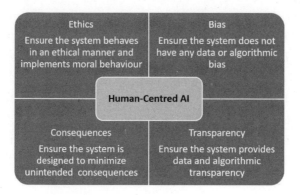

Ethics	Bias
Ensure the system behaves in an ethical manner and implements moral behaviour	Ensure the system does not have any data or algorithmic bias

Human-Centred AI

Consequences	Transparency
Ensure the system is designed to minimize unintended consequences	Ensure the system provides data and algorithmic transparency

Banker, 2016). The FSPB Code of Ethics outlines a set of five broad fundamental principles which institutions and individuals in the financial services industry should adhere to. These include competence, integrity, fairness, confidentiality, and objectivity. The key challenge for AI system developers in the financial sector is how to design systems that implement these principles. For example, a human-centred AI-based loan system should be morally responsible by asking a few questions from different perspectives, such as (a) Is the applicant really in need of purchasing a home? (b) Is the applicant looking for a loan amount that is beyond their financial capacity? (c) Does the applicant have other income sources to repay the loan in case of unstable market conditions? etc., before initiating the loan process.

Another related concept is bias, which creates a cascade effect that affects the quality and outcome of an automated decision-making system and eventually leads to adverse impacts. The bias in AI systems can manifest itself as data bias, algorithmic bias, and model bias. Human-centred AI systems should find ways to overcome these biases and help produce objective outcomes. Interestingly, Klein argues that bias exists in current consumer lending practices, and this can in fact be reduced by incorporating new data and harnessing AI to expand credit to consumers who need it on better terms than are currently provided (Klein, 2020). His proposal is to price financial services based on the true risk the individual consumer poses while aiming to prevent discrimination (e.g., race, gender, marital status, etc.). For example, using an applicant's actual bank balance over some timeframe is preferred over basing it on whether the applicant had credit in the past, and if so, whether they were ever in delinquency or default.

The use of AI systems in financial services is bound to create both intended and unintended consequences. Some of the intended positive consequences of adopting AI systems include the following: (a) Redundant cognitive activities such as banks' internal operating activities like knowing their customers, protecting against money laundering, data entry operations, etc., can be converted to fully automated processes. (b) Reduced time needed to perform redundant operational activities that can be done largely without human dependence, thus eliminating human error and improving performance and quality. (c) Human resources can be redeployed for new initiatives by training them on AI technologies and AI culture. (d) Significant reductions in operational costs and increased productivity can be realised (Folarin & Idris, 2020).

However, AI systems are also likely to create unintended consequences. One may classify them as "accidents". For example, chances are very high that an AI-based system rejects valid loan applications due to some parameters such as ethnicity, gender bias, race, or other reasons. Therefore, as AI integration increases, it is imperative to validate its autonomous decisions before they are released. One approach to do this is through "value alignment", where "moral values" can be fed into the AI system as stories and the system can learn from such past unanticipated consequences. For example, a bank can compile stories by consolidating various lending cases that involved fraud and forgery that the bank has handled over the years. Extracting the knowledge from these cases and feeding it to the AI-enabled lending product will help the system make automated decisions similar to that of a human officer. Another approach is to use Reinforcement ML algorithms that help to minimise or predict the unintended negative consequences by training the AI system in interactive situations. For example, IBM has developed a Reinforcement ML-based platform that can make financial trades by computing the reward function based on the loss or profit of every financial transaction.

A major impediment to widespread use of AI in financial services is the general lack of transparency provided by such systems. Users of such systems are mostly required to treat them as black boxes with little visibility to how the system arrived at a particular outcome. For example, though it is a widely accepted fact that an algorithm can behave in different ways based on the volume and type of data used to train it (Stoyanovich & Howe, 2018), end-users are not privy to the data that was used to train the system. Human-centred AI systems help to address the transparency issue by adopting various methods such as providing better data and algorithm transparency, building explainable AI systems that can walkthrough the process used to arrive at the outcome, and interpretable models.

The Way Forward

Nearly 60% of financial institutions in Asia-Pac have implemented at least one AI-enabled system (McKinsey, 2020a). To move past just experimentation with AI on single use cases, banks will need to adopt an enterprise-wide "AI-first" strategy. Customer expectations have increased along with the adoption of digital banking. During the Covid-19 pandemic, the use of mobile banking channels has increased by 20–50%, and this trend is expected to continue once the crisis ends. Digital banks who are now the customer-experience leaders are incrementally raising the bar on personalisation, where they are now able to predict what a customer needs even before the customer is aware, and deliver the right offer or advice, at the right time, through the right channel.

To compete with the new digital banks, "AI-first" incumbent banks must begin to offer financial services which are: (a) intelligent, recommending actions and automating decisions in real-time; (b) personalised, relevant and contextual based on the customer's needs; and (c) omnichannel, spanning contexts across multiple channels and delivering a consistent customer experience. Banks should also aim to embed financial service interfaces into non-banking products and services so that customers are engaged at the point of use/sale, leveraging ecosystem partners' distribution channels for greater customer reach. In such a case, ICICI Bank has embedded its user interface into WhatsApp.

However, incumbent banks must first resolve existing weaknesses inherent to legacy systems before they can implement AI capabilities at scale. Core banking systems are difficult to change without impacting production operations. Automating decisions and delivering personalised offers in real-time to millions of customers across multiple channels requires banks to develop an AI-enabled decision-making layer which can operate at scale. Furthermore, banks will need to establish collaboration between analytics talent and business teams, employing robust model development tools, sound architecture principles around code reuse, dissemination of knowledge across teams via repositories, and change-management planning that addresses shifts in employee mindsets and skills gaps.

Data management must be a key concern for AI-first banks. Data management strategies must ensure "data liquidity", i.e. the ability to access, process, and analyse large amounts of data required for AI models to generate insights and decisions. Data "pipelines" must be put in place to capture data from multiple sources within the bank and from external third-parties such as market data providers, FinTechs, telcos, and social media feeds. Banks will require centrally managed enterprise data platforms that aggregate and maintain a holistic view of customers and enable AI-models to execute in real-time autonomously and continuously.

A human-centred AI system must be capable of understanding human characteristics and making decisions that are understandable to humans. Building a complete human-centred AI application with a human approach is the key challenge in today's AI technologies. For AI applications to gain wider acceptance in the financial sector, there is a need for further research in developing and evaluating human-centred AI systems that take into consideration the four elements of ethics, bias, transparency, and consequences.

Future advancements in AI-enabled financial services include smile-to-pay facial scanning to initiate payment transactions, micro-expression analysis with virtual assistants, detection of fraud patterns and cybersecurity attacks, and even humanoid robots to serve customers at branches for those of us who still prefer the "human" touch. The world is changing rapidly, and the age of AI is upon us. Incumbent banks that fall behind in implementing their AI-first strategy risk losing market share to new digital banking players who have embraced AI.

References

Courbe, J., & Lyons, J. (2016). Financial services technology 2020 and beyond: embracing disruption. In PWC (Vol. 48).

Etzioni, A., & Etzioni, O. (2017). Incorporating ethics into artificial intelligence. *The Journal of Ethics*, 21(4), 403–418.

Folarin, A., & Idris, O. (2020). Effects of Artificial Intelligence on Business Performance in the Banking Industry (A Study of Access Bank Plc and United Bank for Africa-Uba). 22(5), 41–49.

Howard, A., & Borenstein, J. (2018). The Ugly Truth About Ourselves and Our Robot Creations: The Problem of Bias and Social Inequity. *Science and Engineering Ethics*, 24(5), 1521–1536.

Hudson, C. (2018). Ten Applications of AI to Fintech. URL: https://towardsdatascience. com/ten-applications-of-ai-to-fintech-22d626c2fdac

IDC. (2020). Artificial Intelligence in the Asia-Pacific Region [PDF]. https://www.iicom. org/wp-content/uploads/IIC-AI-Report-2020.pdf

Jordan, M. (2018). Artificial Intelligence – The Revolution Hasn't Happened Yet. https:// appsource.microsoft.com/en-US/product/office/wa104382081?desktop=1.19.8-windows-x86-mendeleyciteaction

Klein, A. (2020). Reducing bias in AI-based financial services. https://www.brookings. edu/research/reducing-bias-in-ai-based-financial-services.

Lindberg, C., Zandhers, E., & Middel, S.R. (2018). Hello, How Can I Help You? The Future of Customer Service in Swedish Service Companies.

Linklaters. (2019). Artificial Intelligence in Financial Services: Managing machines in an evolving legal landscape [PDF]. https://www.linklaters.com/en/insights/publications/2019/september/artificial-intelligence-in-financial-services-managing-machines-in-an-evolving-legal-landscape

MAS. (2018). Principles to Promote Fairness, Ethics, Accountability and Transparency (FEAT) in the Use of Artificial Intelligence and Data Analytics in Singapore's Financial Sector [PDF]. https://www.mas.gov.sg/~/media/MAS/News%20and%20Publications/Monographs%20and%20Information%20Papers/FEAT%20Principles%20Final.pdf

McKinsey. (2020a, September 19). AI-bank of the future: Can banks meet the AI challenge? [PDF]. https://www.mckinsey.com/industries/financial-services/our-insights/ai-bank-of-the-future-can-banks-meet-the-ai-challenge

McKinsey. (2020b, October 13). Reimagining customer engagement for the AI bank of the future. URL: https://www.mckinsey.com/industries/financial-services/our-insights/reimagining-customer-engagement-for-the-ai-bank-of-the-future

McKinsey. (2020c, November 17). The state of AI in 2020. URL: https://www.mckinsey. com/business-functions/mckinsey-analytics/our-insights/global-survey-the-state-of-ai-in-2020

Mhlanga, D. (2020). Industry 4.0 in finance: The impact of artificial intelligence (ai) on digital financial inclusion. *International Journal of Financial Studies*, 8(3), 45.

Obuchettiar, Krishnaraj Arul (2021). Human-Centred Artificial Intelligence: Creating a Better Customer Experience in the Banking Sector. Submitted Dissertation Proposal for Doctor of Business Administration. Singapore Management University.

Riedl, M.O. (2019). Human-centered artificial intelligence and machine learning. *Human Behavior and Emerging Technologies*, 1(1), 33–36.

Shneiderman, B. (2020). Human-Centered Artificial Intelligence: Reliable, Safe & Trustworthy. *International Journal of Human-Computer Interaction*, 36(6), 495–504.

Skinner, C. (2014). *Digital bank: Strategies to launch or become a digital bank.* Marshall Cavendish International Asia Pte Ltd.

Stoyanovich, J., & Howe, B. (2018). Follow the data! Algorithmic transparency starts with data transparency. https://ai.shorensteincenter.org

The Asian Banker (2016). Financial Services Professional Board launches Code of Ethics for the financial services industry.

Xu, W., & Corporation, I. (2019). A Perspective from Human-Computer Interaction. Acm, 1072–5520.

* * *

Dr. Alan Megargel is an Assistant Professor of Information Systems (Practice) at Singapore Management University. He has 30 years of industry experience, including serving as Chief Technology Officer at TIBCO Software Asia, Vice President and Head of Service Oriented Architecture at OCBC Bank, and Senior Enterprise Architect at ANZ Bank. His current areas of specialisation include enterprise architecture in banking, service-oriented architecture (SOA), payments technology, and FinTech alternative financial services. He is a Member of IEEE, the Singapore Computer Society and the Association of Information Systems (AIS).

Dr. Venky Shankararaman is a Professor of Information Systems (Education) and Vice Provost of Education at Singapore Management University. He has 30 years of experience in the IT industry in various capacities as a researcher, academic faculty member, IT professional and industry consultant. His current areas of specialisation include business process management and analytics, enterprise systems architecture and integration, and education pedagogy. He has published over 80 papers in academic journals and conferences. He is a Member of IEEE, the Singapore Computer Society and the Association of Information Systems (AIS).

Index

About the Author

Dr. Anton Ravindran has been in the IT industry for three decades, working for IBM, CA, Singalab and Sun Microsystems before venturing into entrepreneurship. He is currently the Founder CEO of legal tech startup SmartLaw Pte Ltd and GICT Training Pte Ltd, and has been featured in the *Straits Times*, *Business Times*, Channel NewsAsia, and CNBC. He was formerly Co-Founder and CEO of Genovate, which operated in 7 countries and 13 cities. He has won several awards, including the Entrepreneur Award and E&Y Enterprise 50 (E50), for himself and Genovate, respectively.

He holds a bachelors (US), a masters (US) and a doctorate (Australia), all in IT. He is a Chartered Fellow of the British Computer Society as well as a Fellow of the Singapore Computer Society and a Chartered Engineer UK. He was a Visiting Professor with the University of Bedfordshire (UK) and Birla Institute of Technology and Science (Dubai campus).